The Rise of Independent Study

The politics and the philosophy of
an educational innovation, 1970-87

Derek Robbins

The Society for Research into Higher Education
& Open University Press

For Diana
(and Coleridge)

Published by SRHE and
Open University Press
Open University Educational Enterprises Limited
12 Cofferidge Close
Stony Stratford
Milton Keynes MK11 1BY, England

and
242 Cherry Street
Philadelphia, PA 19106, USA

First Published 1988

British Library Cataloguing in Publication Data

Robbins, Derek
    The rise of independent study: the
    politics and the philosophy of an
    educational innovation, 1970-1987.
    1. Great Britain. Higher education.
    Independent learning
    I. Title
    378'.17943'0941

    ISBN 0-335-15848-X

Typeset by Time Graphics, Northampton
Printed in Great Britain by St Edmundsbury Press, Bury St Edmunds

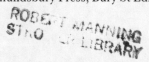

Contents

Acknowledgements

I am indebted to Professor Donald MacRae for his support and encouragement in the last decade. He urged me to write a book on Independent Study and I hope he will not be disappointed with the product. The sympathetic understanding of Dr Robert Murray was invaluable in the final stages of completing the text which is, I hope, clearer as a result of my attempts to accommodate his critical comments. My researches for Part 2 – the historical account of the development of the School for Independent Study – were made much easier by the conscientious cataloguing of the School's 'archives' carried out by two students, Clive Downing and Tony Kent. Although I suspect he may not now like what this book says, I wish also to acknowledge my indebtedness to Professor Tyrrell Burgess. Working with Tyrrell between 1973 and 1978 enabled me to develop an understanding of the political meaning of educational innovation. They were good years and, as I hope this book will show, important years for comprehending current problems.

Introduction

The introduction of the Diploma of Higher Education at North-East London Polytechnic in 1974 occasioned considerable comment in the educational press. Here was a new course, emanating from the most notoriously 'left-wing' institution of the new polytechnics, that deliberately challenged the assumptions which sustained the domination of the universities within the British higher education system. It attacked academic values and argued that students who would be socially useful could be produced more effectively within a different kind of two-year diploma than within a traditional, subject-centred three-year degree. The course was itself an action project that enacted solutions to problems which only reached the agenda of public discussion later in the decade in the Great Education Debate.

But 1974 was a long time ago. The history of the intervening period now appears to this participant as a variation on the theme of the siege and fall of Troy. We insinuated our new course behind the battlements of higher education but, as we gradually emerged from the stomach of our horse, we discovered that Troy had been gradually capitulating to another aggressor. Then there was the double disappointment. Noticing that many of our slogans were remarkably similar to those being used by the occupying forces – noticing, perhaps, that they had been borrowed from us in the first place, we tacitly capitulated as well. Far from claiming Troy for ourselves, we are left instead with the embarrassing sight of our hollow, deserted horse which haunts us as we celebrate our current successes.

The proposal for the DipHE insisted that higher education should be available to the whole population and should, consequently, concentrate on enabling that population to become competent. It was more important that people should be able to act than that they should possess knowledge. The acquisition of knowledge should not be an end in itself. Knowledge should be acquired in order to aid action and should only be retained in as much as it remained instrumentally useful. In principle, academicism was an easy target. Academicism was highly vulnerable to the charge of self-indulgence, but, in practice, academic institutions were able to ignore with contemptuous ease the ideological challenge issued by a trivial diploma course in one of the upstart and inferior new polytechnics.

It took the Government to change the universities. By the time that we had emerged from securing final approval of our diploma course and our post-diploma degree course in 1979, the walls of the universities were beginning to crumble and our horse was redundant. The Government was talking about competence and personal and vocational skills and insisting on the economic accountability of institutions of higher education. It was suddenly disconcerting that so much of what had been 'left-wing' thinking was now 'right-wing'. Not wishing to collaborate in the Government's appropriation of our original vocational critique of academicism, we unconsciously re-defined 'competence' in a libertarian way to mean personal independence. The cultivation of the 'personal' was apolitical and we proceeded to acquiesce in the neutralization of our original political purposes. Meanwhile we have powerlessly witnessed some of the unintended consequences of our thoughts and actions. It was in the soil we tilled that the seeds of current policies germinated, both for higher education and schools.

I have come to believe that the mistake we made was to identify an attack on academicism with an attack on intellectuality. By concentrating on developing the capacity of students to act, we devalued rationality. By encouraging the view that 'bodies of knowledge' should be used, we fostered an attitude of intellectual entrepreneurism which undermined the norms of rational, scientific enquiry and the values of intellectual integrity. These degradations are now written large in our system of higher education. Those who are familiar with the efforts of departments in higher education institutions to recruit overseas students in order to acquire full-cost fees or to secure remunerative consultancy contracts will recognize how little space now exists rationally to question the value of such commercial enterprises. Paradoxically, this book tries to make space to conduct a rational analysis of an educational development which has itself tended to emphasize the irrational.

About 20 years ago, Pierre Bourdieu reminded his readers, by allusion only, of the story of the birds of Psaphon. Psaphon was a Libyan who kept a number of birds in captivity and taught them to say 'Psaphon is a god'. He then liberated them and, in consequence, the Africans paid divine honours to Psaphon. In a world where pressure exists to market courses like products, there is a temptation to produce a book which repeats the formula that 'independent study is good' for an audience which is disposed to be persuaded.

The choice of *The Rise of Independent Study* as a title carries with it the risk that the book might be thought to comprise an incantatory celebration offered by a once captive bird. The chances are that it will only attract people involved in some form of 'student-controlled learning' or those culturally disposed to be interested in developments in 'progressive education'. The danger is still that a book about 'independent study' might be dismissed by 'academics' as readily as the diploma course itself in the 1970s. This book, however, tries to talk both to those who regard themselves as 'converted' to some form of independent study and to those academics who see themselves as, increasingly, fighting a rearguard action to save the values which they esteem in higher education. The account contained within *The Rise of Independent Study* suggests that mechanisms can be devised to democratize the intellect without degrading it, and the book has been given a sub-title in the hope that readers will realize that it contains an attempt to reveal the true character of Psaphon.

An initial difficulty, of course, arises from the adoption of the term 'independent study' to indicate the nature of the innovation at North-East London Polytechnic. It must have been one day some time in June or July 1974, when Tyrrell Burgess rang the extensions of the members of staff of North-East London Polytechnic who were seconded to the Diploma of Higher Education Development Unit. He asked them what name should be given to the permanent unit which had just been established by the Academic Board to run the new course in the Autumn. 'How about the School of Independent Studies or for Independent Study?', he asked. There followed a certain amount of semantic debate: the School of Independent Studies might imply, falsely, that the School would be prescribing and providing courses of independent study, whereas the School for Independent Study might convey an acceptable ambivalence – that the School would encourage students to develop a capacity for independent study and would also offer a context within which that acquired independence might be exercised. The word 'independent' had not been used throughout the year in the discussions of the Unit and had barely appeared in the documentation submitted to the CNAA. In so far as we were aware of them, however, we thought that its connotations were congenial and could do no harm.

Some of us had already dipped into Dressel and Thompson's *Independent Study. A New Interpretation of Concepts, Practices and Problems* (Jossey-Bass, 1973) which then rapidly went the rounds of the staff of the incipient department. With what was, in retrospect, a form of cultural prejudice, it seemed to us a typical Jossey-Bass publication – large print and intellectually slight – and redolent of the ethos of the contemporary American commissions on higher education which had every appearance of being heavily funded but analytically lightweight.[1] 'Independent Study' was a convenient label when a label was needed, but in no sense were we attempting to adapt or import American practice and neither was our understanding of our purposes shaped at all by American educational thinking. Our innovation was homegrown. It arose out of the attempt by a group of staff, who had themselves experienced different kinds of English higher education in different disciplines and in different institutions, to respond to the challenge of developing new practices in a new polytechnic institution.[2] In the debate over the title for the new department, for instance, we knew that it followed from the logic of our course planning that we should not be called the School of Individual Studies, but we had not articulated a rationale for this position as clearly as Dressel and Thompson:

> Individualization can be a first step toward independence, but if individualization is always accompanied by detailed task specification, it

may actually deny an individual even the degree of independence implicit in the anonymity of the traditional class. Properly used, individualization fosters self-discovery and the development of motivation for independent efforts, but as that independence develops, the obligations and privileges of adaptation must be transferred from the teacher to the student.[3]

Equally, we had not explicitly acknowledged or even become corporately aware of Dressel and Thompson's formulation that

Independent Study is the student's self-directed pursuit of academic competence in as autonomous a manner as he is able to exercise at any particular time.[4]

Notions of 'self-discovery', 'self-directed learning' and student 'autonomy' barely entered our framework of thinking in the early 1970s. We talked at length about 'competence' but in a way which assumed that the idea of 'academic competence' was self-contradictory nonsense. The School for Independent Study was established in 1974 to run, in the first instance, a course leading to the award of a Diploma of Higher Education. At some point in the next few years the idea crept into the language that the NELP DipHE was a DipHE 'by independent study'. This labelling was almost certainly the result of the CNAA's inclination to differentiate NELP's DipHE as 'experimental' from all other DipHE courses. It was only with the introduction of the BA/BSc (Hons) by independent study in 1976 that the title of the School became formally associated with one of its courses. This nominating tendency was reinforced by the publication in 1980 of Percy and Ramsden's *Independent Study. Two examples from English higher education* (SRHE).

This comparative analysis was based upon two case studies – one by John Lewin on *Independent Studies at the University of Lancaster* and the other by one of the co-authors, Paul Ramsden, on the DipHE at NELP, which was presented as a report to the staff of the School for Independent Study. The completed research reports are dated, respectively, 1976 and 1975, and Ramsden emphasizes that his findings are based on comments made by students and staff in the first four terms of the operation of the course (September 1974 until December 1975).[5] A fourth chapter summarizes the developments at Lancaster and NELP up to 1979 and is complemented by postscripts written by those responsible for the operation of independent study in both institutions.[6] The first chapter offers an introduction to the case studies in which Percy and Ramsden seek to represent 'The Idea of Independent Study'. Even though the authors readily acknowledge the differences between the Lancaster School of Independent Studies and the NELP School for Independent Study and, indeed, spend some time in spelling out these differences in careful detail,[7] the effect of their efforts might well, nevertheless, have been to reify an 'idea'. The echo of Newman in the first chapter's title is immediately reinforced by an attempt to offer him as an early advocate of independent study:

Over 120 years ago, Cardinal Newman argued that 'self-education in the most restricted sense, is preferable to a system of teaching which, professing so much, really does so little for the mind'.[8]

Evidence derived from research undertaken by researchers at Lancaster (Entwistle and Percy, 1974,[9] and Brennan and Percy, 1977)[10] and from the findings of the Nuffield Foundation's Group for Research and Innovation in Higher Education[11] is introduced to suggest that 'independence in learning' might secure the transformation of what Newman called 'notional assent' into 'real assent'. In this view, independent study should be seen to be an efficient method of maximizing student motivation.[12] In spite of their discussion of a distinction between 'individualized' and 'independent' study and of their consideration of independent study and 'self-knowledge' as goals of higher education, Percy and Ramsden's approach to independent study adheres to a pedagogical orientation. It is the 'idea' of independent study as a device for promoting student motivation and learning which is abstracted from the complex practices revealed in the two case studies. The authors go as far as to conclude that

> on the basis of the studies of NELP and Lancaster, we agree with Dressel and Thompson (1973) that all students should have the opportunity and experience of becoming independent learners during a part of their course of undergraduate study. We propose, then, that one unit of all degree and diploma courses should be taken in a school of independent study.[13]

This recommendation might have had some force if there had been an alliance of 'independent study' practitioners who could have accepted the characterizaton of the 'idea of independent study' superimposed by Percy and Ramsden. In fact, contacts between NELP and Lancaster were minimal throughout the 1970s and, apart from occasional forays, both sets of practitioners remained behind binary barricades.[14] At NELP we already thought that we were in the vanguard of a national movement associated with the introduction of a new, short-cycle award – the Diploma of Higher Education – into the British higher education system. Lancaster was separate from that movement and our allies were those other colleges which introduced the DipHE in the mid-1970s and which joined together to constitute an Association of Colleges Implementing the DipHE (ACID).[15] From 1976, however, the School for Independent Study at NELP did not solely run a course leading to the award of the DipHE, and from that point onwards it became less interested in sustaining solidarity with ACID and more interested in establishing an identity for 'independent study' as a 'brand image' for the pioneering activities of the School.

The revised CNAA documentation for the NELP DipHE of 1976 sought to give a new centrality to the notion of 'independence' in the course's philosophy and, in the late 1970s, there was a clear attempt within the School to tighten control and to establish conformity amongst the diverse ideological orientations which had hitherto flourished and co-existed. This process culminated in the organization in 1979 of a conference – 'The NELP Experience of Independent Study'[16] which sought to offer a public presentation of the School's innovative work. Although the School's attempted self-definition in this period coincided with the production of Percy and Ramsden's book, there was no significant cross-fertilization. The title of the NELP conference is indicative. The School for Independent Study was seeking to characterize itself in terms of its own practice and experience rather than by reference to abstract educational models or by comparison with innovations in other institutions. The self-examination of the late 1970s remained as homegrown as the original development of the early years of the decade.

The self-regarding insularity, which could have been the product of confidence or obstinacy, conceit or defensiveness, is currently in decline. The School is now willing to accept a plethora of labels. It is happy to be associated with a list of descriptors which reads like a catalogue of Jossey-Bass titles: independent study/learning; individualized study/learning; project work; self/peer assessment; experiential learning; non-traditional study; non-directive study; contract learning; self-managed learning; student planned learning; competence seeking; self-directed study; self-directed learning; student-centred learning; peer-group learning. The School's willingness to acquiesce in the cultural invasion which this terminological babble represents, and to resist the discriminations between labels which might give them some precise meaning, only reflects a powerful trend in current thinking about adult and higher education where the rise of independent study or its associated 'synonyms' seems irresistible. Dressel and Thompson's comment of 1973 on the American situation rings painfully true about our present position in the United Kingdom:

> Few areas in higher education today are so vaguely eulogized, yet so little understood, so loosely defined, and so inadequately researched as self-directed learning.[17]

Their response was to define 'independent study', to survey college practices, and to identify problem areas for institutions which might want to introduce their own programmes.

The response of this book, by contrast, is to give an account of the development of one educational innovation in one institution of higher education. It is, crucially, a personal account. I have already spoken about the course which 'we' introduced in 1974 and have imputed motives to colleagues and offered interpretations of our joint actions. I have no right to represent the intentions and motivations of others. This text has not been discussed with any colleague and it therefore makes no attempt to establish a canonical version of 'independent study' or to coerce colleagues into conformity with that version. The intention is not to define and market an innovative educational product. I have participated in the events which I describe – in many instances positively as a protagonist. I helped in the preparation of the Diploma of Higher Education course in 1973 and was mainly responsible for the submission to the CNAA which gained approval for the BA/BSc by Independent Study in 1976. I was the first Course Tutor for the BA/BSc from 1976 until 1979 when I was asked to take responsibility for research within the School for Independent Study. I was fortunate in being able to create an analytical distance from my own involvement in a year of secondment to the LSE, but I returned to the School to see its proposal for an MA/MSc by Independent Study through the CNAA in 1984 and to become its first Course Tutor from 1984 to 1986. My subsequent reversion to my research role within the School has given me the time to write this book and to consolidate the perspective which I began to articulate whilst at the LSE. Although I have tried to achieve an analytical detachment in my text, the account which I offer is unavoidably partial and partisan. It should not be difficult to detect the logical connections between the positions which I adopted within the historical process and my present interpretations of it. Nevertheless, these connections should be made explicit, not least because they help to explain the way in which the book is organized.

The Rise of Independent Study first surveys, in clusters, a selection of the 'surfeit of synonyms' which threatens to disengage NELP's concept of independent study from its institutional roots. Part 1 considers 'experiential learning', 'self-managed learning' and 'contract learning'. It starts from the position that these are all forms of learning which are usually thought to have affinities with independent study. The three chapters indicate the links which exist with the current practice of the School for Independent Study but they also seek to point out the inadequacies of the explications of these modes of learning which are discussed. The intention of Part 1 is to locate independent study alongside the practices of many who may have been drawn to read the book by its title. My assumption, however, is that these versions of independent study are aberrations which have little reference to the social and political contexts which first generated the practice of independent study at North East London Polytechnic.

By contrast, therefore, Part 2 tries to situate the rise of independent study at NELP within its immediate context. It attempts to represent the internal logic of the development of the School for Independent Study. It focuses on the internal logic of the development because it seeks to isolate the process as if it were a piece of diplomatic history. It analyses course documents, institutional politics, and negotiations for approval and it defers, as far as possible, until later, any detailed consideration of the intellectual or cultural positions which might have motivated the actors in the events described. It charts the development, first of all, of the DipHE, then of the BA/BSc by Independent Study, and, finally, of the MA/MSc by Independent Study. It shows that ideological positions tended to become associated with specific courses, but, even more, it exposes sets of fundamental polarities between which the practice of the School in all its courses has seemed to oscillate. Part 2 would seem to imply that there have always been basic oppositions between regulators and non-regulators; credentialists and non-credentialists; advocates of cognitive and advocates of affective objectives; advocates of professional qualification and advocates of personal development; defenders of course objectives and defenders of personal goals; upholders of public criteria and supporters of personal growth.

Part 3 is able to assume the reader's knowledge of the specific institutional context of the rise of independent study and proceeds to explore the politics and the philosophy of the educational innovation. The suggestion is that three general trends of thought and action in the last decade have been locked in conflict and underlie the apparent polarities. The development of the DipHE was part of a campaign for educational reform which sought to extend comprehensivization to higher education by challenging prior assumptions about student access, academic course content, and student assessment. This was the emphasis of the 'old left' which found itself affected by influences derived from co-counselling practices and the thinking of humanistic psychology. The second chapter in this section describes the penetration of higher education by the 'personal growth movement' and the associated drift of the 'old left' towards social democracy. The third chapter presents my personal interpretation of the significance of the BA/BSc by Independent Study. It analyses the incursion into the practice of teaching and learning in higher education made by the 'new directions in the sociology of education', following, in particular, the publication of *Knowledge and Control* (1971), edited by M. F. D. Young. The concern of that movement with the social process of legitimizing knowledge was important to the BA/BSc by Independent Study, but the chapter acknowledges that the 'new directions' lost direction in about 1977 and that the BA/BSc by Independent Study lost some direction with it.

The conclusion resolutely tries to transform what might otherwise seem a lament for past hopes into an outline prescription for a remedy for our present troubles. The 'new directions' failed adequately to reflect on the institutional conditions which generate and sustain bodies of knowledge. The thinking behind the BA/BSc by Independent Study inherited this inadequacy. It foolishly believed that it could establish within an institution a mechanism which would be institutionally neutral and would become the locus for rational dialogue between staff and students about the legitimacy of proposed programmes of study. This fallacy has become more apparent as Government actions destroy the ideological neutrality of educational institutions. The conclusion tentatively advances a modernist solution which might also be a 'new left' solution. There seems now to be no possibility of reversion to an absolute belief in 'academic autonomy' or 'academic freedom'. We have to generate our functional autonomies and our consciously sponsored locations for free and rational dialogue. In the terms used by Habermas, whose work is discussed, we now desperately need to create a 'public sphere'. We now need new contexts within which we can deliberately stand apart from those traditional institutions which constrain us. There is still some hope that individual intellects may there maintain a channel of communication between the 'life-world' and the 'system-world'. The acts of negotiating and registering proposals for study as they have developed within the Degree by

Independent Study may yet be paradigms for the de-institutionalized processes which we shall need in order to counter the influence of partisan institutions and to intercede between the personal and the political.

Notes

1 This was certainly my reaction and one which I remember sharing.
2 It would be interesting to analyse these differences in detail. One explanation of
the innovation, for instance, might be that it was an attempt to introduce an
Oxbridge tutorial system to an institution in which the construction of CNAA
'courses' had already reinforced the regimented teaching practices of the consti-
tuent technical colleges.
3 P. L. Dressel and M. M. Thompson, *Independent Study. A New Interpretation of Concepts,
Practices and Problems,* Jossey-Bass, 1973, p. 5.
4 ibid. p.l.
5 See his footnote 10 in K. Percy and P. Ramsden, *Independent Study. Two examples from
English higher education,* SRHE, 1980, p. 31.
6 John Stephenson for NELP and Jane Routh for the University of Lancaster.
7 See Percy and Ramsden, op. cit. pp. 63-4.
8 Percy and Ramsden, op. cit. p. 3. The quote is from J. H. Newman, *On the Scope and
Nature of University Education* (1852).
9 N. J. Entwistle and K. A. Percy, 'Critical thinking or conformity? An investigation
of the aims and outcomes of higher education', in *Research into Higher Education 1973,*
London, SRHE, 1974.
10 J. L. Brennan and K. A. Percy, 'What do students want? An analysis of staff and
student perceptions in British higher education', in A. Bonboir (ed.), *Instructional
design in higher education,* European Association for Research and Development in
Higher Education, I, 125-152, 1977.
11 Nuffield Group, *Towards Independence in Learning: Selected Papers,* London, Nuffield
Foundation, 1975.
12 For a critique of the relevance of Newman's thinking to independent study, see my
review of a new edition of Newman's *The Idea of a University:* 'The Power of the Idea',
in *Higher Education Review,* Spring 1977.
13 Percy and Ramsden, op. cit. p. 65.
14 The first director (1973/4) of the Lancaster School of Independent Studies –
Professor Frank Oldfield – was for a short while an external examiner for the
NELP DipHE. Professor Alec Ross of the University of Lancaster was Chairman
of the CNAA working party which approved the NELP submission in 1976 for the
BA/BSc by Independent Study and he was also Chief External Examiner for the
BA/BSc by Independent Study from 1976 until 1979. For an account of the ways in
which Professor Ross's 'Lancaster' views of independent study impinged on
NELP practice during the experimental phase of the BA/BSc by Independent
Study course, see E. Adams, D. Robbins and J. Stephens, Research Paper 3, July
1981, op. cit. pp. 43-57.
15 ACID was established in 1973/4 before the approval of any DipHE course. It still
exists as a lobby for the DipHE and its secretary is John Davidson, Bristol Polytechnic.
16 *The NELP Experience of Independence Study,* A collection of papers and documents

prepared and compiled for the first conference on independent study by the
School for Independent Study, 18-20 April 1979. Available from the archives of
the School for Independent Study, Livingstone House, London E15 2LL.

17 Dressel and Thompson, 1973, op. cit. p. vii.

Part 1

A Surfeit of Synonyms

There is no concealing the fact that the title of this Part is pejorative. I mean to convey the impression of a conceptual orgy in which thinking becomes fuddled. I want also to convey the impression of a 'hype' in which productivity and demand are both stimulated by an artificial differentiation between brand labels. In short, this Part is an attack on what 'independent study' has mostly come to mean. It is an aggressive salvo and prelude to a more reasoned attempt to reconstruct a meaning which is in decline. The subsequent reasoned argument develops on the basis of an account of a historical progression. Part 2 traces the growth of the School for Independent Study from the small beginning of one innovative course and its origins in 1970 until the present time. Part 3 traces the same growth from a different perspective. It tries to locate the development of the School within a history of ideas of the same period. The orientations of key participants at the 'micro-level' of the School are linked to larger movements of ideas. But the emphasis of Part 1 is different. It starts from the present and works backwards. An explanation for this can itself be found historically. At the beginning of the 1980s – or more precisely 1982-3 – there seems, in retrospect, to have been a moment of disjunction or discontinuity in the development of the School. Certainly, I experienced such a discontinuity subjectively on returning to the School from my year of secondment in the Autumn of 1983. But the disjunction was also objective. As the School grew in size during the 1970s there was, of course, a gradual augmentation of staff. The gradualism at this time was significant. New staff gradually adapted to the practice of the School without making essential contributions to the thinking which supported that practice. In the early 1980s, however, there was a large influx of new staff – mainly on internal transfer within the polytechnic – to cope with the increase in student numbers. These staff often had preformed ideas of 'independent study' derived from the literature on 'experiential learning' which was then current in a way that it had not been 10 years earlier. Part 1 moves backwards from these preformed ideas in an attempt to bridge the chasm of discontinuity between the present and the past. At the parochial level, this Part seeks to reopen the channels of communication between the thinking of present practitioners and adherents of 'independent study' within the School and the thinking of the 'founding fathers'. In a much wider context, this Part prepares the ground for a juxtaposition of the philosophies of 'old' and 'new' forms of progressive education.

The Part does not aim simply to make connections or to juxtapose. I want to argue that the discontinuity has harmed the potential of 'independent study'. I want to articulate the meanings of variants of experientialism in order to expose them. What kind of criticism of experientialism, however, is possible? It is one of the essential elements of experientialism that it cannot accept the legitimacy of the grounds which might establish its illegitimacy. Experience is assumed to be self-validating. Attempts to verify or falsify the claims of the experientialists become reduced by them to issues of personal assertion and counter-assertion. I am not trying, therefore, to discredit the experientialist positions as such by assembling, for instance, empirical evidence from research in educational psychology. I simply use two approaches which try to cast doubt on or raise queries about experientialist assertions. I question the internal logic of some claims whilst, in other cases, I suggest that claims which purport to be empirically-based have been politically pragmatic. What emerges, however, is, I hope, an exercise in understanding rather than demolition. It follows from the sociological character of my own analysis that I accept that intellectual positions cannot be 'demolished' by reference to absolute criteria of truth. Criticism can only be persuasive if it arises out of a dialogue which, in turn, is made possible by shared assumptions of discourse. The common discourse in this book is, tacitly, the social and intellectual history of the last 20 years. What emerges from Part 1, for instance, is that the slogans of contemporary experientialism have their roots in movements of ideas which surfaced vigorously in the United States of America in the early 1970s. The pre-history of these current international synonyms for independent study was contemporaneous in the United States with the essentially autonomous development of independent study within the School for Independent Study. The shared discourse in the following pages can only be fully grasped when the reader realizes that the positions described in Part 1 are logical extensions of the one strand of independent study which is analysed in the second chapter of Part 3 and which has gradually achieved dominant power during the sequence of political events described in Part 2.

I was privileged, as an undergraduate, to attend some 'practical criticism' seminars given by F. R. Leavis, first of all in a bare, desolate-seeming room in Downing College and then in the refuge of his home in Bulstrode Gardens, bulging with books and papers. In confrontation with a text, he insisted, criticism always could not be anything other than social and collaborative. It had to take the form of a dialogue in which one reader would say: 'This is so, isn't it?' and the other reader would refine the perception by affirming the grounds of agreement and then modifying: 'Yes, but . . .' This Part offers three vignettes about 'experiential learning'. I try to represent the three positions and then to intimate my reservations. This is my own initial 'Yes, but . . .' The whole book incorporates these small sketches into a larger canvas in which they are shown to be miniature manifestations of post-Enlightenment anti-rationalism which has had dire social consequences in the twentieth century. This text offers a personal response to social and intellectual developments in the form of a statement and asks for confirmation: 'This is so, isn't it?' The reader is asked not to ignore the question. He or she is asked to undertake the difficult task of formulating a 'Yes, but . . .' in reply.

(Readers will realize at the end of the book that this account of the form of its argument is meant to be consistent with the substantive position which is finally advanced. I share Alasdair MacIntyre's contention that a distinctive feature of contemporary society is that, in ethical matters, the problem is not just that we all disagree but that we do not agree on what would constitute the grounds on which agreement might be possible. Discussions of 'experiential learning' as a concept and whether any 'learning' can be said to have occurred by 'experiential learning' both seem to be what MacIntyre would call 'interminable' discussions. As will be clear from a reading of the Conclusion, I do not want to associate myself with MacIntyre's anti-democratic solution; instead I suggest that we need to work hard to preserve mechanisms which, through sustained dialogue, will safeguard the equal participation of all members of our society in its continuous self-construction. The content of the book leads to the suggestion that the registration process adopted by the BA/BSc by Independent Study might be a model for the institutional structure needed in our society. Equally, however, it is hoped that the book may open rather than close arguments in such a way that it will exemplify what it recommends.)

1

Experiential Learning

The first 'International Conference on Experiential Learning' took place at the end of June 1987, at Regent's College, London. Of the six conference organizers, two were staff of the School for Independent Study at NELP and three others had been in some contact with the work of the School.[1] This combination was an accident, but it indicates the School's willingness to be associated with the 'experiential learning' label. A key speaker was the Head of the School for Independent Study and one of the conference workshops was a visit to the School to observe its practice. Papers and workshops were organized around six main themes: 'Humanistic and wholistic approaches'; 'Student autonomy, non-traditional learners and independent study'; 'Assessment of prior experiential learning and accreditation'; 'Teaching methods'; 'Institutional responses'; and 'The Social Context'. Titles of papers included 'Experiential Learning and Group Process: approaches derived from dramatherapy'; 'Emerging approaches to inquiry and experiential learning'; 'Critical factors in facilitating learner autonomy in formal educational settings'; 'Experiential Learning at a Distance'; 'Learning Through Doing: introducing experiential learning methods into courses'; 'Facilitating Problem-based Learning'; 'Outdoor Activities and Experiential Learning: an orientation program for entering students'; 'Degree Credits, Academic Learning and Job Mobility for Adult Students through Field Experience' and 'Access Collaboration as a Source of Change in Higher Education'.

In short, 'experiential learning' now rivals, or has already ousted, 'independent study' as the most popular, overriding catch-all label for a range of progressive educational developments. The key to its successful terminological colonization is to be found in the short note which introduces the Call for Papers for the conference:

Rapid change in society demands innovation and change in the structures and practice of formal education to meet the needs of life-long learners. One major innovation has been the emergence of experiential learning. Although non-traditional adult learners have perhaps thrown into clear relief the limitations of traditional approaches to teaching and learning, the benefits to learners of all ages are immense. Programmes based on experiential learning bring about changes in both people and systems and these changes are influencing traditional practice in all fields of education.[2]

'Experiential learning' has shifted away from the simple educational recognition and accreditation of prior experience towards the prescription of educational practice which is itself based upon experiential principles. In the middle of the June international conference, the Learning Experience Trust, in association with the Experiential Learning Network, also organized a one-day national conference in London on the general theme: 'Prior Learning – how to identify it and assess it'. This conference was underwritten by the Further Education Unit whose Chief Officer, Jack Mansall, was also one of the speakers. This was the fourth successive national conference and it used an FEU document on 'Assessing Experiential Learning', prepared by Norman Evans with eight members of the Network.

Evans is a key figure in the English acculturation of experiential learning. A decade of writing and research has culminated in his appointment as Director of the Learning from Experience Trust. The establishment of this registered charity which has recently been grant-aided by the Department of Education and Science marks the attainment of institutional status by what previously had been a movement. The Trust has Sir Charles Carter as Chairman of a board of trustees which includes Dr Edwin Kerr, Sir Richard O'Brien, and the Rt Hon Shirley Williams as members. It has Regional Associates and both a National Associate and an Editorial Associate. As the first brochure isued by the Trust in November 1986 indicates:

> The idea of having Regional Associates is to provide reference/contact points in as many parts of the country as possible and to provide a connection with the Trust. This should be particularly important in providing a two-way flow of ideas about staff training, development projects and research, both from members in institutions to the Trust and vice versa.[3]

It is clear that this growing organization does not wish to become enmeshed in the diffuse confusion of the First International Conference. The brochure expressly disclaimed any association:

> Then I need to clear up any misunderstanding there may be about a pamphlet you may have received concerning the 'First International Conference on Experiential Learning'. The fact that it is being held at Regent's College has suggested to some people that this conference is something to do with the Learning from Experience Trust and myself. It is not. Nor is it something organized through the Network. Nor is it anything to do with CAEL in America. I knew nothing about it until I took premises for LET in Regent's College in September. The Trustees have taken this confusion very seriously – one received a pamphlet through the mail. At the last Trustees' meeting I was instructed to write

to the heads of institutions represented on the organizing group to clarify the status and standing of the proposed conference.

As you can see the Trust and the NELN are in the early stages of planning an extensive national and international programme and we will notify you of all events which we endorse and/or sponsor.[4]

The manifest organizational protectionism of this note reflects the Trust's awareness of the need to delimit precisely the connotations of the term 'experiential learning'. The proponents of an undefined independent study seem currently to have thrown in their lot with the exponents of an undefined experiential learning, but there was a time when the work of the School for Independent Study seemed to coincide in intention with the clearly defined understanding now adopted by the Learning from Experience Trust. That understanding is firmly based on the pioneering American work in the 1970s of the Council for the Advancement of Experiential Learning (CAEL).

A Jossey-Bass publication of 1976 by Morris T. Keeton and Associates – *Experiential Learning. Rationale, Characteristics, and Assessment* – provides a background to the American development:

By 1973, there had emerged a widespread movement toward the increased use of experiential learning to meet the needs of post-high school learners. The creation in 1971 of the Commission on Non-Traditional Study, headed by Samuel Gould, was testimony to the importance of this movement. In its conclusions, the Commission emphasized the need for development of sound assessment and credentialing practices and standards. The Cooperative Assessment of Experiential Learning (CAEL) was a direct response to this need.

CAEL was broached as an idea in August 1973 to an invitational meeting of individuals and representatives of institutions concerned with the need for action on recommendations of the Commission on Non-traditional Study. A smaller meeting in November brought together representatives of the Educational Testing Service, some innovating institutions of higher education, and some individuals influential in mainstream institutions of higher education to consider a specific proposal for what turned out to be the CAEL Project. This proposal, after modification, was funded by a grant from the Carnegie Corporation of New York. The organizing meeting for the project took place on March 3-4, 1974.[5]

In the next few years the project team produced working papers which included a survey of existing practices and a compendium of assessment methods, and theoretical papers were also commissioned which might deepen the understanding of the phenomenon of experiential learning whose practical implications were being explored and charted so rapidly. The focus of the activities of CAEL was resolutely on the problems and possibilities of assessing work and life experiences as equivalent to, and, hence, as grounds for exemption from, structured study within an educational institution.

Although Keeton's own contribution to the 1976 volume of theoretical papers anticipates the elision now current in England from the retrospective evaluation of prior learning experience to the prescription of experiential learning strategies, he was certain that it was the need to make evaluations which generated the CAEL project:

> The pendulum-swing back towards greater uses of extra-classroom experiential learning antedated CAEL. CAEL arose primarily because of the fact that experience is no guarantor of learning. . . . One must know what has been learned and what, among various modes of experiential learning, may in the future best be employed as strategies of learning.[6]

Another contributor – Melvin Tumin – affirmed that this emphasis was crucial. In doing so he clearly articulated a perception of the social context which made the recognition of valid prior learning experience such a moral imperative for the realization of an equal society:

> CAEL's emphasis on assessment of experiential learning can be interpreted as focusing precisely on this question of functionally equivalent achievement. Simply put, one rationale for trying experiential learning and assessing its outcomes is provided by the presence in American society of an academically alienated and an academically disadvantaged population in the midst of a largely academically oriented one, and by the fact that certification of academically equivalent achievement is indispensable for access to the middle and upper-class careers available in our society. If, therefore, we desire success for such people, and want to try to make life more richly available to them, then of course we must try to see what other forms of learning experiences can take the place of traditional forms.[7]

It must have been sentiments of this sort which attracted Norman Evans to the work of CAEL which he encountered for the first time in 1977:

> A colleague fell sick, so in 1977 I accompanied a group of Bishop Lonsdale students to Keene State University in New Hampshire as part of a student exchange that I had set up. Quite by chance, I noticed on someone's shelves a row of publications concerned with the assessment of experiential learning (learning acquired from work and life experience). . . . This was my introduction to the work of CAEL (the Council for the Advancement of Experiential Learning).[8]

In that year Evans ceased to be the Principal of British Lonsdale College of Education, Derby, where he had steered the institution through the post-James Report negotiations to new charitable status as the Derby Lonsdale College of Higher Education, and took up, instead, a post as Research Fellow at the Cambridge Institute of Education. He had originally served 10 years as Headmaster of Senacre Secondary School, Maidstone, one of Kent's Newsome experimental schools which had pioneered a Work Experience

Programme for 15 to 16 year olds in 1959, and his work enabled him to explore systematically the ways in which experiential learning might be acknowledged within the higher education system.

Evans's initial research was confined to issues raised by developments in teacher training. *Beginning Teaching in Professional Partnership* (1978) offers accounts of several schemes which were offered from 1966 onwards in colleges and universities as part of the initial course of training of teachers. Its main theme is that

> much can be done to develop an effective Induction Year for teachers in their first year of teaching without extensive special programmes and considerable additional resources.[9]

This was because there was a growing recognition of the similarity of the requirements for providing an induction year for beginning teachers and in-service training for others. Both kinds of provision should be grounded in professional experience in schools and, therefore, a 'training partnership' between schools and colleges and universities was essential. From 1977 until 1980 Evans undertook a preliminary evaluation of in-service B.Ed degrees financed by the Department of Education and Science. He was able to explore the problems and possibilities of a 'training partnership' through the detailed analysis of six case studies. *Preliminary Evaluation of the In-Service B.Ed Degree* (1981) concludes:

> The claim now made on the basis of evidence derived from the case studies is this: that a programme is effective as a contribution to further professional training to the extent that teachers are convinced it is based on their own store of knowledge, skills and experience. If it begins where they are, they are more likely to think about going somewhere else.[10]

This recommendation of experience-based professional training is the outcome of a straightforward evaluative enquiry still concerned only with the teaching profession, but Evans had already broadened his exploration. In 1980 he edited *Education Beyond School. Higher Education for a Changing Context*, which included contributions from Charles Carter, Harold Silver, George Tolley, Stephen Bragg and Sir Monty Finniston, all of whom considered ways in which higher education might become more responsive to the changing needs of industry and society. Evans's own introduction suggested that pressure might be brought to bear on institutions if the system of payment of tuition fees could be arranged so as to make the student more of a customer and less of a captive banker.[11] His conclusion argues that

> Ours is becoming a learning society. Bookshops and lists of titles from publishers, television and radio programmes and their ratings, do-it-yourself shops of every kind, travel agencies and their bookings; the dividing line between entertainment and learning is now almost impossible to draw. More individuals are wanting to know more about more

things; they are wanting to learn. Society's most precious resource for learning remains higher education. We need a better match between the two.[12]

It was this thesis that he elaborated in *The Knowledge Revolution. Making the Link between Learning and Work* (1981). The long fourth chapter of this book – 'Today's Students in the USA' – offers specific examples of the work of the American Council for Education (ACE) and of CAEL. Evans follows CAEL in emphasizing the importance of accrediting prior experiential learning. It is this orientation towards the assessment of prior learning as a basis for exemption from elements of institutional instruction which may effect a closer match between formal educational provision and society's educational demands:

> The main emphasis in this chapter has been on the development in the US of means of matching the provision of higher education to the conditions of adult life and simultaneously extending the service of higher education to its constituents and securing its own future. The case is made for the value of experiential learning for mature adults. There is just as strong a case to be made for younger students.[13]

Evans argues that the British higher education system must be much more amenable to open access for students – a development that would involve the introduction of sophisticated methods of establishing prior learning, which should be based on the expertise acquired by CAEL. 'Eligibility and entry to college or university is where the search for a better match has to begin', argues Evans, but he also contends that

> Extending the access is only the beginnings of an attempt to alter the perceptions: similar extensions must be made to the kinds of study available. Here experiential learning can be seen as a means of enriching the curriculum.[14]

Writing in 1981 in *The Knowledge Revolution,* Evans is prepared to give the label of 'independent study' to the range of curriculum developments which sponsor experiential learning within courses as an appropriate progression from prior, unsponsored, and exempting experiential learning:

> There are many ways that 'uncertified' knowledge can be used as a basis for further study and Independent Study can be a helpful compendium description of them all.[15]

Citing Percy and Ramsden (1980) Evans particularly commends the practices of the University of Lancaster and of North-East London Polytechnic in offering students opportunities to found their studies on their prior experience. His subsequent work, however, has concentrated much more, in the CAEL tradition, on methods of assessing prior learning.

In May 1983, the Further Education Unit published a project report – *Curriculum Opportunity – A map of experiential learning* – resulting from a study carried out on its behalf by Norman Evans and funded by the DES PICKUP programme. The Introduction offers a helpful clarification of terminology. Evans's brief was to present a 'map of experiential learning in entry requirements to higher and further education award-bearing courses' and the first paragraph of his opening review of the concept of experiential learning forcibly confirms this delimitation:

> For this project, experiential learning means the knowledge and skills acquired through life and work experience and study which are not formally attested through any educational or professional certification. It can include instruction based learning, provided by any institution, which has not been examined in any of the public examination systems. It can include those undervalued elements of formally provided education which are not encompassed by current examinations. It is a definition specially designed to identify a category of learning which can be included among others as evidence on which decisions can be taken for admission to award-bearing courses in further and higher education. It refers only to learning acquired according to the definition before entry to any course. It does not refer therefore to any form of experiential learning which comes from planned experience and is somehow assessed as part of a course by an education institution. It is not concerned with opportunities for using experience for participatory learning. It is concerned with opportunities for entering courses, and for gaining remission of study to shorten a course.[16]

In this paragraph the distinction is clear between the notions of 'prior learning' or 'unsponsored learning' and 'sponsored learning'. When the CNAA established a working group on Admission to consider how far its 1980 statement on the *Extension of access to higher education* was affecting the admissions policies of member institutions, it was natural that Norman Evans should be asked to undertake an investigation of institutional practices under the supervision of a Project Committee which met between April 1982 and September 1983.[17] The outcome was *Access to higher education: non-standard entry to CNAA first degree and DipHE courses* (1984) in which Evans again advocates that the British system should learn from American experience. The emphasis is still upon the need to make an assessment of prior learning, but he recommends that institutions should make that assessment in response to the presentations made by students themselves of their own credentials:

> The theory and practice of the assessment of experiential learning in the USA is highly instructive, whatever the differences between the two systems. There it is found effective to ask prospective students to prepare a fully documented learning autobiography which includes, alongside a record of formal education and any qualifications gained, an account of all other learning, showing how it was acquired. This can be supported by whatever evidence the candidate thinks pertinent. Written work and artefacts drawn from employment, voluntary work or

home-making, references for verification – all can go into a portfolio for consideration by admissions tutors.[18]

There is certainly the sense that affective learning is to be given due consideration as much as cognitive learning. Evans had raised this issue in the introduction to *Curriculum Opportunity:*

> Everyone's learning includes affective as well as cognitive learning. The assessment of experiential learning raises questions about both. Just as it is difficult to think of any learning which does not have an experiential element, so it is difficult to think of any learning which is not a mixture of the cognitive and the affective. The assessment of what has been learned from experience focuses attention on affective learning because of the nature of experience itself. So attempts to assess experiential learning will tend to pay more attention to affective knowledge than is commonly done in assessments of classroom learning.[19]

But if learning itself is experiential, the 'assessment' of experiential learning becomes a charade because it is tautological. Evans asserts in the concluding paragraph to *Curriculum Opportunity*'s first chapter that

> It is important to distinguish between experience and learning. Learning is under consideration; not any experience which may have generated learning. Without that distinction, discussion about experiential learning is confused.[20]

However, in claiming that all learning is a combination of affective and cognitive learning and that the assessment of prior experiential learning is necessarily an assessment of the affective component of whole learning which has hitherto been neglected, Evans undercuts the view originally expressed by Tumin in 1976 that the attempt to assess experiential learning must only be an attempt to establish the equivalence of unsponsored learning as a basis for progression through a system of sponsored, non-experiential learning. In spite of Evans's insistence on a distinction between experience and learning, it appears, nevertheless, that his agenda includes the transformation of structured educational experience:

> Those who are worried by, if not downright suspicious of, the concept of the assessment of experiential learning can argue that experience is not an acceptable academic criteria for admission to courses. They then tend to assume that is the end of the matter, that they have demolished the case for the academic assessment of the experiential learning. They have done nothing of the kind. They have simply not accepted that it is the learning from experience which matters, not the experience itself. That distinction between experience and what has been learned through experience is the beginning of the matter for experiential learning. Thus, to set out to assess experiential learning is to begin to reassess education itself.[21]

To take this approach is to discard the productive evaluation of the equivalence of prior learning and, instead, to enter the minefield of sponsored experiential learning. That is the arena of terminological confusion which has now been appropriated by the First International Conference of Experiential Learning. Much of that confusion has been engendered by the confluence of the CAEL stream of experiential learning with a different stream which has developed contemporaneously in management training. 'Self-managed learning' is currently regarded as synonymous with 'independent study' as much as is 'experiential learning'.

Notes

1 Dave O'Reilly and Colin Mably (SIS); Ed. Rosen who is an external examiner on the DipHE; Susan Weil who has done research on student expectations at SIS; and Eric Wilcocks, Dean of Antioch University in London who has had long connections with SIS and NELP.
2 The First International Conference on Experiential Learning to be held at Regent's College, Regent's Park, London, England, 18-25 June 1987, Call for Papers, Experiential Learning: an International Perspective.
3 Letter from Norman Evans, Director, Learning from Experience Trust, to Members of the National Experiential Learning Network, 26 November 1986, p. 1.
4 ibid. p. 3.
5 M. T. Keeton and Associates, *Experiential Learning. Rationale, Characteristics, and Assessment,* Jossey-Bass, London, San Francisco, Washington, 1976, p. xvi.
6 ibid. p. 4.
7 ibid. p. 43.
8 N. Evans, *The Knowledge Revolution. Making the link between learning and work,* Grant McIntyre, 1981, p. vii.
9 N. Evans, *Beginning Teaching in Professional Partnership,* Hodder & Stoughton, 1978, p. 1.
10 N. Evans, *Preliminary Evaluation of the In-Service B.Ed Degree, with particular reference to further professional training,* NFER-Nelson, 1981, p. 158.
11 N. Evans (ed.) *Education Beyond School. Higher Education for a Changing Context,* Grant McIntyre, 1980, p. 12.
12 ibid. p. 249.
13 N. Evans, *The Knowledge Revolution,* op. cit. p. 94.
14 ibid. p. 103.
15 ibid. p. 138.
16 N. Evans, *Curriculum Opportunity. A map of experiential learning in entry requirements to higher and further education award bearing courses,* Further Education Unit, 1983, p. 5.
17 The Project Committee under the chairmanship of Mr P. Toyne comprised Prof. J. H. Calderwood; Mr L. J. Herbst; Mr J. Stephenson (SIS, NELP); Mr R. Waterhouse; and Mr W. J. Callaway.
18 N. Evans, *Access to higher education: non-standard entry to CNAA first degree and DipHE courses,* CNAA Development Services Publication 6, 1984, p. 17.
19 N. Evans, *Curriculum Opportunity,* op. cit. p. 7.
20 ibid. p. 9.
21 ibid. p. 9.

2

Self-Managed Learning

In January 1976, a monograph on 'Experiential Learning' by a lecturer in Management at Sheffield City Polytechnic – Tom Boydell – was published as one of a series of publications on aspects of Adult Education by the Department of Adult and Higher Education of the University of Manchester. Boydell began by admitting that the meaning of the term was confused:

> A few months ago, I ran a seminar on 'experiential leaning', which I introduced by saying that I wasn't sure what experiential learning is. This is still reasonably true, whilst I am attempting to write this monograph, not, I hope, because I don't know anything about the subject, but because the more I look into it the more I find that different people seem to take the phrase to have different meanings.[1]

The confusion which he had witnessed bore no relation to the contemporary American concern to recognize and accredit unsponsored learning. It was a confusion which seemed confined to what might be meant by the process of sponsored, experiential learning. Boydell found that when management teachers or trainers were asked what they meant when they said that they used 'an experiential approach', they offered a variety of answers:

> Some say that actually they teach from a certain book; others talk about non-directive methods, the use of structured exercises, participative approaches, action learning, the use of projects, discovery learning, games and simulations, substitute-task exercises, learning communities, the non-use of lectures.[2]

The purpose of Boydell's monograph, therefore, was to explore some of the concepts used in learning theory so as to distinguish clearly the significance of 'experiential learning' as practised in management education. This exploration followed closely Ausubel's[3] distinction between 'rote' and 'meaningful' learning and, more particularly, between 'expository' and 'discovery' learning. In the former, according to Ausubel, 'the entire content of what is to be learned is presented to the learner, in its final form', whereas in the latter 'the principal content of what is to be learned is not given but must be discovered by the learner'.[4] Within this dualistic framework, Boydell works towards a placement of 'experiential learning' within the general category of 'meaningful-discovery' learning types. He argues that all the techniques subsumed under the heading of 'experiential learning' have two features in common:

(i)   they lead to meaningful learning and
(ii) this learning is achieved by the learner sorting things out for himself – i.e. he restructures his perceptual experiences and hence gains insight, or learning.[5]

Boydell quotes from an article of 1970 by A. W. Wight in which 'experiential learning' is defined in terms of a model

> which begins with the experience followed by *reflection, discussion, analysis* and *evaluation* of the experience. The assumption is that we seldom learn from experience unless we assess the experience, assigning our own meaning in terms of our own goals, aims, ambitions and expectations.[6]

This insistence that experience only becomes learning if an assessment takes place of what has been learned from experience would seem to be in accord with the position advanced by Morris Keeton and his colleagues in emphasizing the need to evaluate prior learning in order to assign credit and allocate exemption. There is, however, a crucial difference which, in the last decade, has disengaged 'self-managed learning' from 'experiential learning' as represented by the Council for the Advancement of Experiential Learning and its putative British counterpart – the Learning from Experience Trust. Boydell accentuated the crucial difference at once:

> The key here, to me, is the process of assigning our own meaning; from this process, Wight continues, comes
>   . . .the *insights,* the *discoveries,* and *understanding.* The pieces fall into place, and the experience takes on added meaning in relation to other experiences. All this is then *conceptualized, synthesized* and *integrated* into the individual's system of constructs which he imposes on the world, through which he views, perceives, categorizes, evaluates and seeks experience.[7]

CAEL recognized that there was a social need to establish mechanisms whereby unsponsored experiential learning might be objectively assessed and accredited, whereas the understanding of 'experiential learning' adopted by Boydell tends towards a personal evaluation of learning in which the principal criterion of value is that learning's contribution to self-development. Boydell extends his analysis by distinguishing between different 'meaningful-discovery' types. He considers the application of Gestalt-Insight Theories, then claims that 'Autonomous Learning Theory/Strategy' adds to the Gestalt model by adopting a phenomenological approach which stresses that all perceptions are relative, and are dependent on the individual, his goals, self-image, feelings etc.[8]

It follows from this that

Autonomous learning is closely allied to self-actualization.[9]

'Self-actualization' was Maslow's term, but Boydell mentions the terms used by a range of other, primarily American, social psychologists to suggest the same emphasis: 'fully functioning person' (Rogers, 1961);[10] 'adequate personality' (Combs, 1962);[11] 'fully functioning self' (Kelley, 1962);[12] 'self-actualization' and 'maturity' (Argyris, 1957);[13] 'creative becoming' (Allport, 1955);[14] and, again, 'self-actualization' (Wexler, 1974).[15] The states of being which are thus given authoritative status by the conceptualizations of experts can be realized in three different approaches. Boydell first recommends 'The Learning Community Approach' and then the process of 'learning from one's everyday experiences'. The third type of experiential learning takes the autonomous learning strategy a stage further. This can be done

by becoming wholly real-problem oriented, to the extent that the learning takes place at the manager's job.[16]

The target of Boydell's exposition of learning theories is still the management training practitioner, but already there is a hint of a wider application. Boydell recounts that some critics of the 'Learning Community Approach' tell him that all he is after is self-actualization whereas they are interested in professional competence, and he admits that

Here all I can say is that I see no real difference between self-actualization and professional competence.[17]

The key to managerial competence is the capacity to manage other people, which is dependent on possessing the capacity to manage oneself. This position is sustained within the management context in *A Manager's Guide to Self-Development* (1978), collaboratively produced by Boydell and Mike Pedler and John Burgoyne. This book is introduced as 'an aid to management self-development' and it asserts that it is based on the simple fundamental premise

that any effective system for management development must increase the manager's capacity and willingness to take control over and responsibility for events, and particularly for himself and his own learning.[18]

It offers a range of hints and exercises for the use of managers themselves. Part I, for instance, devoted to 'Setting and meeting goals for management self-development', has chapters which present a 'life planning activity', 'some ideas about management and the qualities of successful managers' and guidance for 'assessing yourself and setting some goals for self-development'. Many of these notes of guidance had already been adopted more generally in the Planning Period which constituted the first term of the

Diploma of Higher Education course at NELP in the autumn of 1974. The language used by the authors in introducing readers to how their book should be used is similar to that used by the staff of the School for Independent Study in helping all students to embark upon the process of planning their own programmes of study:

> If you are interested in having a go at this self-development programme you will need first to take some time thinking about where you are now and where you want to be in terms of work and career activities, in thinking about the skills you have and those you need to develop, and in working out learning goals and planning a personal learning programme.[19]

In the mid-1970s the practitioners of independent study at NELP judiciously used management techniques and procedures for their own educational purposes. Self-development was a means to an end in which students would be able to articulate independently what they needed to learn, but, by the end of the decade, the means was well set on the path to becoming an end in itself. The fluctuating relationship between 'independent study' and 'self-managed learning' at NELP is discussed in detail in a later chapter, but the stages by which 'independent study' and 'self-managed learning' have come to be regarded as synonymous in the national context can be indicated by the progression in the work with which Boydell has been associated. The publication of *Management Self-development. Concepts and practices*, edited by Boydell and Pedler, in 1981 marks the point at which the commitment to 'self-development' threw off the constraints of an exclusively 'management' ethos. The editors interestingly indicate in their own preface the process of self-development which had led them away from blinkered 'training' formulae:

> Approximately ten years ago we were both heavily involved in a 'systematic' approach to management education. This involved us in taking great pains to identify the needs of our 'target population', specify behavioural objectives for them, plan teaching activities, devise objective tests, and so on.
>
> Gradually, however, for reasons we didn't fully understand, we became dissatisfied with all this trainer-centred activity, which treated the learners as cohorts of homogeneous passivity. Together with one or two close colleagues, we moved into what we dubbed a 'learning community' approach . . .[20]

To judge by the dates of publications this transition was taking place between 1976 and 1978. *Management Self-development* is the product of work during the 1978 to 1980 period which consolidated this transition. As Boydell and Pedler themselves put it:

> We gradually became aware that our new approach was, perhaps, part of something much wider – that some of the underlying ideas could find

other forms of practical expression. It seemed that a useful generic title for this wider field was 'self-development', and hence we started to use the term and to play with (i.e. think about) the concept. In so doing we were involved in the preparation of a programme of structured activities for self-development (Pedler *et al.*, 1978), a brief overview of a number of approaches (Burgoyne *et al.*, 1978), and an annotated bibliography (Boydell and Pedler, 1979). Thus we encountered a number of attractive people and their work, and we felt it would be helpful to bring them together.[21]

The grounds for inclusion of articles in this volume, therefore, were that contributors were actively involved in 'self-development' practices and were in a position to make comments which might assist in determining the nature of 'self-development'. Some of the titles of contributions reflect synonyms for 'independent study' which are in common usage and which can be clustered under the label of 'self-managed learning', although this term itself has diminishing currency. In particular, for instance, there is a contribution from Reg Revans in which he discusses 'Action learning and the development of the self' and another contribution from John Heron on 'Self and peer assessment'.

Revans's work in management education gained significant publicity in 1977 as a result of the adoption by GEC of an action learning programme. One of the essential characteristics of the approach outlined by Revans in Casey and Pearce's account of the events at GEC was that

> In action learning the majority of time is given both to diagnosing in the field what the problem may be (so challenging the value systems of those caught up in it) and to applying any solutions to the problem that may be suggested (so challenging the validity of such proposals.) In traditional programmes held away from the field, diagnosis is generally assumed and application necessarily ignored.[22]

This formulation was wholly compatible with the 'action-oriented' and 'problem-centred' approach of independent study at NELP in the mid-1970s, but Revans's 1981 contribution to *Management Self-development* goes further and is in alliance with the experiential tendency in which independent study has also became enmeshed:

> There is a distinction between verbal acquaintance with something (such as correctly stating the height of the world pole vault record) and realizing something, in whole or in part, at some specific here-and-now (such as getting within ten centimetres of that record while a brass band is playing on August Bank Holiday, 1980, at Wath-on-Dearne). If the distinction is overlooked or ignored – as it often is in a culture such as ours, whose literate bureaucracy is paid more for writing letters about jet engines than are its engineers for making them – we may fall into serious error.[23]

Similarly, John Heron describes his own commitment to enabling students to acquire 'self-determining competence' – dating back to his *The Concept of a Peer Learning Community* of 1974,[24] in terms which have affinities with the rationale for independent study adopted by the School for Independent Study at about the same date:

> I have long argued . . . that an educated person is an aware, self-determining person, in the sense of being able to set objectives, to formulate standards of excellence for the work that realizes these objectives, to assess work done in the light of those standards, and to be able to modify the objectives, the standards or the work programme in the light of experience and action, and all this in discussion and consultation with other relevant persons.[25]

But the willingness to acquiesce in a process in which 'objectives' and 'standards' are continuously modified 'in the light of experience and action' betrays an experientialism which had originally been latent and is now rampant.

If the notion of 'independent study' has been hijacked by various versions of experientialism, some of which are represented in *Management Self-development*, the editors' opening chapter on 'What is self-development?' offers a discussion of the issues which provides clarifying categories as usefully as did Boydell's 1976 exposition of 'Experiential Learning'. Boydell and Pedler now realize that the introduction of 'self-actualization' as a goal of experiential learning confused the discreet spheres of 'learning' and 'development'. A distinction between 'of-self' and 'by-self' helps them towards this tentative conclusion. Reflecting, perhaps, on the 1976 Boydell article, the editors write:

> Earlier it seemed clear that when people were talking about self-improvement à la Dale Carnegie or self-actualization after Maslow, then they were primarily concerned with the *of* self dimension which construes self-development as a goal or a series of ascending goals. On the other hand there are in common usage several meanings which have to do with development *by* self, e.g. learning without a teacher; independent study; distance learning and the learner taking responsibility for making decisions at all stages of the learning process. In these meanings, the term refers primarily to a process rather than a goal.[26]

In these terms, the NELP independent study of the mid-1970s was a 'by-self' process. However, Boydell and Pedler argue from their experience of 'learning communities' that 'by-self' processes have 'of-self' implications and they assert that

> Once people question the traditional stereotypes of teacher and learner, once they have experimented with new forms, there can be no simple going back.[27]

In moving relentlessly forward towards an acceptance of all 'of-self' implications, however, Boydell and Pedler usefully jettison the 'learning' claims of experientialism. The distinction between 'of-self' and 'by-self' which they found difficult to sustain only arose because they had falsely been talking about 'learning' when they should have been talking about 'development', and they continue:

> To distinguish briefly between the two . . . we may say that learning has more to do with the incremental acquisition of knowledge, skills and abilities than with the qualitative transformational progression of the whole person. It is in this sense of *learning* – i.e. as not normally affecting/transforming the self – that the by-self/of-self dichotomy stands proud and easily seen. With the concept of *development* the dichotomy does not stand: development by self implies an of-self dimension; development of-self implies the active by-self agency. (Or does it? Can the self be developed in a non-self responsible way?)[28]

It follows from this that practices developed in the field of management education and training which had, by the early 1980s, made substantial inroads into mainstream education should now be applied beyond the constricting context of educational institutions, where students still tend to be required to acquire some 'not-self' learning. At the beginning of their own contribution to *Management Self-development*, Boydell and Pedler had commented that it

> now seems uncomfortably constraining to limit the concepts of development and self-development to the field of management education. These ideas belong to all people everywhere and not just to managers.[29]

A fortiori it has become constraining to limit these concepts to formal teaching/learning situations and, hence, Pedler and Boydell's Fontana paperback: *Managing Yourself* (1985) in which, they claim, their fundamental assumption is

> that anyone who wants to improve the way they manage others must first learn to manage themselves. If we can create order in ourselves then we have taken the first step to creating order amongst others and in the environment in which we work. Thus, we need to learn to manage from the inside out, starting with managing yourself (i.e. *managing me*) and then moving out to managing the people and world around us.[30]

In so far as this is a managerial or an entrepreneurial society, the self-developmental extension of 'self-managed learning' can lay claims to being its appropriate form of 'humanities' learning. Independent study is now caught up in this process of extravagant appropriation. If Boydell is right, however, in showing that the logic of his exploration in the last decade of experiential learning must lead, in the end, to a choice between experience or development and learning, then the School for Independent Study's titular attachment to the notion of 'study' should prove an embarrassment to those supporters of 'independent study' who have followed a similar intellectual route.

Notes

1 T. Boydell, *Experiential Learning*, Manchester Monographs, 5, 1976, p. 1.
2 ibid. p. 1. Boydell comments that the 'certain book' is usually D. A. Kolb, I. M. Rubin and J. M. McIntyre, *Organisational Psychology: An Experiential Approach*, Prentice-Hall, 1971, or H. R. Knudson, R. T. Woodworth and C. H. Bell, *Management: An Experiential Approach*, McGraw-Hill, 1973.
3 See D. P. Ausubel: 'In defence of verbal learning', in *Education Theory*, II, pp. 15-25, 1961, and D. P. Ausubel, *Educational Psychology: A Cognitive View*, Holt, Rinehart, Winston, 1968.
4 Ausubel, op. cit. p. 22, quoted in Boydell, op. cit. p. 5.
5 Boydell, op. cit. p. 17.
6 A. W. Wight, 'Participative Education and the Inevitable Revolution', in *Journal of Creative Behaviour*, 4, pp. 234-82, 1970, quoted in Boydell, op. cit. p. 17.
7 Boydell, op. cit. p. 17. The quotation is from A. W. Wight, op. cit.
8 Boydell, op. cit. p. 38.
9 ibid. p. 39.
10 C. R. Rogers, *On Becoming a Person*, Houghton-Mifflin, 1961.
11 A. W. Combs, 'A Perceptual View of the Adequate Personality', in Association for Supervision and Curriculum Development: *Perceiving, Behaving, Becoming*, 1962.
12 E. Kelley, 'The Fully Functioning Self', in *Perceiving, Behaving, Becoming*, op. cit.
13 C. Argyris, *Personality and Organization*, Harper & Row, 1957.
14 G. W. Allport, *Becoming: Basic Considerations for a Psychology of Personality*, Yale U.P., 1955.
15 D. A. Wexler, 'A Cognitive Theory of Experiencing Self-Actualisation and Therapeutic Process', in D. A. Wexler and L. N. Rice (eds), *Innovations in Client-Centred Therapy*, Wiley, 1974.
16 Boydell, op. cit. p. 67.
17 ibid. p. 64.
18 M. Pedler, J. Burgoyne and T. Boydell. *A Manager's Guide to Self-Development*. McGraw-Hill. 1987. p. 1.
19 ibid. p. 4.
20 T. Boydell and M. Pedler (eds), *Management Self-development. Concepts and practices*, Gower, 1981, p. vii.
21 ibid. p. vii.
22 D. Casey and D. Pearce (eds), *More than Management Development. Action Learning at G.E.C.*, Gower, 1977, p. 3.
23 Boydell and Pedler, op. cit. p. 209.
24. J. Heron, *The Concept of a Peer Learning Community*, University of Surrey, Human Potential Research Project, 1974.
25 Boydell and Pedler, op. cit. p. 112.
26 ibid. p. 7.
27 ibid. p. 7.
28 ibid. p. 8.
29 ibid. p. 6.
30 M. Pedler and T. Boydell, *Managing Yourself*, Fontana/Collins, 1985, p. 11.

3

Contract Learning

It is significant that Tom Boydell's monograph on 'Experiential Learning' of 1976 was published by the Department of Adult and Higher Education of the University of Manchester in a series of publications on aspects of Adult Education. In the last decade, 'experiential learning' and 'contract learning' have both come to be regarded as particularly appropriate for adult learners. This point was made to the School for Independent Study in the mid-1970s when it became clear that a large number of applicants to the DipHE course were in the CNAA 'mature student' category, but the School resisted identification as an 'adult education' course on the grounds that this would reduce its potential impact on conventional higher education practice. There is no longer any grounds for fearing such marginalization and, indeed, by contrast, an ideology of adult education is now beginning to influence all educational practice in ways which are in accord with independent study. In the United States one man – Malcolm Knowles – is the doyen of the adult education movement, and the background to the changing influence of that movement can be traced by reference to the development of his career and thinking.

Knowles offers an account of this development in the introductory chapter of *Andragogy in Action. Applying Modern Principles of Adult Learning* (1984), entitled 'The Art and Science of Helping Adults Learn'. He tells how he became director of adult education at the Central YMCA in Chicago in 1946 and how the experience he gained there led to his first book, published in 1950, under the title of *Informal Adult Education*. He remarks of the title that he

> had been trying to identify the essence of adult education, the thing that made it different from traditional education; and the best I could come up with was 'informal'. I still had not developed a comprehensive, coherent, integrated theory. But it was a step in that direction.[1]

There is an element of post hoc rationalization here, because the historical evidence would seem to suggest that Knowles first experienced the need to differentiate adult education from 'mainstream' higher education in order to sustain the existence of the adult education movement and that he only secondarily developed a coherent theory as part of a process of legitimization. In 1951, for instance, he became executive director of the newly formed Adult Education Association of the USA and the knowledge gained in this post informed his account of *The Adult Education Movement in the United States* (1962). As the preface to this book indicates, the years in which he held the post of executive director (1951-9) also provided him with ample evidence of a disorganized adult education movement. He writes:

> this writer shared intimately both the hopes and frustrations of those who were seeking to bring some sort of order out of the adult educational chaos.[2]

The way out of this chaos, he argued, was to find a distinctive social function for adult education. Knowles's historical account in which he describes the 'emergence of institutions for the education of adults' and the 'shaping of a field of adult education' is redolent of a desire that the movement should become firmly institutionalized and should receive proper recognition.

The third part of the book – 'The nature and future of the Adult Education Movement' – moves from history to manifesto. The historical argument is that as differences between the learning needs of youth and adults became increasingly recognized

> the programs offered to adults tended to be constructed less and less on the basis of traditional academic principles of subject organization and more and more on the basis of the problems of individuals and of society; and even in the traditional educational institutions the curriculum for adults burst out of the academic boundaries. New institutional forms were created, including the continuing education center, the training laboratory, the community college, the coordinated course, the college of general studies, and others, in order to better fit the needs of adult learners. The methodology of adult education tended to move away from traditional classroom methods in favour of methods that would make greater use of the experience of the adult learners, such as group discussion, role playing, case method, book-based discussion, the unstructured group method, and various combinations of methods in workshops, conferences, and institutes. By 1960 adult education had become quite different from youth education in both form and substance.[3]

Nevertheless Knowles realized that adult education would remain peripheral – 'doomed to advance only in the technology of meeting ephemeral needs and remedying gaps in the existing equipment of adults'[4] – if there were no concurrent changes in youth education. Adult education would only be able to play a full part in a system of 'life-long' education if youth education reduced its pre-emptive commitment to the view that the function of education is to transmit culture from one generation to the next. The argument of the manifesto, therefore, was that there was one central challenge before the modern adult education movement. According to Knowles, the movement must educate adults about the new meaning of education, and especially it must help the educators of youth to re-examine the effects of what they do in the schools on the quality of the learning their children engage in when they become adults. The highest priority subject matter for adult education in the immediate future is education about education. If that succeeds, then all education would become unified into a 'lifelong education movement'.[5]

It would seem that it was only after this campaign platform had been identified that Knowles gave serious attention to the development of a supporting theory. An opportunity presented itself when he was invited, in 1960, to Boston University to start a new graduate programme in adult education. As he remarks of that appointment in his 1984 retrospect:

During the next fourteen years, I had a laboratory where I could apply principles of adult learning in a university setting. . . . During this period a theoretical framework regarding adult learning evolved.[6]

He picked up the label of 'andragogy' from a friend in 1967 and, since it made sense to him 'to have a differentiating label', he started using the term in 1968, notably in an article which appeared in 'Adult Leadership' in April of that year entitled 'Andragogy, Not Pedagogy!'[7] A year later he gave the new term greater currency in a survey which he was commissioned to undertake on *Higher Adult Education in the United States. The Current Picture, Trends, and Issues.* There he offered the following explanation:

Derived from the stem of the Greek word for mature male, *Aher (Andros)*, this label distinguishes the study of adult learning and teaching from the study of youth learning and teaching symbolized by the label *pedagogy*. There is developing, accordingly, a coherent and comprehensive theory of adult learning and a differentiated technology of adult education.[8]

Writing in 1984, Knowles claims that Houle's *The Inquiring Mind* (1961) stimulated a great deal of research by adult educators into the unique characteristics of adults as learners, but that this research was rapidly supplemented by findings from other fields of enquiry. He cites the work of specific clinical psychologists and psychiatrists, developmental psychologists, social psychologists, and sociologists to substantiate the view that

Clearly, by 1970 – and certainly by 1980 – there was a substantial enough body of knowledge about adult learners and their learning to warrant attempts to organize it into a systematic framework of assumptions, principles, and strategies. This is what andragogy sets out to do.[9]

And this was what *The Modern Practice of Adult Education* set out to do in 1970. An extract from this book – 'Andragogy: An Emerging Technology for Adult Learning' – is reprinted in Volume I of the Open University reader, *Education for Adults* (1983), edited by Malcolm Tight. Within the same collection is an account by John Stephenson of the practice of the School for Independent Study.[10] The similarity between the tenets of andragogy and the assumptions of independent study is striking. Knowles first gives a general account of the assumptions about the characteristics of adult learners upon which andragogy is based which differentiate it from those assumptions about child learners upon which pedagogy is based. He lists four. As a person matures:

> 1) his self-concept moves from one of being a dependent personality toward one of being a self-directing human being; 2) he accumulates a growing reservoir of experience that becomes an increasing resource for learning; 3) his readiness to learn becomes oriented increasingly to the developmental tasks of his social roles; and 4) his time perspective changes from one of postponed application of knowledge to immediacy of application, and accordingly his orientation toward learning shifts from one of subject-centeredness to one of problem-centeredness.[11]

He then elaborates the distinction between andragogy and pedagogy in relation to each of these categories. A selection of his instances with respect to the first category – differences of 'self-concept' – clearly indicates the strong unison that currently exists in the descriptive languages of 'experiential learning', 'self-managed learning' and 'andragogy'. The selection also suggests how readily 'andragogy' can seem to be in accord with 'independent study'.

Knowles differentiates between andragogy and pedagogy in respect of their different diagnoses of the needs of learners:

> The adult's self-concept of self-directivity is in direct conflict with the traditional practice of the teacher telling the student what he needs to learn . . . In andragogy, therefore, great emphasis is placed on the involvement of adult learners in a process of *self-diagnosis* of needs for learning.[12]

Similarly, he differentiates in relation to the 'planning process':

> Teachers of adults who do all the planning for their students, who come into the classroom and impose preplanned activities on them, typically experience apathy, resentment, and probably withdrawal. For the imposition of the will of the teacher is incongruent with the adult's self-concept of self-directivity.[13]

and, again, in relation to the conduct of 'learning experiences':

> In traditional pedagogical practice the function of the teacher is defined as 'to teach' . . . In contrast, andragogical practice treats the learning-teaching transaction as the mutual responsibility of learners and teacher.[14]

or, finally, by way of example, Knowles distinguishes between the pedagogical and the andragogical attitudes towards assessment:

Probably the crowning instance of incongruity between traditional educational practice and the adult's self-concept of self-directivity is the act of a teacher giving a grade to a student. Nothing makes an adult feel more childlike than being judged by another adult; it is the ultimate sign of disrespect and dependency, as the one who is being judged experiences it.

For this reason, andragogical theory prescribes a process of self-evaluation, in which the teacher devotes his energy to helping the adults get evidence for themselves about the progress they are making toward their educational goals.[15]

As we have seen, these recommended practices and attitudes to be adopted in the 'teaching' of adults are introduced by Knowles on the authority, so he claims, of at least 20 years of research into the specific learning needs of adults. Knowles's work stimulated the research of Allen Tough in Canada, which is described in his contribution, 'Self-planned learning and major personal change', to Malcolm Tight's collection of essays, and the andragogical approach has been particularly influential in the work of the Nottingham group in the UK, whose work is represented in the collection by Paula Allman's 'The Nature and Process of Adult Development'. Her research has been refreshingly critical, but it remains difficult to avoid the suspicion that the supposed learning peculiarities of adults have been appropriated in the service of a larger educational campaign in the United States. The social psychological 'evidence' for andragogy and andragogical practice have been mutually reinforcing in support of an inter-personal counter-culture.

The evidence from Knowles's writings is sufficient to suggest that the needs of adults only offer pseudo-authority for the experiential practices which he advocates. At the time when he was advancing the notion of andragogy, Knowles was already recommending implicitly andragogical principles for adoption at all levels by learners of all ages. He wrote in 1969:

If it is true that the time span of major cultural change is now less than the lifetime of a human being, the needs of society and of individuals can no longer be served by education that merely transmits knowledge and is concentrated in the years of youth. *The new world requires a new purpose for education – the development of a capacity in each individual to learn, to change, to create a new culture throughout his life span.* The central mission of elementary, secondary, and collegiate education must become, then, not teaching youth what they need to know but teaching them how to learn what is not yet known. The substance of youth education, therefore, becomes process; the process of learning and the substance of adult education becomes content – the content of man's continually expanding knowledge.[16]

Invoking the support of A. N. Whitehead, Knowles made the same point in his reprinted contribution to *Education for Adults* , but, here, he is overtly hostile to pedagogy:

Another problem with pedagogy is that it is premised on an archaic conception of the purpose of education, namely, the transmittal of knowledge. As Alfred North Whitehead pointed out a generation ago, it was functional to define education as a process of transmittal of what is known so long as it was true that the time-span of major cultural change was greater than the life-span of individuals.[17]

With amazing ingenuousness Knowles finally exposes in 1984 the spuriousness of the authority for andragogy to be found in developmental psychology. He describes the way in which his 1970 book – *The Modern Practice of Adult Education* – was originally subtitled *Andragogy Versus Pedagogy* and he continues:

> The 'versus' was in the title because at that point I saw the two models, pedagogy and andragogy, as dichotomous – one for children, the other for adults. During the next ten years, however, a number of teachers in elementary, secondary, and higher education who had somehow been exposed to the andragogical model told me that they had experimented with applying (or adapting) the model in their practice and had found that young people learned better, too, when the andragogical model was applied. On the other hand, many teachers and trainers working with adults cited circumstances – especially in basic skills training – where the pedagogical model seemed to be required. So the revised edition of the book, published in 1980, had the subtitle *From Pedagogy to Andragogy*.[18]

The alteration to the subtitle seems an inadequate response to information which potentially demolishes the andragogical edifice. For the proper deduction from the information would seem to be that different teaching methods are appropriate for different kinds of learning irrespective of the developmental stage of the learners. The inescapable logic for the practitioners of independent study must then be that a close identification of independent study with the andragogical approach must limit the scope of possible study.

Notes

1 M. S. Knowles and Associates, *Andragogy in Action. Applying Modern Principles of Adult Learning*, Jossey-Bass, 1984, p. 4.
2 M. S. Knowles, *The Adult Education Movement in the United States*, Holt, Rinehart & Winston, 1962, p. vii.
3 ibid. p. 255.
4 ibid. p. 279.
5 ibid. p. 280.
6 Knowles, 1984 op. cit.
7 M. S. Knowles, 'Andragogy, Not Pedagogy!', in *Adult Leadership* 16 (April 1968), pp. 350-86.
8 M. S. Knowles, *Higher Adult Education in the United States. The Current Picture, Trends, and Issues*, 1969, p. 28.

9 Knowles, 1984 op. cit. p. 6.

10 This is a reprint of Stephenson's 'Higher Education: School for Independent Study' which had been first published in T. Burgess and E. Adams, *Outcomes of Education*, Macmillan, 1980.

11 M. Tight (ed.), *Education for Adults*, Vol. 1, *Adult Learning and Education*, Croom Helm in association with The Open University, 1983, p. 55.

12 ibid. p. 58.

13 ibid. p. 58.

14 ibid. p. 59.

15 ibid. p. 59.

16 Knowles, 1969 op. cit. p. 23.

17 Tight (ed.), op. cit. p. 53.

18 Knowles, 1984 op. cit. p. 6.

Part 2

The Innovation

Part 2 is, I think, unproblematic. If Part 1's critique of versions of experientialism has aroused the question: 'What, then, was the "independent study" which developed at North-East London Polytechnic?', Part 2 tries to give a factual, chronological account of what has happened since 1970. The account works from documents. The scope of the discussion is deliberately and narrowly circumscribed. The first chapter indicated that the earliest proponents of the DipHE saw the development of that course as more than simply a course development like thousands of others which were being designed within polytechnics in the early 1970s. They saw the development of that one course as part of a national campaign to transform our higher education system. It is important to clarify the intended significance of the course in order to justify the concentrated attention on small details of curriculum innovation in the following chapters. The progress of the ideas of educational reform which first stimulated the DipHE, however, is analysed in detail in the first chapter of Part 3.

These four following chapters recount a simple story. At the outset a small pressure group of staff within NELP made proposals for the introduction of a course leading to a new national award. The intention was that the new course would embody 'left-wing' ideals for polytechnics. It would be a continuous change-agent within NELP and would maintain a pressure for change within the higher education system generally. The pressure group effectively defined the parameters of the proposed new course before the formal establishment by Academic Board of a Unit which was charged with the task of preparing a course submission for validation by the CNAA.

Even within the pressure group there were chinks of disagreement which widened later. Although Eric Robinson took the initiative in establishing the original working-party, the submission to the CNAA bore the hallmark of the thinking of Tyrrell Burgess. There was tacit conformity to a 'leftist' position such that shades of difference were discounted. The first chapter which follows culminates in an assessment of the proposal made by the first working party. I was not a member of that working party. The views which I express here are not significantly different from those which I expressed in January 1973, when I joined the extended working party. The Development

Unit which was set up for 1973/4 had to be task-oriented. It had to sustain the momentum from the original working party and it wanted to retain ideological continuity. It was inevitable that the process of preparing the DipHE course submission should be one of staff induction to introduce new staff to those ideas already fully developed within the original working party. Equally inevitably, there were those members of the Development Unit who were reluctant to accept that they would have to take responsibility for defending views which had already been finalized. This tension remained under control from 1973 until 1975 but changing circumstances meant that from 1976 some differences of attitude began to acquire institutional existence and status.

The second chapter concentrates on the immediate context of the DipHE submission to the CNAA of 1974. The analysis of the documentation is designed to point out the nuances which indicate the transition from an 'old-style' vocational course to a 'new-style' student-centred proposal. It tries to indicate the intrinsic difficulty of making that ideological adjustment. The third chapter is crucial for an understanding of the emergence of the three strands of influence which are explored in detail in Part 3. The first strand is substantially the 'leftist' position which was the legacy of the original working party. The process of planning the details for the course originally proposed had shown, however, that it would not be easy to operationalize the intention of making students 'generally competent'. Surreptitiously, the Development Unit admitted defeat on this issue, and made a virtue out of necessity. Competence could not be taught. It could only be acquired experientially. Learning objectives could not be devised by staff for students and, hence, the process of devising their own objectives which was offered to students was justified by staff as being itself an experiential process which developed competence. The acquisition of measurable skill and the assessment of levels of attainment both became submerged in a person-centred interpretation of student-centredness. The capitulation of the original position of the reforming Left to the values of personal growth was gradual.

The third chapter shows that between the years 1976 and 1979 the influence of 'personal growth' which was at first confined to the Central Studies component of the DipHE extended to the whole course through the introduction of the part-time DipHE in 1976. The fourth chapter suggests that the victory of the 'reforming left' over 'personal growth' in the managerial subordination of the part-time DipHE to the full-time DipHE in 1979 was more apparent than real. My judgement here is that the re-assertion by the full-time DipHE of structural rigidities which had been suspended by the part-time course was only a pseudo-regulatory stance. Indeed, I would go further and suggest that there has been a consistent tendency for the reformist position to be pseudo-regulative. It adopts structural requirements which have no intellectual rationale. These requirements are cosmetic. They are designed to secure 'credibility' rather than quality. The third strand in operation within the School in the 1970s is given most prominence in the third chapter. The BA/BSc by Independent Study emerged out of an attempt to secure national recognition for the achievement of students who had gained the NELP DipHE. As the DipHE seemed to relinquish any criterion-reference as a course, the progression of students towards publicly recognized degrees had to be based on their individual attainments and the quality of their individually articulated intentions for further study. The registration procedure for the BA/BSc by Independent Study was established to make the judgement of level and quality which the DipHE Assessment Board was resisting. In 'taking over' the personal growth strand of the School's work institutionally, the reformist strand had, almost unconsciously, surrendered to it ideologically. The intellectualist strand, embodied in the BA/BSc by Independent Study, was the only remaining threat to the triumphant alliance.

The fourth chapter sketches the movement from 1979 until the present. My suggestion is that the inclination of the reformist tradition to acquire public acceptance by acquiescing in regulatory procedures to which it has no real commitment – and which it clandestinely subverts – is again recurring in respect of the operation of both the BA/BSc by Independent Study and the MA/MSc by Independent Study. It is precisely because I sense that the distinctive values of the 'intellectualist' stance are in danger of being subsumed and neutralized by the de-politicized remains of the old-left position of the original working party that I have wanted to write this book to explore the possibilities for the preservation of an intellectualist reformism. This Part tries to present the background in course developments – the skeleton – which is then given flesh in the detailed analyses of the three strands offered in Part 3.

4

Nineteen Seventy – Nineteen Seventy Three

In 1968, Eric Robinson's book, *The New Polytechnics*, discussed the challenge posed by the proposed introduction of about 30 new higher education institutions in the United Kingdom. He argued:

> It is unlikely that universities and polytechnics will exist side by side permanently. The essential issue at stake is 'What type of universities will this country have in the future?' One of the essential components of this question is 'What type of student and what type of course of study will the universities provide?' One might interpret the polytechnic policy as an attempt to change the concept of the British university and in particular to replace the concept of the boarding school university by that of the urban community university. The essential feature of the polytechnic as an urban community university, as a people's university, must be its responsibility and responsiveness to democracy rather than its insulation from it.[1]

Eric Robinson became Deputy Director of NELP at its inception in 1970. One year later, Penguin Books published *Patterns and Policies in Higher Education*, with contributions from George Brosan, Charles Carter, Richard Layard, Peter Venables, and Gareth Williams. One of George Brosan's essays – 'A Polytechnic Philosophy' – presents the contrast between universities and polytechnics more scientifically by borrowing the phrase 'social dynamics' used by Thurman Arnold to describe the behaviour of social institutions. In contrast to the creed of universities, he writes,

> There is another creed in the institution of education, which, put simply, is that people should be trained to do jobs. This crude vocational need first made itself manifest on a significant scale during the first industrial revolution, and as a consequence the institution of education split into two parts: the universities did not absorb the need to train mechanics, plumbers and so on; they were dealt with separately in their mechanics' institutes. This is the first example of one of the laws of social dynamics, which states that where there is acute conflict between the ideals and the practical needs of an institution – in this case the institution of education – the institution will split into two

parts. One will represent the ideal, and the other will cater for the practical activity which contradicts the ideal. Over the years the social need for educating people has gradually become more respectable; the aristocratic prejudice against education both declined and was seen to be dysfunctional. It was quite predictable that the organization representing the ideal, i.e. the universities, would have a higher place in the social hierarchy than the organization doing the practical job.[2]

Formerly Principal of Enfield College of Technology, George Brosan had been appointed the first Director of NELP at its inception. The institution, therefore, which emerged out of the amalgamation of Barking Regional College of Technology, West Ham College of Technology and South-West Essex Technical College and School of Art (at Waltham Forest), was led at the outset by two men who held precise and pronounced views about the nature and future development of polytechnics within the British system of higher education. Robinson's book, indeed, was a deliberate attempt to make a statement about that future development in advance of the designation of the new institutions. Both men sought to present North-East London Polytechnic as a blueprint for the introduction of change into the higher education system, and, as a consequence, their attitudes and actions were never parochial. A great deal was thought to be riding on the introductory, formative years in the conglomeration of scattered buildings and dispersed sites east of the East End of London.

The strongest attitude was one of opposition, or even hostility, to academicism. The fourth chapter of *The New Polytechnics* indicates Robinson's perception of 'vocational, liberal and academic education':

> We used to think of liberal education of the elite and vocational education of the mass but this is now outdated. In contemporary society everybody needs both – the manager needs technical expertise as well as clear thinking, the worker needs understanding as well as manual skill. The great problem is not in the conflicting demands of the concepts of vocational and liberal education. It is the conflicting demands of these concepts on the one hand, and that of academic education on the other. This educational conflict can be resolved only by breaking the domination of the whole educational system by universities which are devoted to the academic ideal.[3]

Vocational education is, by definition, something which in contemporary society is liberal. The enemy is not liberal education, therefore, but academic education. By 'academicism', Robinson means the cultivation of knowledge for its own sake. Associated with his hostility towards the self-perpetuating cultivation of academic knowledge was Robinson's hostility to those 'academics' who sought to maintain positions of social power and status as a result of sustaining the exclusivity of their knowledge. The best way to deal with universities was not to try to transform them but to ignore them and hope that they would gradually disappear.

Practical actions followed from this fundamental state of mind. As the three former colleges were restructured to establish a new, united polytechnic, departments were given titles which diminished any academic image. There were, for instance, new departments of Applied Biology, Applied Economics, and Applied Philosophy. More importantly, however, as Deputy Director in charge of course development, Robinson initiated a programme of course design which would free the institution from subservience to the University of London. But it was not enough to cease to teach University of London external degrees and to secure approval for new courses from the Council for National Academic Awards. Robinson instituted internal procedures for validation which would ensure that NELP's new courses would conform to his liberal/vocational conception of higher education and, by extension, would ensure that NELP became the pioneering kind of institution for which he had hoped in his book.

One of Robinson's first acts was to establish a Course Development Unit (CDU). All course teams which might be set up within departments to prepare proposals for new Degree courses were obliged to submit their proposals initially to this Unit. A small group of staff was seconded to the Unit to build up expertise in course design. It offered advice, but it also exercised tight control. Its first report, issued in November 1970, insisted that

> The function of the Unit is developmental, not juridical; its aim is to assist, not to frustrate.[4]

But, as one member of staff commented in response to a subsequent questionnaire which sought to evaluate the first year of operation of the CDU:

> there is an important ambiguity of function, between the advisory role of the CDU, which by definition Departments can make use of at their discretion, and Mr Proctor's responsibility to approve or not approve new courses, which affects the way the CDU is seen by Departments. Without the sanction of Mr Proctor's vetting function, the CDU might be used less. On the other hand protestations of wishing to be advisers only, having no policy etc., are not altogether convincing when Mr Proctor is in the key role as both CDU Chairman, and Assistant Director Course Planning.[5]

Undoubtedly, the CDU sought to enforce a particular model of course design, which was labelled a 'systems' approach. All course teams developing courses in the polytechnic were required, first of all, to consider what kinds of student they were expecting to come onto the course, and, secondly, to consult with industry and potential employers to establish what sorts of graduate student they were looking for. This was expressed in terms of 'input' and 'output'. Staff were required to define the projected student input and output for their proposed courses and, where possible, to conduct appropriate 'demand' and 'needs' analyses to justify their projections. It was only then that staff should plan the course content, which had to be seen as a process which would enable the projected student input to become the desired output. As summarized in the CDU's statement of the *Principles which the Unit has taken as basic to the Development of all Courses* (1973), this formula seems bland enough:

1 Specification of an educational need which may or may not correspond to recognized subject disciplines.
2 Substantiation that there is a demand for the course.
3 Characterization of the probable entrant.
4 Statement of course objectives, in terms of the need and the likely applicants.
5 Determination of the type and length of course (degree, non degree etc.)
6 Specification of a curriculum (whether some students will require additional courses; teaching methods; examination methods in relation to course objectives etc.)[6]

but it did aggressively operationalize Robinson's anti-academicism. The course design assumptions of the 'new' universities in the late 1960s, for instance, had appeared to be completely different. The ostentatiously innovative 'inter-disciplinarity' of new courses at Sussex, or Essex, or Warwick, had originated in the perceptions of the staff about how they themselves thought their subjects or disciplines should develop. It was the result of a refinement of content conducted by academics without reference to any perception of what their likely students might bring to that content or derive from it.

In the first two years of its existence (July 1970 to July 1972), the CDU played a major part in the development of the polytechnic. In that period, academic approval for 17 course submissions was sought from the CNAA, and only two proposals were rejected. This was largely to be attributed to the work of the Unit which reported, in July 1972, that it had considered 42 courses to date and had held a total of 74 major meetings with staff responsible for course proposals.[7] Nevertheless, the Unit was attacked within the polytechnic from opposite extremes. There were, first of all, staff who were inclined to adopt an academic view of course design. Subject specialists were confident that they knew what the content of their subject was without reference to any input/output model. Indeed, it was irrelevant what kinds of student were going to receive the information which they themselves possessed and were employed to transmit. Subjects represented discrete bodies of knowledge and it was the function of staff to pass on, or hand down this organized knowledge. On the other hand, there was, secondly, a Marxist opposition to the 'systems' model. It was argued that by transforming content into process, the Robinsonian emphasis inevitably subordinated education to the existing structure of capitalist society. For the Marxist, 'academic freedom' left open the possibility that educational institutions might foster a stance which could criticize capitalism rather than be managed and manipulated by it.

The CDU was in the middle of the opposition between educational ideologies of the 'left' and the 'right'. Additionally, by 1973, it was not able to cope with the quantity of course development within the polytechnic. Central ideological control over course design faded. By the autumn term, 1973, the CDU became part of a new Centre for Curricular Development and surrendered its direct link with the directorate in the internal validation of new course proposals.[8] Well before that date, however, Eric Robinson had established an alternative mechanism for maintaining the purity of the polytechnic's progress. The establishment of a new course within the polytechnic leading to a new national award – the Diploma of Higher Education – might create a continuing change-agent within the institution which would safeguard its future more successfully than could a unit which solely vetted new courses at inception.

Towards the end of 1970, a committee under the chairmanship of Lord James of Rusholme had been appointed by the Secretary of State for Education and Science, Mrs Margaret Thatcher, to carry out an intensive study of the education, training and probation of teachers. In particular, the committee had been briefed to consider what should be the content and organization of teacher training provision, whether a large proportion of intending students should be educated alongside other students, and, in this context, what should be the role of the colleges of education within the framework of higher education in Britain as a whole. The James Report was published on 25 January 1972. It recommended that teacher education should be split into three cycles. The first would be a degree course or two-year course for a Diploma of Higher Education (DipHE), open also to non-teachers; the second would consist of two years of professional preparation, the second year to be spent mainly in the schools; and a third cycle of in-service training. The intention was that the proposed new course would be broad in scope, both so as to allow students to gain a general training and education which would prepare them for a range of possible professions, and also, simultaneously, at the institutional level, so as to stimulate the integration of educational studies with studies in other disciplines. The existence of a qualification which would be equivalent to the first two years of an Honours degree and which would be preparatory to a range of professional training would, it was supposed, give colleges of education the opportunity to become multi-purpose institutions instead of being restricted to the single function of training teachers. As the Report put it:

> The course would be broad in scope and would include, for all students, a substantial element of general studies, occupying about a third of the time combined with rigorous study of normally two special subjects, one of which might or might not be related to educational studies, chosen by the students from a range of options.[9]

One advantage of the proposal, therefore, was thought to be the fact that the supply of teachers could be controlled at the point of entry to the second cycle, without wasting two years of higher education for those for whom teaching posts might not be available. Indeed, the Committee envisaged that diplomates might become more readily employable than graduates from many university degree courses: it argued that the diploma

> would offer a 2 year course consisting of both a general education and some specialized elements, which themselves might look to future occupational choices, for example, languages or economics for students thinking of a career in business. It has been suggested that such a qualification would be welcomed not only by business, industry and the public service but also by the schools. The schools may see it, for many of their sixth formers who require higher education, as a welcome alternative to the present university courses which are not necessarily well suited to the aptitudes and aspirations of all those who are formally qualified to take them.[10]

It was this relevance of the proposed new award to social needs beyond simply the structure of teacher training which was endorsed by the Government White Paper of December 1972 – *A Framework for Expansion*. The government recognized the need for a two-year course that was not vocationally specific. It therefore approved the introduction of two-year courses leading to a DipHE. These courses were to serve a wider purpose than that envisaged in the James Report, the White Paper claimed, but the nature of this wider purpose was not articulated.[11]

If the government tentatively saw the new award as one means to release higher education from the stranglehold of the academic orientation of the universities, it is not surprising that Eric Robinson should have seen it even more clearly in this light. There was obviously an opportunity to introduce a new course which might strike at the heart of the three-year academic degree nationally, and, within North-East London Polytechnic, might constitute the crucial development from which all other courses would take their vocational bearings. The James Committee had provided anti-academic ammunition, but there seemed a real danger, in 1972, that its recommendations would lead to the introduction of anaemic 'liberal' or 'general' studies courses. The essence of Robinson's philosophy was that the old alliance of liberal and academic should be replaced by a new alliance of liberal and vocational. He wanted to strip liberal education of many of its academic aspects and to insert into it a much greater vocational orientation. It seemed that the underlying assumption of general education in the James Report was that it should involve the acquisition of general knowledge. By contrast, Robinson wanted to insist that the vocationalist dimension for the new course would only be secured if its goal could be the attainment in students of general competence rather than the acquisition of general knowledge. Just as the publication of *The New Polytechnics* in 1968 had been an attempt to make a pre-emptive statement about the future development of the new institutions, so, in 1972, it became clear that a comparable pre-emption would be necessary in respect of the future development of the DipHE. Accordingly, a working party of seven polytechnic staff was set up by the Director of North-East London

Polytechnic in the Spring of 1972 'to formulate proposals for a programme for DipHE which might be established at the Polytechnic in the near future'.[12]

This working party produced an Interim Report in October 1972 – several months still before the publication of the Government White Paper. The introductory paragraphs confirm both that the planning of the DipHE at NELP had a larger political significance and that, internally, it was intended that it should exemplify Robinsonian principles of course design. The second paragraph makes it explicit that the work of the seven members of staff

> had two purposes, one internal to the Polytechnic, the other external. For the Polytechnic the Working Party has begun the discussion and preparation on a new educational programme. At the same time it has sought to make a contribution to the national discussion about the DipHE. These two practices have been found to be wholly compatible, since the working party has tried to see how the broad proposal for the DipHE could be worked out in the context of the policies and circumstances of a particular institution.[13]

The fourth paragraph outlines the process of course design which had led to the interim statement:

> An important principle of NELP policy is to design courses to cater for the needs of prospective students rather than to seek students to fit courses that NELP would like to run. Having defined the DipHE concept the working party, in accordance with this policy, then sought to identify, for planning purposes, types of potential student for whom the programme was intended so that their estimated needs would form the basis of detailed planning.[14]

The balance of the content of the report which follows these introductory remarks reflects the above interpretation of the input/output model in favour of the prime significance of the characterization of input. Almost two pages are devoted to the consideration of the Student Intake, while less than half a page is given to the discussion of Output. That half page can hardly be said to indicate a 'needs' analysis since the expected career choices of the hypothetical output are already contained within the character of the hypothetical input which the working party has already selected as its target. The half page somewhat ingenuously states:

> Output
>
> Most of the students of the types listed who pursue a course of general education can be expected ultimately to proceed to careers in which a general education is highly valued and which do not require specialist technical expertise that must be acquired by several years of specialist study.

On this basis, and on the basis of an appraisal of the destination of many such people in the past, we identify the following major career areas:
(a) business and public administration;
(b) teaching;
(c) social work;
(d) communications.

The DipHE is not intended to provide an adequate terminal qualification for entry to any career in these fields, nor are these fields the only ones for which DipHE would provide an adequate general education. It is hoped that the programme will make a significant contribution to the provision of highly skilled recruits for employment in North East London.[15]

The input/output model stands exposed as a specious framework which justifies special provision for a different kind of student intake. Input is wagging the output tail. Equally, as the earlier characterization of the student intake makes clear, the working party was determined to ensure that A levels would not wag the input tail. The James Report had recommended that the normal entry requirement for the DipHE should be the possession of two A levels, but that there should be 'generous provision for exceptions in the case of mature entrants and those applicants who, although possessing different formal qualifications, are strongly motivated to teaching and give promise of becoming effective teachers'.[16] The working party's document chose, therefore, to emphasize that the admission of the holders of any A levels minimized the extent to which subject specialism would influence the characterization of input:

> A programme open to all students with 2 passes in GCE A level can presume no subject knowledge or skill that all students have developed to A level.[17]

It also chose to emphasize that the weight which the James Committee was prepared to give to student motivation should be extended, for a general education, beyond the demonstration of a motivation only to teaching:

> Generous provision for exceptional admission should be made for applicants who produce evidence of strong motivation to further education.[18]

The document does not, in other words, provide evidence derived from any analysis of student demand. On the contrary, it singles out the kind of student demand which it finds congenial and for which the preconceived course content will be an appropriate response:

> A sixth form course or FE college course designed with organic unity should be given greater weight for entry to DipHE than conventional academic courses that depend on specialist subject knowledge to GCE A level.[19]

Similarly, the account of the employment possibilities for diplomates is thin and imprecise because, in fact, the working party was committed to a view of the intended general characteristics of all students which, it believed, would make them generally employable. After specifying its approach to course content, the working party's document admits that it is based on an assumption or, even, a belief:

> This approach depends on the validity of an assumption that there is a wide range of skills that can be defined and assessed which constitute a common base for the employment and/or further education and training we have postulated for DipHE students. We believe that this is so and that these basic skills are common to all forms of academic and professional work.[20]

The justification for this commitment to the transmission of 'transferable skills' is

> the observation that criteria of skill rather than those of knowledge are the most appropriate in the selection of candidates for employment or further education and training in the fields with which we are mainly concerned.[21]

This value judgement that the recognition of skill ought to be the basis for selecting candidates in the chosen professions is not substantiated by any evidence derived from employers that this is observably the case. The document's comments simply embellish the working party's determination to effect an interpretation of the James Report which will emphasize competence rather than knowledge. This position is made explicit at the beginning of the discussion of content:

> Objectives
>
> The student's objectives in the programme are conceived as those of a general education defined in terms of skills relevant to the ultimate vocational objectives. The working party attaches great significance to the choice of this approach to the definition of general education rather than the more conventional one, followed by the James Committee, of definition in terms of subject knowledge. It recognizes that programmes based on either definition will have much in common but believes that the distinction is an important one of principle. In particular it means that the student's successful completion of the DipHE will depend upon tests of what he can do rather than tests of what he knows.[22]

Having carefully selected its ideal types of student and their consequent prospective career outcomes, and having stated its conviction about the general vocational appropriateness of possessing transferable skill, the working party could be confident of the congruence between its own agenda of intentions and 'the student's objectives in the programme'. Its main problem, therefore, became, as it states,

> the definition of these skills and the means whereby students with a wide range of background and interest may acquire them.[23]

The document first offers a tentative definition of the necessary transferable skills:

(a) the ability to develop alternative ideas about a situation;
(b) the ability to formulate objectives and to do so in terms of the means for achieving them;
(c) the ability to relate this thinking to established bodies of thought and knowledge and thereby to make use of these;
(d) the ability to identify within a situation personal problems of value judgement and decision;
(e) the ability to work in association and collaboration with other people;

associated skills of communication and social relationships including

(f) the search, selection and use of written, graphical and oral material;
(g) the techniques of creating and organizing such material, including the skills of writing and speaking with purpose in a variety of situations;
(h) the formal and informal conduct of group activity in committees, seminars and work teams;
(i) the use of mathematical and other formal aids to thought and analysis;
(j) certain rote and mechanical skills.

> It will be necessary for the student to develop the co-ordinated use of these skills in planning and taking effective action in situations with which he is confronted.[24]

The working party accepted that there might be some difficulties with these objectives, but it reiterated its belief that the modern world would esteem more highly those people who possessed the above kinds of abilities than those who might possess specialist knowledge of a subject. The next stage in planning the new course was to consider the ways in which students might acquire the defined skills. The working party was clear here that it was

> essential to our concept of the programme . . . that the student shall be an active participant rather than a passive recipient.[25]

but it was equally clear that this aim was to be achieved by initiating the students into an understanding of the pre-defined intentions of the course:

> From the start every effort must be made to make this a reality by familiarizing the student with the programme, its method and its objectives.[26]

This was to be done in an initial induction period in which students would also have the opportunity to remedy defects in their existing basic skills so that some commonality might be established amongst the diverse intake. After this introduction, each student would be required to pursue a 'special interest' and to undertake 'central studies'. This division followed the recommendation of the James Report that there should be both specialized and general studies, but the working party elaborated its intentions in accordance with its own philosophy. The special interest which each student would have to identify was to be seen as a vehicle for developing the skills of the whole programme and not as an opportunity to acquire some specialist knowledge:

> Each student will be required to identify a field of *special interest* which will form the vehicle for much of his study. This will define his physical location within a department of the Polytechnic for approximately half his time in the programme. In consultation with tutors this field of special interest will be defined so as to permit its pursuit to contribute to the development of all the generalized skills. Thus, for example, a literary interest must be defined so as to include some aspects of scientific and quantitative analysis and a scientific interest must be defined so as to require substantial reading and writing. Each special interest must be defined with an academic and a practical dimension i.e. so that it involves substantial studies within one or more academic disciplines and so that it involves work and study in some contemporary field of practical activity. Generally these requirements will be satisfied by a definition of special interest which is, by the normal standards of both academic and vocational education, a narrow specialist one in that it embraces only a part of the area of study and activity covered in a conventional degree or professional course.[27]

It is obvious from this passage that the students' special interest studies were to be the means by which the institution's academic subject specialists were to be confronted with the need themselves to adopt instrumental attitudes and approaches. The students were meant gradually to succeed where the Course Development Unit had already failed. The intended infiltration into the whole polytechnic by means of special interest studies was to be ideologically sustained and nourished by the central studies component of the course which was to be 'explicitly directed towards the acquisition of the generalized skill objectives of the programme'. The practical arrangements envisaged here were as follows:

> For this work the student will be attached to a central tutor and to a seminar group of students with a variety of special interests. The theme of the central studies will be the formulation and solution of problems of action and decision. Each seminar group will have a programme which includes both a progressive study of problem solving and a study in turn of the development of each of the skills listed in para 11. In

support of this work there will be a range of lecture courses and classes open to all students. These will include non-specialist courses in philosophy (particularly social philosophy and the philosophy of knowledge), sociology (particularly the sociology of knowledge), psychology (particularly the psychology of perception and the psychology of learning), economics (particularly public policy and practical accounting), the use of libraries, reading, writing, graphical communication, the use of modern technology in communication, computing, mathematics, the methods of science.[28]

In these specifications for both parts of the proposed new course, the working party firmly laid the foundations for the subsequent submission to the CNAA. The section devoted to the 'form of the programme' was followed by others which outlined 'Course work and assessment', the 'Organization and control of teaching', the 'Numbers enrolled', 'Cycle 2 courses' and 'Programme Development'. Although some of these were slight and were to be supplemented by appendices which were in preparation, the working party accepted that the bulk of its work was done. It recommended that

after the amendment of the report in the light of comments received and its submission to the Academic Board the working party shall be dissolved. If and when a decision is made to implement the programme a department or division of the Polytechnic should be formed to prepare the detailed programme for formal approval and implementation.[29]

The working party was not, however, dissolved. It was extended. In January 1973, it was augmented by formal representatives of each of the faculties of the polytechnic. At the same time it became known that Eric Robinson had been appointed Director of Bradford College of Technology and would be leaving NELP at the end of the 1972/3 session. These were two important factors which caused some subsequent modifications of the blueprint which the working party had so forcibly prepared.

Notes

1 E. Robinson, *The New Polytechnics. The People's Universities*, Penguin Books, 1968, p. 48.
2 G. Brosan, C. Carter, R. Layard, P. Venables, G. Williams, *Patterns and Policies in Higher Education*, Penguin Books, 1971, p. 61.
3 Robinson, op. cit. p. 92.
4 K. Parker, *The Course Development Unit*, Report No.1 of the Course Development Unit, November 1970, NELP, p. 2.
5 K. J. Shave, *A Sample Evaluation of the Work of the C.D.U. over its first session. 1970/1*, November 1971, p. 2.
6 J. Hargreaves, *Principles which the Unit has taken as basic to the Development of all Courses*, NELP, February 1973.

7 J. E. Proctor, *Report to the Director. Activities over the period July 1970 to July 1972 for which the Assistant Director (Course Development) had direct responsibility*, NELP, July 1972, p. 2.

8 See J. Hargreaves, *The Course Development Unit at North East London Polytechnic*, NELP, autumn term 1973, p. 5.

9 James Report.

10 ibid. para 4.19. p. 46.

11 See *A Framework for Expansion*.

12 *Interim Report of the Working Party on the Diploma of Higher Education*, NELP, October 1972, p. 1.

13 ibid. p. 1.

14 ibid. p. 1.

15 ibid. p. 3.

16 James Report.

17 *Interim Report*, op. cit. p. 2.

18 ibid. p. 2.

19 ibid. p. 2.

20 ibid. p. 4.

21 ibid. p. 4.

22 ibid. p. 4.

23 ibid. p. 4.

24 ibid. p. 4.

25 ibid. p. 6.

26 ibid. p. 6.

27 ibid. p. 6.

28 ibid. p. 8.

29 ibid. p. 11.

5

Nineteen Seventy Three – Nineteen Seventy Six

On 24 January 1973, at the invitation of Sir Kenneth Berrill of the University Grants Committee and Dr E. Kerr of the CNAA, representatives from the Committee of Directors of Polytechnics and other bodies attended 'the first trans-binary educational discussions of their kind'. It had been suggested in a joint letter from Dr Kerr and Sir Kenneth Berrill to those invited to join the conference that there might be a group discussion on subjects such as problems of curriculum content, design of courses, and the possible preparation of model DipHE and Degree courses which higher education institutions could adopt if they thought them valuable. The outcome of the discussion was

> Unanimous support for an action programme, involving a DipHE Study Group charged with the formulation of a framework of guidelines which, as far as possible, avoided the 'imposition of exact constraints'.[1]

A 'Trans-Binary DipHE Study Group' was established under the chairmanship of Sir Walter Perry of the Open University. Dr Brosan was a member of this Group which agreed at its first meeting on 27 February to produce 'a short paper embodying a model DipHE scheme' for consideration at its second meeting. On the basis of this consideration, the Group prepared draft guidelines which were agreed in early May and circulated for comment to validating bodies and to the initiating conference. The final 'trans-binary guidelines' were issued in July 1973.

In the first half of 1973, therefore, there seemed a real chance that the government's recommendation of December 1972 that there should be a new two-year qualification in British higher education was going to lead to a major restructuring of course provision in both universities and polytechnics. Since NELP had already prepared a detailed specification of the kind of course it would introduce, which was at once available for discussion by the Trans-Binary Study Group, introduced by Dr Brosan, there also seemed every chance that the national changes might follow the NELP proposals. This was the exciting context of the first meetings of the 'extended working party' at NELP which took place weekly through the spring term. At a meeting of the Governing Body on 25 May 1973, the Governors confirmed that the Polytechnic should develop proposals for the Diploma of Higher Education, and much of the remainder of that academic year was devoted to establishing formally a group which would be responsible for this task. In July, the Academic Board took the unprecedented step of establishing a unit – the DipHE Development Unit – which would enable a limited number of staff to be released from teaching commitments so as to prepare the necessary documentation for a CNAA submission. After the departure of Eric Robinson, Tyrrell Burgess became the Chairman of the working party and, on August 2, he advised members of staff that they would hear officially during the summer vacation about their internal transfer or secondment. His letter also pointed out that the submission would need to be completed by the middle of November and, to this end, it also included a list of over a dozen tasks to be undertaken in the autumn about which members should reflect during the summer.

The DipHE Development Unit met formally for the first time on 17 September 1973. It comprised a core of staff who were internally seconded full-time to the Unit and a larger group which was made up of staff who had been given a limited time allowance for the DipHE development work. The full Unit sustained the composition of the 'extended working party' in that there were members who were drawn from all the faculties of the institution. Full meetings of the Unit were held weekly while the central core staff prepared papers, drafts, or reports which were considered at these meetings. The first meeting set up working parties for a range of Cycle 2 programmes and also established three working parties for the DipHE itself – on special interest studies, assessment, and central studies. These three working parties were active throughout the autumn term, 1973, while the whole submission took shape in the weekly meetings. These were inevitably concerned primarily with the process of preparing a document while educational arguments took place in the working parties. The outcomes of many of these arguments were deferred in order to reach agreement on a main text on schedule. An agreed text of 100 paragraphs passed through the polytechnic's internal committees in December 1973, and was formally submitted to the CNAA on 15 January 1974.

Following the publication of the 'Trans-binary guidelines', the CNAA had also been busy in the autumn of 1973 in making preparations to receive possible DipHE submissions from institutions. Early in December, the Senior Assistant Registrar discussed the establishment of a 'special group along the lines of a Subject Board, to consider all college applications for approval of courses leading to DipHE'[2] Members for such a group were sought before the end of the year. James Porter, then Principal of Berkshire College of Education, was asked to be chairman of the Group in the light of his experience as a member of the James Committee and of the Trans-Binary Study Group. The first meeting of the Diploma of Higher Education Group took place on 14 March 1974. The Group received a paper entitled 'The Validation of Proposed Diplomas of Higher Education', setting out its terms of reference, and it also received applications for approval of DipHE courses from NELP, Huddersfield Polytechnic, Crewe and Alsager College of Education, Berkshire College of Education and from Portsmouth Polytechnic. It was, therefore, at the first meeting of the CNAA validating group that the NELP main text was considered. The NELP DipHE Development Unit considered the CNAA response to the main text at its meeting of 29 March. A reply to these comments and the substantial appendices to the main text were all forwarded to the CNAA in April. A visit of representatives of the CNAA DipHE Group took place on 17 May, and it offered a report on its findings to the second meeting of the DipHE Group on 18 June. It was the recommendation of this meeting that the proposed course at NELP should be approved for an initial intake in 1974. It was agreed that a vital part of the monitoring of the course would be a further visit to the Polytechnic in November or December 1974, when 'the choices of the first students, the staffing implications, the contracts and the likely post-diploma programmes could be considered by the Group'.[3]

18 June was a day for celebration at the DipHE Development Unit, NELP. Many of the hopes of early 1973 were unrealized. The 'Trans-binary guidelines' had not positively embraced NELP's interpretation of the James Report but had, instead, issued guidelines which passed responsibility to the validating bodies. In the university sector there was no evidence to suggest that courses would be developed which would need to be validated, while the CNAA approach was highly cautious. It had ensured that a conventional, subject-based DipHE proposal would be approved at the same time as NELP's and it was clear that NELP's proposal was to be regarded as an exception rather than as the norm and was to be scrutinized very closely and sceptically as an 'experiment'. Nevertheless, the plans that had commenced as far back as spring 1972 had at last come to fruition. However much NELP might now have been prevented from pioneering a development which might alter the course of British higher education provision, and however much the precise intentions were circumscribed or to be monitored, there would be a course in autumn 1974. There would, at last, be an intake of students which was not hypothetical.

The main text of the successful proposal to the CNAA was presented in ten chapters:

1 Introduction.
2 The Philosophy of the Programme.
3 Aims and Objectives.
4 Entry Requirements and Procedures.
5 Structures.
6 Nature of the Programme.
7 Validation and Assessment.
8 Programme Organization and Control.
9 Resources.
10 Staff.

Some of these re-state the positions of the earlier working paper of 1972, but some important new developments contributed to the emergence of independent study at NELP.

Whereas the explicit starting-point for the working party document of 1972 had been the recommendations of the James Committee, the DipHE submission begins, instead, with the Government White Paper of December 1972. It deduces from the Government's response to the James Committee in favour of a wider purpose for the DipHE than had been envisaged in its Report that

> it is clear that the Government wishes to encourage the creation of new kinds of programmes at this level, and we believe that the need for such programmes becomes more urgent as numbers in higher education grow.[4]

The Government had undoubtedly recognized the need for greater flexibility in higher education, but the above sentence tries to represent this recognition as the same as an awareness of the different needs which must arise in educational provision as a result of greater student numbers. This point is immediately reinforced in the following sentence:

> Briefly, if there is to be a transition from elite to mass higher education, this must almost by definition imply the creation of new programmes and new routes to qualification.[5]

The next sentence fully confirms that the underlying motivation of the DipHE submission was to meet the requirements of new higher education customers:

> In designing the present programme we have acted on the principle that new and different groups of people will be going into higher education.[6]

Whereas the working party document had tried to emphasize the need of society for a vocationally flexible manpower, the DipHE submission emphasizes more that higher education must be different in a society where it is available to all. It takes its cue from the title of the Government White Paper to develop further its position:

> In brief, the expansion of higher education seems to demand an explicit decision about the kind of education that is to be provided. We accept that there are broadly two traditions of higher education which have been characterized as the 'autonomous' and 'service'. . . . The distinction relates to the purpose and mode of study, not to distinctions between institutions. Many of the courses in Britain's 'autonomous' universities are in the service tradition. Public sector institutions extend and develop their studies 'autonomously'. This present programme lies explicitly in the 'service' tradition. Every part of it is directed to the needs of the students and through them to the needs of society. What we seek to do is to increase competence. For this purpose

we have thought it right to reject an approach based upon the demands or the structure of a subject or discipline.[7]

The non sequiturs between these last three sentences demonstrate the way in which the DipHE Development Unit was wrestling with Eric Robinson's ideological legacy. Robinson sustained opposition from Marxists because he had seemed to equate the needs of society with the employment needs of a capitalist state, but the DipHE submission avoids this confrontation by claiming that the needs of society will be met by the proposed course necessarily by meeting the needs of students. Although Robinson had argued that the employment need of society was for vocationally flexible – competent – employees, the DipHE submission, by contrast, is only able to offer the disembodied assertion that the staff seek to 'increase competence' in students. Further, this aim must be achieved by rejecting an approach which is committed to the perpetuation of subjects and disciplines. Contained within this passage, in short, are the signs of a transition from a functionalist approach to the place of education and educated people within society to one which seeks to emphasize the part which people may play, by active participation, in constructing their own social institutions and environments.[8]

Student participation became a key element in the DipHE submission in a way which had barely been foreshadowed by the working party's original determination to prevent students from passively acquiescing in processes which would be organized for them. The submission was politically anxious to be seen to be conforming as far as possible to the guidelines for the DipHE etablished by the Trans-binary Study Group, but it explicitly rejects the 'module', 'credit' or 'unit' approach to course construction which had been cautiously commended in the guidelines. Its reasons for this, which were subsequently elaborated in one of the appendices,[9] were clearly stated in the main text:

> We do this in order to give the student a share of responsibility, not for selecting 'options', but in planning his own programme. It will be for the student to formulate and agree his goals with staff and peers, his methods of reaching them and the means of testing his performance.[10]

This articulation of an opposition to educational practices which represent the provision of opportunities for student choice between options as 'student-centred' exposes the essence of the positive position which underpins the whole submission. It is the process of planning itself, in accordance with a prescribed framework, which engenders competence. The new feature of the submission is the confidence that competence is not a state of being to be reached by students as an 'output characteristic' but is, instead, a developing capacity which is acquired as it is exercised. This position is defended in the following Popperian terms which were specifically elaborated in a further appendix. To assign responsibility for planning to students in traditional courses is claimed to be inappropriate because the student cannot know enough to share responsibility for planning. Confidence in the aptness of our own proposals and in the intellectual rigour of the students' experience derives from an explicit view of the way in which knowledge is advanced and acquired. The logic of discovery is consistent with educational principle. The first and most difficult task is to formulate problems; the second to propound trial solutions; the third to test these solutions with rigour. It is this framework which enables the student to take the responsibility we assign to him, and gives a guarantee that the process is an educative one. We rely, in short, less on content than on method.[11]

Although Chapter 3 of the DipHE submission reproduces with very little change both the section of the working party document which had indicated student stereotypes and the section which had hypothesized the likely objectives of those students, subsequent chapters show, in a new way, the importance of student planning as a mechanism for ensuring that NELP would serve the needs of its local community. The following statement indicates the extent to which the DipHE Development Unit had thrown off the over-riding concern with the production of a vocationally flexible workforce:

The Polytechnic is located in a large urban area where the take-up rate of places in higher education has always been very low. The number of young people with normal minimum entry requirements is also low. This is more related to traditional attitudes to education than to the ability of the young to benefit from higher education. It would therefore be inappropriate for the programme to require of all students evidence of achievements untypical of the area we seek to serve.[12]

The proposed admissions procedures were to be the first stage of a process which would determinedly implement one of the polytechnic's stated objectives – that students should be selected by reference to their likelihood to benefit from the institution's provision. As paragraph 30 of the submission states:

The purpose of our procedures is to ensure that those students who are able to benefit most are not refused a place on the programme. In keeping with the philosophy of our programme, and in particular of our student guidance system, interviews will be mutual. The applicant will be assessing us and we shall be determining how best to help the applicant.[13]

While the working party's document had briefly suggested that students would need to be initiated into the non-academic beliefs of the course planners, the introductory Planning Period proposed in the submission was designed to continue the concentration upon the students' potential for benefit:

> The DipHE programme itself begins with a six week planning period whose object is to enable students to understand their own strengths and weaknesses, to formulate for themselves the capacities which they will have at the end of the programme, to plan, with their tutors, the means of gaining these capacities and to determine what would tell them that they had failed. At the end of the planning period each student will negotiate a contract with his central studies tutor and special interest tutor covering in general terms his objectives and programme of work and in more detail his immediate programme for the rest of the first term. This contract will be available to be called in by the validating board for the programme.[14]

The curious transformation of the Robinsonian 'systems' approach to course design is here complete. The submission proposes that, in the Planning Period, the students should identify themselves as input and as potential output and should devise a programme of study to effect the transition. In ensuring that this took place through a process of guided planning, however, staff would be securing the student competence which, before, had been the course objective. The proposed process of planning, in other words, was now ambivalently both a means and an end. What was to be the status of the objectives which the students would devise if the capacity to devise such objectives was itself to be regarded as an adequate objective?

It appeared that this would be a question for another new feature of the DipHE submission – the validating board. It was proposed that this should be

> a body external to the polytechnic, to guarantee the quality of individual programmes in a situation where it is impossible to prescribe courses in advance.[15]

It would be the function of DipHE tutors to judge whether the programmes proposed by students would be adequate vehicles for the realization of their objectives, and it would be the function of the validating board to assess, 'on a random sampling basis', the judgements made by staff. The criterion for validation was, implicitly, the coherence of the planned programme of study. The submission quickly insisted

> that the external validators will not be the same as any proposed external examiners.[16]

and thereby indicated that it regarded 'monitoring' assessment as of greater significance than 'qualifying' assessment. This orientation was made explicit in the preamble which introduced the chapter on 'Validation and Assessment':

> In keeping with the overall philosophy of the programme, we see the assessment process as providing a framework within which the student becomes aware of and makes his own 'monitoring' assessment of his own capabilities. In terms of this function, assessments external to the

individual student are relevant only in so far as they contribute to his own self-assessment, and provide a feed-back which helps him to identify his weaknesses, and thereby to improve his performance. The process, conscientiously carried out, should ensure that the normal outcome from the programme is success.

Nevertheless we recognize the importance of the traditional function of assessment – that is, the establishment of a 'level of performance' indicated by the award of a diploma. For this purpose a basis of 'qualifying' assessment of the student's competence at the end of the programme is needed.[17]

There was a very clear sense in which the monitoring assessment was regarded as the real assessment and the qualifying assessment as a token compliance with unfortunate political necessity. It was proposed that each student would be given a termly 'profile' statement of his strength and weaknesses. Certified copies of these profiles would be available to the student on completion of the programme 'whether or not he is awarded a diploma'.[18] As far as qualifying assessment was concerned, the submission had recourse to the formula which had been used in the working party document in respect of student objectives:

The basis of assessment will be as agreed during the planning period, but it is expected to include the following criteria:–[19]

Whereas the submission passed the actual specification of objectives to the students, it failed actually to do the same for the criteria of qualifying assessment for the simple reason that the 'expected' criteria were linked to a proposed course struture which was not thought to be negotiable:

(a) The student must demonstrate competence in his agreed skills in the 'set' situation in Term 6 of central studies.
(b) The student must demonstrate competence in his agreed skills in a special interest study which has been pursued for at least three terms.[20]

In spite of the submission's new emphasis on the process of planning, the identifiable structural components of the course – inherited from the James Report – also received considerable attention. The conception of special interest study is fundamentally unchanged from the outline impression given in the working paper document. It was only to be embellished in imaginative detail in the subsequent appendix.[21] By contrast, the conception of the central studies component had developed dramatically in the discussions of the DipHE Development Unit's core staff. While the 1972 working party had envisaged a programme of central studies by means of which students would acquire skills through attending a range of relevant multi-disciplinary lectures or courses, and, equally, had envisaged that students would be involved in seminar groups, the submission placed its emphasis firmly on the student group:

> For a maximum of one day a week in the first year and of two days a
> week in the second, each seminar or activity group will formulate,
> implement and monitor a programme of activities. Such work will also
> involve the group functioning as an organizational and administrative
> unit, as a sub-committee of the central studies committee, and with a
> representative on the latter.[22]

The kinds of provision which had been anticipated by the working party were
now to be assigned a subordinate role. Supporting remedial work and basic
courses were to be provided on demand, and a 'file'[23] of conceptual material,
compiled by staff, would indicate specialist teaching which might be offered
by staff if the topics should prove relevant to the activities in which the
groups might become involved. The expertise of staff was to be regarded as a
resource for students and the determinant of the character of the central
studies component would, therefore, be the activities chosen by groups.
Having surrendered an imposed curriculum for central studies, the DipHE
Development Unit did, however, agree a structure for group activities which
would guarantee that the course's hypothetical objectives would be progres-
sively acquired:

> Initial activity work will involve the formulation and implementation of
> a series of fairly limited tasks requiring and demonstrating in turn the
> 'competence in particular skills' listed in Chapter 3, in the context of a
> number of overall group activities. The group activities will become
> progressively larger and more complex and require the 'competence in
> general skills' listed in Chapter 3, on the basis of an increasingly large
> mix of the skill requirements.[24]

It was insisted that group activities would provide the context within
which skills and competences could be acquired and exercised while, at the
same time, the refusal to set 'projects' for students would in itself ensure that
they would actively develop the capacity to generate problems and the means
to test practical solutions.

Although this new conception of 'activity groups' dominated the submission's representation of central studies, no separation from the original seminar groups was intended. It was proposed that each student would, on com-
mencing the course, be assigned to a seminar group and a central tutor. In
this context the student would make plans in the Planning Period and then,
afterwards, share with other students his interests and skills:

> On the formation of the seminar group there will be an initial justifica-
> tion by each student of his special interest studies and activities as
> vehicles for the meeting of the skill objectives of his course, and of their
> use as a means of examining the different approaches listed in Chapter
> 3. In each of Terms 2, 3, 4 and 5, there will then be group discussion of
> the individual special interest programmes of group members.[25]

Although there was no sense in which the Development Unit wanted the
seminar groups to be inter-'disciplinary', it was intended, nevertheless, that

students should make each other critically aware of the different specialist contexts in the polytechnic in which they were developing their skills. The two components of the course were to cohere because both central studies and special interest studies were only different contexts for developing the common skills of the course as hypothetically stated in Chapter 3. The most tangible integrating principle between central studies and special interest studies was, implicitly, that both should be 'problem-centred'.

The fact that the submission's account of the proposed components of the course makes constant reference to the objectives offered in Chapter 3 of the document suggests that the detailed course planning could not regard the substance of the course process as hypothetical in the way that is implied by the account of the Planning Period and of student planning. The submission enshrines tightly prescriptive structural control as well as, paradoxically, a commitment to student participation. The chapter devoted to the Unit's proposals for the Programme Organization and Control makes it clear that the opportunity should exist for students not only to plan their own programmes of study but also democratically to modify the structure of the situation in which those studies might take place, but the implications for CNAA approval of this potential for the constant adjustment of the course are not explored.

It must, indeed, already have been a formidable task for the CNAA visitors to distinguish the parameters of the proposed actual and the proposed hypothetical in the main text of NELP's DipHE submission. The extended arguments provided in the appendices and the bulk of further detail provided there cannot have removed the initial sense of bewilderment. The DipHE Development Unit exuded enthusiasm and dedication on 17 May 1974, but it is hardly surprising that the CNAA group was cautious in its approval. The document's lack of clarity about the course's intentions in safeguarding a publicly creditable level of student performance in the demonstration of their own skill objectives was a major contributory factor in producing the CNAA group's reserved approval. It was to be an important element in the group's continuing reservations about the experiment which it had unleashed.

During the summer of 1974, the NELP DipHE Development Unit formally became the School for Independent Study. Seventy-two students were recruited for commencement in the autumn. These were assigned in groups of 12 to six central tutors. Tyrrell Burgess became the first Head of School – a position which he held until 1978. The first term was hectic. Central tutors were finding their feet in implementing the submission's intentions in respect of the six-week Planning Period which culminated, on 5 November, in the first visit of the newly established Validating Board comprising Asa Briggs, Frank Hornby, Lord James of Rusholme, Lady Plowden, Cedric Price and Sir Toby Weaver, four of whom were in attendance. Meanwhile, following its intention to monitor the course closely, the CNAA DipHE group visited the Polytechnic again on 27 November. As a result of this visit, the new Registrar at the CNAA, Dr Salmon, was able to write to Dr Brosan:

> The Council recognizes the value of a controlled experiment in inde-
> pendent study and wishes to encourage its continuance and develop-
> ment. . . . thus I am pleased to inform you that an extension to the
> period of approval of the course for one further year has been
> approved.[26]

There were, however, eight conditions to this extended approval. Some of
these related to a continuing requirement that mature entry to the course
without standard entry qualifications should be restricted, and others
related to the need for the provision of post-diploma courses. The School
vigorously contested the CNAA group's position on admission during 1975
with the result that a meeting was arranged for 31 October. The outcome of
this confrontation was reported to a meeting of the DipHE group which took
place on 27 January 1976, when the School's report on its first year of operation was also received. There was clearly much anxiety about the standard of
student performance in the NELP DipHE with the result that the group did
not feel able at that stage to commit itself definitely to further approval. It
was recommended that

> In view of the importance, in establishing standards, attached by the
> group to the advice of the internal Validating Board (whom the group
> were to meet on 30 March), and of the External Examiners which would
> inevitably result in delays, members felt that the outcome of the visit
> (on 9 February) could not include a decision upon a September 1976
> intake of students. The Polytechnic should therefore be advised to
> proceed with its selection and admission of a 1976 cohort once the
> visiting party was satisfied that the selection procedures are both
> appropriate and rigorous.[27]

Members of the DipHE group did register their own distaste for this continuing piecemeal approval, and it was hoped that a firm decision about the
course would be taken in the autumn.

Meanwhile, back in August 1975, NELP's Assistant Director, John
Stoddart, had advised Dr Salmon that the School was developing post-
diploma opportunities and that the polytechnic would be hoping to submit a
proposed programme to the Council for the continuation of independent
study at the post-diploma level, leading to the award of a degree. He wrote:

> If this submission is successful the Polytechnic will have accom-
> modated the legitimate choice which students wish to make in complet-
> ing the Diploma between a process of assimilation to existing courses
> and modes of study, and continuing independence of study.[28]

At the same time, therefore, as the School was engaged in a protracted
defence of its practice in the DipHE, it was also occupied in preparing submissions both for a one-year post-DipHE course leading to the award of a
BA/BSc by Independent Study which would be available to the first cohort of
diplomates in September 1976, and also for the rapid introduction of a part-

time DipHE course to operate alongside the still contentious full-time programme. 1976 was an important year.

Notes

1 Paper CDP72, February 1973, p. 1, quoted in E. Adams, D. M. Robbins and J.
  Stephens, SIS Research Paper 1, *Higher Education for a changing society: issues raised by
  the introduction of the Diploma of Higher Education award,* July 1981, p. 19.
2 ibid. p. 25.
3 E. Adams, D. M. Robbins and J. Stephens, SIS Research Paper 2, *Establishing a new
  course for a new award: issues raised by the development of the DipHe at NELP and at other
  colleges,* July 1981, p. 41.
4 DipHE, NELP, *Submission to CNAA*, November 1973, p. 2.
5 ibid. p. 2.
6 ibid. p. 2.
7 ibid. p. 3.
8 This different political orientation is clear from the elaboration of the argument
  offered in Appendix 2.2: 'The Expansion of Higher Education requires Different
  Kinds of Courses', p. 4:
     Democracy requires political competence of a high order. If power is to be
     shared people need to know how to use it! They need to know how social
     institutions work and how they can be changed. This sort of competence has to
     be learned.
9 Appendix 2.4.
10 op. cit. p. 3.
11 ibid. p. 4.
12 ibid. p. 10.
13 ibid. p. 13.
14 ibid. p. 14.
15 ibid. p. 26.
16 ibid. p. 25.
17 ibid. p. 25.
18 ibid. p. 27.
19 ibid. p. 28.
20 ibid. p. 28.
21 See Appendix 5.5.
22 DipHE, NELP, *Submission to CNAA*, op. cit. p. 19.
23 An outline of the 'file' was provided in Appendix 5.2 and was available in full for
   the CNAA visit.
24 DipHE, NELP, Submission to CNAA, op. cit. p. 20.
25 ibid. p. 20.
26 quoted in SIS Research Paper 2, op. cit. p. 43.
27 quoted in ibid. p. 48.
28 quoted in ibid. p. 46.

6

Nineteen Seventy Six –
Nineteen Seventy Nine

It had always been intended that the DipHE should be recognized as equivalent to the first two years of an Honours degree. This was certainly the intention of the James Committee, the Government White Paper, and the Trans-binary Study Group. The award should have that value, as a terminal qualification, for employers, but it should also have that status for diplomates who might want to pursue their studies to degree level. Just as it quickly became clear, however, that the universities were not proposing to make any significant contribution to the development of the new award, so it rapidly began to seem likely that degree courses which often had only recently received approval from the CNAA precisely because they were thought to be coherent or 'holistic' in design would be unwilling to accept that students might reach the work planned for a third year by an alternative, general route. The Open University had already introduced the notion of credit accumulation to British higher education, but the implications of credit transfer were slow to impinge upon the groups and panels which exercised the CNAA's validating function. The Toyne Report of 1978[1] opened up possibilities for new initiatives in organizing credit transfer arrangements, but it came too late to save the DipHE.

NELP tried to exert pressure on the CNAA to conduct a campaign which would advertise the new award. On February 4 1976, the then Deputy Director of NELP, George Seabrooke, wrote to Dr Kerr requesting that the Council make a public statement emphasizing that the DipHE was in fact comparable to the second year of a degree course. This request arose after students of NELP's first DipHE intake had applied to other institutions to continue their studies at post-Diploma level. Without any reference to the merits of particular students, the response in general terms had been that other institutions would

> accept the diploma as equivalent to an entry qualification to higher education or as giving 'credit' for one year's study.[2]

Dr Kerr argued in response that, notwithstanding the recognition of equivalence, it had been appreciated all along that not every Diploma course would provide sufficient match with an existing degree course for a two-for-two-credit to be acceptable to a receiving institution.[3]

He understood that the DES was about to launch a publicity campaign on behalf of the DipHE, but if this should be too long delayed he undertook to consider unilateral action which might help to sponsor the new award. On 4 May 1976, Dr Kerr did circulate a letter to the Directors or Principals of those institutions which were approved to conduct courses leading to CNAA awards in which he discussed the admission of diplomates of Higher Education to degree courses. The letter emphasized that the Council had been rigorous in its validation of DipHE courses to ensure that they were of a standard equivalent to the first two years of a degree programme, but the remainder of the letter appeared to rehearse the difficulties which institutions might encounter in matching students into a third year. It points out, for instance, that it would be important for institutions to check that

the DipHE programme did not omit any essential topic on which the final year of the degree course is built.[4]

It was easy, of course, to reduce this statement to absurdity. No degree course would be likely to admit that elements of the first two years of teaching were inessential, and, as a result, DipHE courses could only expect to secure exemption in as much as they were virtually identical with the first two-thirds of linked degree courses. The notion of a general Cycle One course which could offer students the opportunity for transfer to a range of Cycle Two courses foundered at this first hurdle. DipHE courses *in* specific subjects began to develop where continued study in those subjects could be guaranteed, or, worse, the DipHE award was one which could be offered to students who did not wish – or would not be allowed – to complete a degree course. Modular degree schemes emerged which accommodated the DipHE but which effectively neutralized it as a discrete course. In summarizing the impact of the DipHE on the national system, Peter Scott wrote in 1984:

Of course, considerable progress has been made with the DipHE. Yet even its most enthusiastic supporters would not claim that it had yet secured a firm foothold in higher education. It is unknown in the universities, and in the polytechnics and colleges is still seen in most cases as a stage towards a degree, and a teacher education degree in many cases, rather than as a qualification in its own right.[5]

The internal situation at North East London Polytechnic mirrored the national one in respect of the recognition of the new course and the new award, but the refusal of the DipHE Development Unit and of the School for Independent Study to allow the NELP DipHE to become subject-centred ensured a unique outcome. As Peter Scott further commented:

Only in a few cases, most notably at the North-East London Polytechnic, has the DipHE been able to sustain an independent existence divorced from the BEd.[6]

The planning of the one year – third year – BA/BSc by Independent Study arose out of the School's fierce resolve neither to be compromised by a process of assimilation to existing degree courses nor to be marginalized by any tacit assumptions that its educational activities were generically different from, or alternative to, the norm.

The DipHE Development Unit had envisaged four possible modes of post-diploma development: 1. direct entry into the third year of an existing course; 2. entry into the third year of an existing course by way of a bridging course; 3. movement to an existing qualification by the design of a new course; 4. movement to a new qualification by way of a new course. By November 1974, the School felt able to identify, on the basis of returns from the rest of the institution, six existing, or proposed, NELP degree courses which would countenance, with conditions, direct entry to the third year; and four existing, or proposed, NELP degree courses which would countenance entry to the third year after a bridging course. There were no offers of new, specially designed, courses which would lead diplomates to existing qualifications, but there were 10 suggestions of possible new courses leading to new qualifications. The neat intentions of the original DipHE Working Party that there should be new 'Cycle Two' courses in areas which corresponded with their 'output stereotypes' – such as Social Work and Communications – which were sustained in working parties throughout the year of the DipHE Development Unit were, however, rapidly modified by the intentions of the first intake of students. As these students began to realize not just that the DipHE award was not going to receive significant national recognition but that, in particular, the emphasis of the NELP DipHE of method rather than content, competence rather than knowledge, was generally unacceptable and incomprehensible, they also began to see the 'opportunities' proposed for them at NELP as obstacles as discouraging as those which were supposed to be on offer nationally. It was logical that the School should identify what kinds of post-diploma opportunity were actually desired by the first intake of students. This it did in November 1974, and a planning paper reported student demand to be as follows:

> 50 students have been prepared to suggest areas in which they might wish to pursue their studies further. Since some students mentioned alternatives, we have a total of 71 possible options. These break down to the following broad areas:
>
> | | |
> |---|---|
> | Art and Design | 14 |
> | Arts | 22 |
> | Business | 3 |
> | Human Science | 13 |
> | Science | 5 |
> | Management | 4 |
> | Institutional Study | 4 |
> | Independent Study | 5 |
> | Librarianship | 1 |
> | | 71[7] |

There were several problems which seemed intractable. It was clear that the students had not internalized, during the Planning Period, the notion of the course planners that their Special Interest studies should be seen as the vehicles for the acquisition of the transferable skills advocated in the course documentation. The students' plans for post-diploma study were conceived mainly as extensions of the specialist content of their individual programmes of study rather than as extensions which built upon the one standard output characteristic of general competence advanced by the course. Since the post-diploma needs of the first intake of students seemed so radically individualized, it appeared to the School that the development of conventional post-diploma *courses* could not fail to be inappropriate. Not only was student demand in the 1974 intake so thinly spread that no 1976 post-diploma courses could be viable, but there was also no guarantee at all that the provision designed in 1976 for the 1974 intake would, in 1977, meet the needs of the 1975 intake. To establish post-diploma courses which were, ostensibly, tailor-made for the NELP DipHE would only have the effect of generating new structures which would constrain students as much as did the polytechnic's existing provision. There seemed a real danger that, within one year of the commencement of the DipHE, the freedom which it offered for students to define their own objectives would be undermined by the imposition of sets of requirements for further study both in existing degree courses and in special post-diploma courses.

At the end of 1974, therefore, the logic of the requirements of students seemed to be pushing the School in the direction of individualized study at post-diploma level. At the same time, the polytechnic's new Assistant Director (Courses) – John Stoddart – had his own plans for sustaining the momentum for change at NELP which had revived with the approval of the DipHE. His intention was that a polytechnic advance on an adult education front might also offer a means of securing a range of post-diploma opportunities. This strategy was introduced in January 1975, when John Stoddart returned from a visit to the States where he had examined community colleges and independent study programmes. A meeting with selected staff was called for 17 January 1975. In advance of that meeting John Stoddart circulated a paper entitled 'Possible Adult Education Programme', which outlined some of the assumptions involved in existing approaches to adult education and concluded that:

> If we accept these assumptions in planning an Adult Education programme, then we must think of education not as a process of transmitting knowledge but as a process of self-directed enquiry.[8]

In practical terms the paper proposed:

1 That the Polytechnic develop a degree programme for adult students (with flexibility in mode of attendance). Such a programme should take as its starting-point the present DipHE structure, which should be critically examined as to its suitability as a base for degree work by individualized study.

2 That the Part-time DipHE should be developed within the framework of the Adult degree programme.
3 That provision be made in the degree programme for the entry of diplomates from the existing DipHE.[9]

It was clear that any further course development initiatives to be taken by the School should be incorporated within a framework which embraced the whole institution. An adult education working party was established with the School heavily represented, but which also involved tutors of part-time courses from all parts of the polytechnic. By April a draft submission for an adult education degree programme had been prepared. It proposed that all entrants to the programme should initially go through a process of planning comparable to that of the DipHE Planning Period on the basis of which they would organize a sequence of studies which would either take advantage of the institution's existing part-time course provision or of opportunities for independent study or of a combination of the two. The emphasis of the draft submission seemed to be in sympathy with the orientation of the School for Independent Study in that students were to be offered the opportunity to use the resources of the institution to plan their own programmes of study to degree level, but, at the same time, it could be thought that independent study might be accommodated and neutralized by incorporation within a structure which was, essentially, modular. The consequences for the School would be that the Planning Period would be extracted from the DipHE while the two components of the DipHE – Special Interest studies and Central Studies – would be offered as separate, free-standing modules within the adult education degree programme.

Although the structure for the new course envisaged by the Adult Education Working Party might be said to offer all students the opportunity to negotiate independent programmes of study, it did also seem to entail the de-construction of the existing DipHE. The School had itself seemed to anticipate this disintegration of the original course structure of the DipHE when, at the beginning of 1975, two of its management committees – the Special Interest Board and the Central Studies Board – were renamed the Individual Work Board and the Group Work Board, but the proposals of the Adult Education Working Party seemed, perhaps, to entail more – the disintegration of the School. Certainly, when the relevant sub-committee of the polytechnic's Academic Board rejected the proposals of the Adult Education Working Party – fearing, perhaps, the creeping infiltration of the whole institution by the ideology of independent study, there were those within the School for Independent Study who were not at all grieved. There were, nevertheless, some clear legacies of the attempt to launch an adult education degree programme. The notion that the faculties of the polytechnic might develop themselves Cycle Two opportunities had faded in favour of the idea, fostered by discussions within the Adult Education Working Party, that a mechanism might be devised which would make the whole institution accessible at post-diploma level to students who might want to negotiate their own programmes of study. The failure of the adult education venture meant that, in May, 1975, the School was formally asked to

> take responsibility for submission of an appropriate scheme and be the responsible agency for its operation.[10]

but it was also an important success of the Adult Education Working Party that the School could not possibly contemplate an introverted post-diploma development. The adult education discussions had preserved the School's engagement with the rest of the institution. The School itself might be secure in its organizational autonomy, but the whole polytechnic had to be its constituency for its students' programmes.

In giving the School formal responsibility for the establishment of post-diploma opportunities in the polytechnic, the sub-committee of Academic Board also ensured that a working party of faculty representatives was established to liaise with the School. This met in July 1975, to consider some 'Notes on individualized Post-diploma opportunities in the Faculties leading to a degree by independent study' prepared by the School. These notes argued that it ought to be considered that students from existing taught courses might wish to transfer to a third year of independent study and that, therefore, a mechanism was needed for this reverse transfer which would parallel the arrangements also under negotiation for securing the admission of diplomates to taught courses. The assumption, in other words, was that

> independent study offers an alternative rather than a substitute way of learning.[11]

While the faculty working party was urged to consider the grounds for 'discipline-based' independent study in the light of the above contention, and while, equally, an 'access procedure' for diplomates wishing to gain entry at the third year to existing courses was under discussion, the School itself concentrated on articulating a justification of study according to its two modes – individual work and group work – at degree level. These strands came together in the autumn term 1975, and the proposal for a degree by independent study was written by the beginning of January 1976. After consideration by several polytechnic committees, a revised document was submitted by the School to the Deputy-Director by 20 February, and submitted by the Polytechnic to the CNAA by the end of February.

The submission to the Council which finally emerged out of a range of rather diverse internal contexts contained an Introduction, two Sections, and 16 appendices. The first Section – 'The Submission' – offered a formal justification for the submission of a proposal for a one-year course leading to the award of a Degree by Independent Study. That justification was expressed in relation to the provision for diplomates required by the guidelines for the Diploma of Higher Education published by the study group under the chairmanship of Dr Walter Perry in May 1973; in relation to the terms of reference of the School for Independent Study; and in relation to the Educational Policy of the School for Independent Study. A statement from the School's

Development Plan was quoted as an indication of the philosophical orientation of the School to which the Degree submission conformed:

> The School is committed to the view that students should plan and be responsible for their own programme of study with the guidance and co-operation of tutors. Great importance is assigned to the process of educational planning by the students. This involves the planning both of the substance of course content and also of the mode of attendance that is most convenient.[12]

The second chapter of the first section of the submission in which 'Its Character' is explained makes it clear that the degree course should provide a means by which students could offer their own justification for their chosen method and content of learning. The degree submission overtly banishes the 'hidden agenda' of staff objectives which underpinned the 'student-centredness' of the DipHE document. It does this by clearly differentiating between the 'course' which is the responsibility of staff and the 'programmes' of study which are negotiated by students:

> As staff, we are designers and controllers of a *course*. Students are the designers of their own course which, for clarity, we shall call their programmes of study. It is the function of the course to validate and facilitate these programmes.[13]

This distinction between 'course' and 'programmes' is crucial for an understanding of the whole submission. The underlying intention of the document was to propose a course structure which would be responsive, without predisposition, to the programme proposals of students. As a consequence, there was nothing that could be said prescriptively within the submission about the kinds of 'programmes' which the 'course' would countenance. The submission was eager to distinguish explicitly between what it could say and what it could not. In introducing the second section of the document, paragraph A.2.4 states:

> We insist that the structure of the course which requires a process of validation is non-negotiable but that there is room for negotiation in the criteria upon which validation is to be based. In the document which follows (Section B. *The Course*), we describe, firstly, our regulations (Chapter 1. The Non-Negotiable Structure); secondly, we describe our anticipation of the situation of informal relationships within which, during the pre-course, programmes will be formulated (Chapter 2. The Predicted Intake); and thirdly, we describe our conceptual predispositions (Chapter 3. Negotiating Guidelines) by hypothesizing justifications for categories of possible programmes and criteria for their validation.[14]

The essence of the non-negotiable structure of the course was that there should be a 'pre-course' operated within the School for Independent Study during which students would prepare proposals for their programme of study. These would be submitted to a Validating Board which would decide whether or not students might be admitted to the course itself. As the submission states:

> After acceptance by interview, students will register initially as members of the School for Independent Study. They will be assigned to a personal tutor within the School for Independent Study and will be offered a dead-line by which to submit proposals to the Validating Board. Until a proposal is accepted by the Board, a student cannot be considered as being on the course. The course which we propose, therefore, comprises two parts – a pre-course for which students are eligible if they satisfy formal entry requirements . . . and for which they must register with the Polytechnic; and the course programme in which students can follow their own proposed programmes of study if these have been submitted during the pre-course and have been approved by the Validating Board.[15]

The degree submission deliberately engineered a situation in which all diplomates would be eligible for entry to the pre-course but in which there would not be an automatic transition to the course. The document followed the approach developed by the Adult Education Working Party whereby the process of planning was to be extracted from the course of study and, in consequence, it gave to its proposed Validating Board a significance which was quite different from that of the body of the same name which operated for the DipHE. The degree submission sought to exercise control at the point of entry to third year degree work which would parallel the control exercised by the tutors of conventional degree courses both inside and outside NELP in considering the requests for access made by diplomates. The crucial difference, however, was that students would not be asked to satisfy the formal requirements of existing degree courses which were normally expressed in such a way that they could only be satisfied by undergoing the first two years of their structured teaching, but, instead, would be offered the opportunity to make their own case for the validity of their proposed programmes and in defence of their own credentials to pursue these programmes. The assumption was, therefore, that if students had acquired competence at a proper level in successfully gaining the NELP DipHE, that competence would be demonstrated in their capacity to develop cogent proposals for programmes of study in which their independence would be exercised rather than gained. The degree submission tacitly rejected the notion that 'competence' or 'independence' constituted the standard output characteristics of all successful diplomates on which a post-diploma course structure might be predicated. It relinquished the implicit course objectives of the original DipHE Working Party and of the DipHE Development Unit and surrendered course control to the Validating Board which would determine the validity of proposed programmes. There was no controlled input to the proposed course but only an open situation in the pre-course in which proposed programmes might be developed for testing on the Validating Board. The document commented that we define input as the total input of students, staff, resources and information which enable the course to operate.[16]

and the attempted characterization of the input explicitly included the curricula vitae of staff and their definitions of independent study as components of the 'attitudinal situation within which we expect negotiation to take place'[17] in the pre-course. But the submission proceeded to offer guidelines on how programme proposals would be presented in order to satisfy the Validating Board and it also offered both general and specific criteria for validation which would be adopted by that Board. It is hardly surprising that the CNAA focused attention on the proposed membership and operation of the Board for the course which, it insisted, should be renamed the Registration Board.

The degree submission gave precise details about the proposed Validating Board:

> The function of the Validating Board is to ensure that programmes proposed by students are such as to merit the award of an Honours degree if they are successfully completed . . . The Validating Board will consist of formal representatives from the Faculties of the Polytechnic, the Chairman of the Group Work Board of the School for Independent Study, three personal tutors from the School for Independent Study and will be chaired by the Course Tutor. One external examiner will sit on the Validating Board in an advisory capacity so as to establish the necessary link between the Validating Board and the Assessment Board. With the exception of the representative external examiner the membership of the Validating Board will be internal to the Polytechnic so as to secure the commitment of the institution to the validated programme . . . Members will be staff with considerable experience in teaching on the degree courses of the Polytechnic or elsewhere and the Validating Board will draw upon external expertise where it is required to reach a judgement of a proposed programme.[18]

This was a clear concession to the CNAA's attitude to the Validating Board for the DipHE where, it was being argued, external examiners were being asked to observe the assessment of the performance of students in meeting objectives which they would not have sanctioned had they been involved in the validating process. But the concession was not yet enough. A CNAA working party met in May 1976 to receive the polytechnic's submission for a Degree by Independent Study. A deputation from the polytechnic was invited to attend the working party's next meeting in early June and it was advised, in advance, that the working party would be

> interested and anxious to discuss the number and role of the external examiners to be appointed if the course is approved, the 'validating board', its role, its membership, its title and the provision within the course scheme for the classification of the Honours award which it is proposed should be the outcome of it.[19]

The CNAA group did push for the early involvement of external examiners at the validation stage as well as in assessment and, in approving the course for two years, it insisted that its chairman, Professor Alec Ross, should be designated Chief External Examiner with the task of reporting on the course direct to the full Council. This he did to the 55th meeting of Council when he gave a verbal report of the first meeting of the Registration Board which had taken place on 8 July 1976, when 12 proposals out of 23 had been approved. The Council's minutes record that Professor Ross

> was therefore firmly of the opinion that the Registration Board should be more formally established, if necessary by Council itself, since the external members could be regarded as acting as validators of individual programmes of study on behalf of Council. They should be given more authority and their position clearly established.[20]

It was as a result of this opinion, clearly, that the polytechnic was informed shortly afterwards

> that the registration of students on programmes of Independent Study is subject to the agreement of the External Examiners.[21]

The CNAA's favoured solution to the problem of the Registration Board seemed to be in the direction of establishing an external body which would scrutinize the internal judgements of the polytechnic. The School fought hard against this apparent trend because it was thought that it would destroy an essential element of the submission's philosophy – that there should be rational discourse between programme proposers and validators such that validation would become the culmination of an intellectual dialogue.

In October 1977, the polytechnic requested

> that the Council, recognizing the satisfactory standard of the first group of graduates, should be prepared to extend experimental approval to an intake for September 1978 at once, pending receipt of a full revised proposal in the New Year for consideration for full approval.[22]

This request was accepted by the CNAA and a meeting was arranged for February 1978, to receive a revised submission. This first revision was referred back to the polytechnic by the CNAA working party with a request for 'a full and comprehensive formal submission for a degree scheme to replace the present experimental scheme'.[23] This was provided and, with other papers, constituted the basis of a meeting between the polytechnic and the CNAA working party in April 1978, which led the working party to recommend to Council that the course should be reapproved for two further entries (September 1978 and January 1979) subject to a series of conditions, one of which was that the scheme should continue to be monitored by the working party. In order to make monitoring observations of the course, the CNAA working party visited the polytechnic in February 1979. After observations, it was prepared to terminate its monitoring role as long as it could receive a definitive document outlining the scheme. The submission was, therefore, again redrafted and submitted for the consideration of the working party in June 1979 and the polytechnic was informed in September that the approval of the Degree by Independent Study had been extended for three years.

During the course of this arduous series of meetings and visits, the polytechnic had resisted throughout the attempt to take the Registration Board outside its own walls. Instead, sub-registration boards were established in each faculty to make specialist recommendations to the main Registration Board. Specialist external examiners were members of the appropriate sub-board while the Chief External Examiner remained a member of the full Registration Board. Additionally, the CNAA working party had pressed the polytechnic to formulate more explicit validating criteria. Even though the working party accepted that more refined and definitive criteria would emerge during the operation of the course, it was so satisfied by the polytechnic's response that, after three years of discussion, it was now felt that the standard of the Degree by Independent Study as an Honours degree had been safeguarded by the agreed procedures and criteria of the Registration Board.

Although the process of securing final approval for the Degree by Independent Study was a major preoccupation for the School for Independent Study between 1976 and 1979, there were other important activities which shaped the subsequent development of the School and its conception of 'independent study'. This was the period in which, first of all, full approval was secured for the full-time DipHE course, and in which, secondly, a new approval was gained for a part-time DipHE course. A deputation from the polytechnic met with a working party of the CNAA DipHE Group in September 1976, to discuss both these issues, and the polytechnic received formal notification on 1 November 1976, that the Group had approved both the full-time and part-time modes for five years from 1977. The Group's approval for the full-time course was based on the papers submitted by the School for Independent Study, which proposed modifications to the original course intentions made in the light of the experience gained in operating the course for two years. The DipHE Group perceived that there were 11 significant changes to the original course proposal. Some of these – an extended two-stage planning period; a strategy of 'diminishing dependence'; and making explicit what was previously the 'hidden curriculum' in the form of a list of objectives – are best elaborated by reference to the definitive booklet about the NELP DipHE, which was produced in mid-1977 following the lodging with the CNAA of the definitive course document in the early part of that year.

Whereas the original DipHE submission of 1974 had made no explicit reference to 'independent study', the new document which superseded the old in 1976/7 contains a new section devoted to an explication of the 'General Concepts' governing the operation of the DipHE:

> Central to the philosophy of the programme are our concepts of Independent Study, Independence, Competence, and Transferability.[24]

Each concept is elaborated in turn. Assertions are discreetly modified by careful caveats or constraints. Independent study, for instance, involves

> freedom from the obligation to be totally reliant on established academic solutions or academic traditions. Students may use such solutions or parts of such solutions as part of their own programme but do so only because of their relevance and not because they are imposed.[25]

Nevertheless,

> In order to do this, students need to become familiar with the nature and status of established knowledge and traditional educational solutions.[26]

Similarly, 'Independence' is

> the demonstration of general competence without the direction of others.[27]

but, follows the caveat,

> 'Independence' has never been taken by the School to mean complete *freedom*. Rather, it is interpreted as meaning personal responsibility.[28]

This, in turn, requires the student

> to recognize and accommodate the constraints of life. These include resources and the need to obtain a publicly recognized Diploma.[29]

The constraints on 'independence' are intrinsic to the definition of the concept, but the constraints on 'competence' are explicitly imposed:

> The School has always sought to define competence in two types of context: as an individual working in a context which is largely the individual's own choosing, and secondly within the constraints imposed by membership of a group.
>   Working with other people involves being prepared to, and having the ability to:
> (a) relate and adjust one's own individual interests and requirements to the needs of the group and other members in it;
> (b) make positive contributions to successful group problem formulation and solution testing;
>   and
> (c) work with people of different academic, vocational and personal backgrounds, and on problems not directly related to one's own immediate expertise.[30]

This formulation, in other words, provides a rationale for the existing dual characteristics of the course. Whereas the developments in 1975 associated with the Adult Education Working Party had seemed to imply a bifurcation of the School between individual and group studies, the revised DipHE submission of 1976 which met with CNAA approval sought to advance a notion of independence which might re-integrate the existing components of the existing course. The revised document similarly tried to impose a meaningful structural pattern in the planning processes which had, in practice, followed from the original submission's advocacy of a six-week Planning Period. For the second intake of students in 1975 the staff of the School had already recognized the practical need to allow the opportunity to develop 'interim' and then 'final' planning statements. What might have become a process of drift was to be regulated by the following overt rationale:

Progress through the programme has three broad phases:
- Dependence, in which an intellectual, administrative, and social framework is provided within which students can formulate their own immediate educational problem within the Programme's and Polytechnic's constraints, and devise an appropriate solution. (Up to final validation.)
- Semi-dependence in which students work on their solutions with tutorial feedback from a wide variety of sources. (Between validation and the pre-assessment term.)
- Independence in which he practices and demonstrates his ability to operate without external support. (Final 2 terms.)[31]

Finally, and most importantly, the revised document at last clarified the relationship between the course objectives and the objectives which might be formulated by individual students. It argues that the 'general Concepts' already described 'together constitute the nature of a NELP DipHE' or, more explicitly:

they represent *programme* objectives for all students who wish to gain a DipHE.[32]

Students were still to be offered the opportunity to articulate their own objectives which were still, hypothetically, those identified in the original submission, but these were now clearly to be negotiated in relation to six standard criteria. The document states that the programme objectives are that

AT THE END OF THE PROGRAMME the students should, without depending on external support, be able to:
1 formulate their own education problems, and propose their own solutions;
2 implement such solutions without imposed dependence upon the traditional;
3 monitor and subsequently re-adjust when necessary the progress and direction of their solutions;
4 judge the success or failure of their solutions and to engage in external dialogue on the validity of their judgement;
5 work in collaboration with others on the formulation of problems related to the needs of the community;
6 work with people and on projects not directly related to their own immediate expertise.[33]

These six 'objectives' have, subsequently, been the controlling statements of the NELP DipHE. They give the appearance of imposing order and of enforcing standardization but, in spite of the references to public recognition and accountability for the Diploma award, these 'objectives' are little more than extrapolations from the procedural practices of the School which, by their overriding concentration on process rather than content, simply obfuscate the question of what might constitute a standard 'level' of achievement. It is not clear, for instance, whether students are to advance solutions to their problems which are judged to be 'good' solutions in order to satisfy the programme's objectives or whether it is sufficient for them to advance, implement, monitor and modify their solutions without regard to their objective worth. Similarly, it is not clear whether the fifth objective might be met by solely working 'successfully' in collaboration with others or by achieving an objective level of performance as one of a group of collaborators.

It was precisely because the DipHE moved towards a revised submission in 1976 which was speciously regulative that the submission for the BA/BSc by Independent Study sought at the same date to construct a mechanism – the Registration Board – which would evaluate not simply whether students could prepare proposals for a further year of 'independent study' but whether the proposed programmes of study themselves were intellectually valid as equivalents to traditional third year studies for Honours degrees. Nevertheless, if the supposed standardization of the output from the DipHE was, for the purposes of the Degree, vacuous, the procedural rigidity imposed by the revised submission's regulating objectives was thought excessive by some staff and considered by them to be in conflict with their notion of independent study. A non-regulatory orientation found a focus in the opportunity offered by the proposal for a part-time DipHE course.

The development of a part-time DipHE submission had been delayed by the activities of the Adult Education Working Party in 1975. Like the momentum for the post-diploma development, that for the part-time diploma was regenerated immediately after the collapse of the adult education proposals. A part-time DipHE submission was ready in February 1976 at the same time as the degree submission, but consideration of it was deferred to coincide with the September review of the full-time DipHE. As a result of these delays, the first part-time intake to the DipHE did not take place until April 1977. The submission to the CNAA for the part-time DipHE at first sight contains only minor amendments to the original, 1974, full-time document. The main text of 1974 is reproduced while alterations are highlighted in an initial explanatory page. As the introduction states:

Where there are differences these are usually for one of two reasons. Either:
(a) because different attendance patterns and potential students dictate different organizational procedures
or:
(b) because we have included improvements made in practice in the

operation of the full-time DipHE. . . .[34]

The main difference proposed – in the organization of the course – arises from a combination of these two reasons. The part-time submission proposes that the course will operate in three phases which it calls 'diagnostic', 'development', and 'demonstration'. The document elaborates in the following way:

> In the diagnostic phase the student will go through a planning period similar to that for the full-time programme. . . . In the development phase the student will work through his agreed programme using the group work and individual work modes (as appropriate) to develop those abilities he has indicated in his 'statement'. In the demonstration phase the student will be required to show that he has gained the abilities he set out to learn, and convince his tutors and the assessment board of the programme of this.[35]

This account clearly reflects the same kind of thinking which was to lead later in 1976 to the adoption by the full-time DipHE of phasing in terms of 'dependence', 'semi-dependence', and 'independence'. The crucial difference, however, is that the part-time submission envisages that students will be able to deploy group work and individual work modes of study 'as appropriate' in order to meet their personal objectives, while the full-time revised submission proceeds to construct course objectives which necessarily entail that students should employ both modes in the required proportions. The part-time DipHE submission wishes to emphasize the objectives of students and, to that end, is prepared to be party to the tendency to de-construct the DipHE that became apparent in the Adult Education Working Party discussions, while the revised full-time submission seeks to arrest that tendency and to consolidate, instead, the prescribed structure in the guise of establishing course objectives. The degree submission was a response to the situation which deliberately rendered the structure of the diploma irrelevant. The non-regulative orientation of the part-time submission is reinforced in its recognition of the particular needs and difficulties of part-time students. Although its formal presentation of individual work and group work is the same as that of the original full-time submission, the part-time document implicitly accepts that the structure of each student's course must be negotiable as a result of a series of practical constraints. Whereas both the degree submission and the revised full-time DipHE submission moved towards a formal and operational distinction between 'negotiable' and 'non-negotiable' elements of course structures, the circumstances in which the part-time course would operate inevitably emphasized the importance of negotiability. It was accepted that for individual work the student would have to negotiate with his tutor to attend at mutually convenient times, while

> For group work, students will need to arrange to be in attendance at set times which will be dictated not just by the time availability of tutors, but also of other students.[36]

The document naturally added that

> As numbers on the programme increase . . . the choice of meeting times will be greater.[37]

However, numbers of students on the part-time DipHE did not increase rapidly. As a result the incipient divergence of the part-time DipHE from the full-time norm was accentuated rather than diminished by the practical implementation of its proposals.

A flavour of the extent of the divergence between the two modes of the DipHE can be gained from an internal review of the part-time DipHE conducted by its Course Tutor in autumn 1978. He offered a comparison between the theory of the original scheme and the practice of the course. From the outset, the core unit for part-time students had been called the 'set' and the Course Tutor described its theoretical function as being

> to act as a Personal Tutor group where the overall progress of the student is to be monitored and is seen to act as a mutual support group and acts as an effective 'anchor' for the student. The set is particularly concerned with the transfer from dependence to independence with the tutor taking a Counsellor/trainer role creating an environment in which genuine creative criticism can take place.[38]

It had not actually been able to fulfil this function in quite these terms, however:

> Originally I think the set was envisaged as remaining constant or relatively so over the three year period of the course. In practice this has not been possible, particularly due to declining student numbers, making mergers of sets necessary. This reduces the numbers of sets and restricts students' choice of time. Consequences of this are that mixed intake sets are appearing.[39]

Circumstances of this sort pushed the part-time DipHE towards an emphasis of peer group learning and student self-managed learning.

Other organizational factors within the polytechnic also contributed towards the separation of the part-time from the full-time DipHE. As a result of a rationalization of the faculty structure of the polytechnic, the School for Independent Study became a part of a new Faculty of Humanities as from 1 January 1978. Simultaneously and consequently, Tyrrell Burgess resigned from his post as Head of School and was replaced by John Stephenson who had been a member of the original DipHE Working Party and, since 1976, had been the Course Tutor of the full-time DipHE. In recognition of the absorption of the School within the Faculty of Humanities, which was mainly based at the Barking site of the polytechnic, the part-time DipHE was based at Barking while the rest of the School remained at the Holbrook Annexe of the West Ham site. Until the whole School moved to Barking in July 1979, the geographical separation of the part-time DipHE accentuated a growing ideological rift.

As far as CNAA course approvals were concerned the School for Independent Study seemed finally to be in a secure and stable position when it was notified in Autumn 1979 that the BA/BSc by Independent Study was approved for three years. Since the full-time DipHE had been approved in autumn 1976 for a further five years and, with it, the part-time DipHE for the same period, all three courses operated by the School were, therefore, not due for re-approval until 1982. This consolidated position inaugurated a period of steady expansion which was, however, not without tension as the latent differences concealed within the three course documents occasionally manifested themselves.

Notes

1 P. Toyne, *Educational Credit Transfer: Feasibility Study*, funded by the DES, Final Report, May 1979.
2 quoted in E. Adams, D. M. Robbins and J. Stephens, *Establishing a new course for a new award: issues raised by the development of the DipHE at NELP and at other colleges*, SIS Research Paper 2, July 1981, p. 50.
3 ibid. p. 50.
4 ibid. p. 51.
5 P. Scott, *The Crisis of the University*, Croom Helm, 1984, p. 222.
6 ibid. p. 223.
7 quoted in E. Adams, D. M. Robbins and J. Stephens, *Establishing a new course for a new award: issues raised by the development and negotiation of the Honours degree by Independent Study at North East London Polytechnic*, SIS Research Paper 3, July 1981, p. 11.
8 ibid. p. 13.
9 ibid. p. 13.
10 ibid. p. 20.
11 ibid. p. 23.
12 *Submission of proposals to the CNAA for a Degree by Independent Study*, February 1976, p. 3.
13 ibid. p. 4.
14 ibid. p. 4.
15 ibid. p. 5.
16 ibid. p. 4.
17 ibid. p. 7.
18 ibid. p. 19.
19 Adams, Robbins and Stephens, SIS Research Paper 3, op. cit. p. 43.
20 ibid. p. 45.
21 ibid. p. 46.
22 ibid. p. 54.
23 ibid. p. 64.
24 *The Diploma of Higher Education 'red' book*, NELP, 1977, par. 21.
25 ibid. par. 22.
26 ibid.
27 ibid. par. 23.
28 ibid.
29 ibid.
30 ibid. par. 24.
31 ibid. par. 26.

32 ibid. par. 28.
33 ibid.
34 *Submission of proposals to the CNAA for a part-time Diploma of Higher Education*, February 1976, p. 1.
35 ibid. p. 15.
36 ibid. p. 19.
37 ibid. p. 20.
38 Paper of 30.11.1978 prepared by Part-time DipHE Course Tutor (Bob Lusty) to be found in the Archives of the School for Independent Study, box 51.
39 ibid.

7

Nineteen Seventy Nine –
Nineteen Eighty Seven

The period since 1979 has certainly witnessed a marked acceleration in the growth of the School for Independent Study. For the first intake to the DipHE in 1974 there were 72 students. In 1979, 100 students entered the full-time DipHE while 40 enrolled on the part-time DipHE and 16 commenced their studies leading to the award of a BA/BSc by Independent Study. By 1984, the full-time DipHE intake had risen to 199 students while the part-time DipHE intake had dropped to 34 students. In the same year, 59 students commenced on the full-time mode of the degree and 28 students on the part-time mode. The current norm is for an annual DipHE intake of about 200 students, while the degree recruits about 100 students annually and the recent course leading to the award of an MA/MSc by Independent Study admits about 30 students each year. At any one time, therefore, the School is likely to comprise about 500 students, which represents about 10 per cent of the student numbers for the whole institution. In autumn 1983, the Head of School reviewed the School's recent recruitment pattern in order to make recommendations to the polytechnic for its consideration in relation to the first set of specific requirements issued by the National Advisory Body. He was able to summarize the expansion of the School in the following way:

> Student numbers on the full-time DipHE have increased from 100 in 1980 to 183 in 1983. The number of full-time Degree students has risen even more rapidly, from 22 in 1980 to 51 in 1983. Expansion has also been evident in the part-time programmes during the past two years. In 1982 the part-time DipHE had only 10 students and this number has increased to 17 in 1983. The part-time Degree, which had only 2 students in 1981, grew markedly to accommodate 17 students in 1983 and continued expansion seems likely.[1]

and was able to project that

> assuming the recommended courses of action are followed, we may expect populations of 518 full-time and 390 part-time, including 280 Pre-Course, Independent Study students . . . by November 1986.[2]

Even though this ambitious projection has not materialized, the steady growth of the School for Independent Study has been remarkable. The increased size and, especially, the gradual change in the weighting within the School of separate courses, generated new organizational difficulties which were themelves expressions of ideological differences. While in 1980 there were about 20 degree students to 200 Diploma students, the degree course could still be considered a minor element of the work of the School. In so far as the rigour of the degree Registration Board was thought to threaten the claims made by the DipHE for its diplomates, that threat could still be considered negligible. At the end of 1979 the far greater threat to the uniformity of the School for Independent Study had seemed the tendency towards separate development evinced by the part-time DipHE. During the academic year 1979/80, however, the School was again physically reunited on one site at Barking and, as a result of a process of internal reorganization carried out during 1979, the management of the full-time and the part-time DipHEs was brought under the control of one course committee from the beginning of January 1980. If the orientation of the major, full-time DipHE course can be characterized, as evidenced by the revised submission of 1976, as one towards regulation and standardization, while the orientation of the minor, part-time DipHE course can, conversely, be characterized as one towards deregulation and openness, the irony of the situation subsequent to 1980 was that the ideology of the minor course became prevalent. This was nowhere more obvious than in the development of the Group Work component of the course.

The revised DipHE submission of 1976 had reiterated the contention of the original documentation that Group Projects were to be

> used as vehicles for the development of the students' transferable or general competence skills in collaboration with others.[3]

By spring 1980 it is clear, however, that the status of the 'collaborative context' has changed. Notes of guidance issued to students about Central Studies Project Work indicate the criteria to be adopted for projects. Most of these are in accordance with original practice, but the sixth suggests that in general, projects should

> Provide a forum in which the skills of collaborative working can be identified and practised, e.g. inter group communication, group leadership, decision making, group organization etc.[4]

The new feature was not just that collaboration was in the process of becoming an end rather than a context for the development of other ends. More importantly it was that students were now expected to articulate a theoretical perspective on their own group behaviour:

> Apart from the demonstration of practical and collaborative skills and intellectual achievement, students should indicate that they can relate practical problems in groups to theoretical models. Individual reports should therefore show evidence of reading and understanding groups and organizations. A short list of recommended books is attached.[5]

It is not surprising, therefore, that the Renewal Proposal of February 1982 –
written in order to secure further CNAA approval – sounds a new note in its
representation of the philosophy of the programme. It claims, first of all, that
in the eight years of operation of the course

> the philosophy of the programme has, at a fundamental level, remained
> remarkably consistent with the principles underpinning the first sub-
> mission to the CNAA in 1973.[6]

To substantiate this claim, the document proceeds to assert that 'now as
then' the School emphasizes

> A view of learning in which students acquire a general competence . . .
> which is consistent with their own experience and intentions.[7]

It is arguable, by contrast, that the original DipHE Working Party had,
rather, a view of the function of the higher education process that it should
enable students to attain a general competence consistent with *its* perception
of the needs of society. In continuing to insist on the consistency of its
relationship with the past, the 1982 document only confirms the suggestion
that there was a shift away from a conception of 'competence' as a measurable and demonstrable capability towards one of it as a personality trait
dubiously synonymous with 'independence':

> our purpose is still to provide students with an educational experience
> that enables them to become generally competent and independent. By
> this we mean that they should be capable of coping with a wide variety
> of different situations, many of them unfamiliar, both as individuals
> and as members of a community, without needing to be dependent
> upon the direction of others.[8]

The Popperian position is similarly almost unconsciously experientialized.
The evidence which is produced in confirmation of the original allegiance to
Popper indicates, instead, an operational interpretation which trivializes:

> We are further confirmed in our view of the nature of learning and the
> ways in which knowledge is extended. At its simplest level we believe in
> learning by doing which in this case means directly involving students
> in their own learning processes. We believe that trial and error is a
> natural and effective method of learning, involving an original tentative
> shot at setting out the nature of a problem and a possible solution;
> having a go to see if it works; and in the light of information gathered
> and experience gained producing a more sophisticated statement of the
> nature of the problem. People who are competent at learning in this
> way are more likely to be capable of coping with changing circum-
> stances without dependence upon others to show the way.[9]

The imprecise usage of 'learning' diminishes the status of the dimension of
'objective knowledge' here, while the following paragraph makes it clear that
the course had really embraced an alternative solution to the problem of

equipping students with the capacity to cope with change and with the unfamiliar:

> We wish also to give recognition to the importance of the affective domain in education. The ability to cope with the unfamiliar is as much dependent upon self confidence as it is on problem solving and other related skills. We continue to believe, therefore, that a process of self analysis supported by tutor and peer group guidance helps to stimulate purposeful personal development, and that the achievement of personally set goals leads to the development of self confidence.[10]

With this new emphasis of confidence rather than capability it was inevitable that the tension inherent in the 1974 DipHE submission between monitoring and qualifying assessment should revive. One external examiner had asked, in his 1979-80 report on the course:

> By what criteria can the students, tutors, and assessors judge the attainment of second year undergraduate studies *through* the objectives?[11]

and the 1982 renewal document responds:

> The difficulty has been that the learning goals which students have set themselves, and which have been considered to be valid in terms of their previous experience and future intentions and their need to gain a Diploma, have not necessarily been easily assessable in isolation. The 1976 Submission document did not sufficiently clarify the relationship between legitimate learning goals for the students and performance for the award of a Diploma with the effect that their learning goals were being used as the basis for assessment rather than as means of preparing students for their assessment. This has been a particularly difficult problem in the context of collaborative skills.[12]

This response accurately diagnoses the problem and the document indicates that it seeks to resolve the difficulty by clarifying the different roles of validation and assessment. By following the document's internal referencing, it is possible to unravel the clarification which is offered. Chapter 4 highlights the main changes which have been made to the 1976 submission, the second of which involves the production of an explicit distinction between the roles of the validation and assessment processes:

> We therefore propose to clarify still further the respective roles of Validation and Assessment. The former is concerned with the validity of students' programmes of study in terms of their own experience, future intentions, and available resources, whilst the latter is concerned solely with the award of the Diploma. By making a clearer statement of what is required for the award of the Diploma (as in a) above), the way is open for students to see their own objectives as personally set learning goals which in turn will determine their own programmes of study. As a

consequence, monitoring assessment and the Transcript . . . will both become much more important, the latter describing students' experience and achievements on the course, including the award of the DipHE.[13]

The intended separation of personally valid but non-assessable and non-credit-worthy activity from activity which would meet the objectives of the course which itself acted as the guarantor of their public validity seemed completely clear. There was a strong sense that the option which might not involve the acquisition of the Diploma was the purer one, and it is clear that the document offers a formula which accommodates both regulators and non-regulators in an attempt to create the conditions for the harmonious co-existence of credentialists and non-credentialists. In fact, however, the accommodation was more complete because the regulatory stance was vacuous and in only spurious conflict with the non-regulatory. Why, otherwise, were there not students emerging from the School clutching only Transcripts and not Diplomas? The explanation is discerned in the paragraph a) which purports to offer the 'clearer statement of what is required for the award of the Diploma'. It reads:

> Our proposal clarifies the status of the Programme's overall objectives (paragraph 8) and requires students to demonstrate all four in the contexts of their overall programme of study including Validation, an individual specialism, and a collaborative project on an unfamiliar topic. These programme objectives are appropriate to second year honours degree level (and higher) and apply to all students irrespective of area of study.[14]

The reduction of the programme objectives from the six of 1976 to four is significant here. The four objectives still emphasize that students should be able to plan and monitor their own programmes and the wording only deviates from that of the first four objectives of 1976 by diminishing Popperian overtones, but the fifth and sixth objectives of 1976 have now become two out of the three 'contexts' in which the four objectives should be demonstrated. Whereas the 1976 document stipulated that students should absolutely be able to

(5) work in collaboration with others on the formulation of problems related to the needs of the community;

(6) work with people and on projects not directly related to their own immediate expertise.[15]

the 1982 document instead states that the four 'process' objectives must be demonstrated in the context of:

(i) the student's own overall educational development by means of the validation and successful completion of an appropriate programme of study, and in the specific contexts of:

(ii) a relevant specialist area, and

(iii) an area outside their specialist expertise, on problems related to the needs of the community, in collaboration with others.[16]

In short, students will satisfy the programme's objectives if they do the programme. The course, therefore, has a relentlessly tautological character. Since students devise their own programmes of study, both in Individual Work and in Group Work, and submit them for validation, and since the criterion for validation is explicitly that the proposed programmes should meet the personal needs of the proposers, it follows that there is no logical difference between 'what is required for the award of the Diploma' and the personally set learning objectives of the students.

Nevertheless, the CNAA group which visited the polytechnic in May 1982, was impressed by the School's clarification of the aims and objectives of the DipHE course. The Background notes to the two-day visit of representatives of the Inter Faculty Studies Board reviewed the history of negotiations between the CNAA and the polytechnic in respect of the DipHE:

> Some eight years on, various working parties and visiting parties, including the working party of the Inter Faculty Studies Board which had considered the latest submission and discussed it with staff at a meeting in February 1982, felt that the School's procedures had been greatly improved: The procedures for admitting students, for ensuring that their Statements are properly formulated and validated, for providing a range of group activities and support courses, for providing academic and personal counselling, and for assessing the students' work at the end of the course, are now much clearer than in the early years. Moreover, the course aims and objectives, and the School's policy in admitting mature students without formal qualifications equivalent to A level, have been revised and clarified.[17]

It was agreed that the CNAA visit should concentrate upon the review of the operation of the DipHE, while a brief consideration of the progress of the BA/ BSc by Independent Study might raise issues which could be resolved subsequently. There was, therefore, every intention to review thoroughly the whole work of the School before the end of the 1981/2 session. The conclusion of this intensive scrutiny was that the DipHE should

> continue in approval for intakes from 1982, subject to satisfactory progress review visits at regular intervals of six years as requested by the Polytechnic.[18]

Within this general approval, there was, however, some indication that the CNAA group appreciated the inherent tension in the distinction between the objectives of students and the objectives of the course. It was felt that the solution to this problem might be found either, operationally, in a closer working relationship between the external members of the Validating and Assessment Boards, or in a further clarification of the course documentation:

The visiting party wishes to underline the need for a good understanding between the Validating Board and the Assessment Board, particularly between the external members. This must be centred on an understanding of the programme objectives ... The staff may in fact see some value in clarifying and reformulating these objectives, but the visiting party does not require this. It does however underline the importance of ensuring that the students are given very clear signals about how their own proposals relate (or not, as the case may be) to the programme objectives ... and are then given an element of formal feedback on their progress at the end of the first year.[19]

The CNAA group did, in other words, accept the distinction between course and student objectives, but it did not expose the inadequacy of the demarcation between the two offered in the School's revised submission. The group similarly recognized the key position of the Registration Board in the BA/BSc by Independent Study in maintaining public Honours degree standards, but, in this instance, was less readily satisfied by the School's presentations. Full consideration of the degree course was deferred to July when the group received a deputation from the polytechnic to speak on behalf of the School's request that the degree course should be brought into continuing approval and that it should also be given permission to extend admission to the pre-course to students who had followed a variety of two or three year programmes at other institutions. Until 1981, the CNAA had restricted admission to the pre-course to NELP DipHE holders or to students following CNAA degrees at NELP who would successfully have completed the first two years before the date of the Registration Board. In 1981, this approval had been extended to DipHE holders from institutions who were able to attend the pre-course in the months prior to the June Registration Board. In 1982, the polytechnic sought to extend further the entry categories to the pre-course to accommodate any holder of a DipHE or any student who had completed the first two years of a CNAA honours degree course; to holders of an appropriate number of Open University credits, or of an appropriate Certificate in Education; to holders of an ordinary degree from any UK higher education institution; and, exceptionally, to any student in a position judged equivalent to any of these. The polytechnic also sought permission to allow admission on an experimental basis to holders of an HND or equivalent award, and to holders of European or North American two-year university qualifications. If successful, this bid would clearly have two simultaneous effects of enormous significance. Permission would open the way for the first time to national and international access to the one-year course in its own right and, therefore, potentially destroy the 'special relationship' between the NELP DipHE and the BA/BSc by Independent Study.

In contemplating an approval which, in the view of critics, would surely 'open the flood-gates' for the degree course, the CNAA group focused attention on the pre-course to the degree and on the procedures of the Registration Board. Importantly, the group first established that the staff responsible for the degree course saw the pre-course arrangements and the process of registration and validation of student proposals, as safeguarding both the standard of the degree course itself, and the interests of students on the course.[20]

In the report of the meeting there is also the further affirmation that, in the light of the discussions which had taken place about admissions, registration, and assessment,

the working party was convinced that the Registration Board played an absolutely crucial role in setting and maintaining academic standards for the degree course, perhaps even more so than the Assessment Board, since it was the Registration Board not the Assessment Board that decided what form assessment should take, as well as deciding whether prospective students and their study proposals were of honours degree potential.[21]

As a consequence, the CNAA group concluded that they would wish to observe a meeting of the Registration Board on the occasion of its next visit to the polytechnic. This CNAA visit would take place in Autumn 1984 to coincide with the polytechnic's internal review of both the DipHE and the degree. In the meantime, the course was given continuing approval for intakes of students from September 1982, subject only to the submission of satisfactory reports from external examiners for the period from 1980 to 1982, some of which were lacking in the documentation considered in July 1982. The polytechnic was also asked to redraft its proposals for extending the entry to the degree and to submit these to the CNAA for confirmation. The outcome here was that a limited number of non-NELP students entered the degree in October 1982 and thereafter. The formal recognition of a set of extended entry requirements was delayed, however, until after the visit of the CNAA to the polytechnic in December 1984. It was after this visit that the CNAA group was able to conclude, in general, that

The School for Independent Study is clearly running a successful degree programme by Independent Study.[22]

and to comment, in particular, that

The Polytechnic's own review documentation (including the external examiners' reports), the observation of the Registration Board meeting, and the discussions members had with staff and students all served to confirm the fact that the Honours degree course by Independent Study continued to be very successful. Members were impressed by the rigour with which the administrative procedures established for its operation and management were carried out.[23]

While the degree course was securing this endorsement of its activities between July 1982 and December 1984, the School had also been taking steps to provide opportunities for independent study for graduate students. A proposal for a course to provide opportunities for programmes of study leading to the awards of MA/MSc by Independent Study, and Post-Graduate Diploma by Independent Study was submitted to the CNAA in May 1984 and approved in July of that year. The proposed structure for the course was very similar to that in operation for the BA/BSc by Independent Study – a pre-course or Orientation Phase was to precede admission to the course itself, whch might only be secured by the approval of individual programmes of study given by a Registration Board. Unlike previous submissions from the School for Independent Study, however, the attention of the MA/MSc submission was directed more towards the course's potential contribution to the practical management of the whole institution than to a specification of the School's educational philosophy. It is significant that the submission argues:

> Higher SSR's and tighter control of resources are presenting a major challenge to NELP's teaching/learning strategies in all areas of its work. Independent Study makes a signifcant contribution to the Poly-technic's solution to these problems by putting responsibility for learn-ing onto the student, by recruiting students to specialist areas related to research and consultancy not normally supported by taught courses, by increasing student usage of under-studented course components, by making more intensive use of the Polytechnic's libraries and other learning resources, and by exploiting specialist resources outside the Polytechnic including students' own workplaces where appropriate.[24]

Although the submission acknowledged that it completed the natural progression of the course development of the School for Independent Study, it was also at pains to announce that it would provide a mechanism which could rescue threatened post-graduate work throughout the institution. At the same time that the submission was ostentatiously celebrating the achievement of the kind of incorporation within the whole institution which had been sought, unsuccessfully, in 1975 by the polytechnic's Adult Educa-tion Working Party, it also sought to offer a representation of a unified School. An important opening chapter attempts to make a statement about 'independent study' which accommodates diversity:

> Independent Study in the School for Independent Study has developed over a period of 12 years in response to the contributions of its various academic staff in the context of changing circumstances and of a variety of philosophical perspectives.[25]

The different approaches of the DipHE and the BA/BSc by Independent Study are briefly highlighted, but, in conclusion, the unifying feature of independent study is confidently advanced. Independent study does not provide simply a course of the gaps of the institution but occupies an intellec-tually defensible position between the extremes of post-graduate taught courses and research degree registration:

> The common feature of the thinking which encouraged the develop-

ment of the DipHE and of the Degree by Independent Study was the view that the function of the teacher is to enable students independently to formulate problems and confront phenomena to be explained and to exercise their own judgement of the validity, or usefulness of traditional views and solutions. Many post-graduate students are likely to be seeking to use the course as an opportunity to further their own personal and vocational developments. They may want to design programmes of study which arise directly from their experiences in employment. They will need to be aware of the language and explanations of academic disciplines which impinge on their particular problems, but they may not need to be in receipt of the organized knowledge of any one discipline. Equally, their projects will be particular to their own situations but not necessarily original in the conventional sense understood in registration for higher research degrees. The proposed course, therefore, allows for an extension of the practice of the School for Independent Study which can fit appropriately between the taught post-graduate course on the one hand and the research degree on the other.[26]

The submission to the CNAA for the MA/MSc by Independent Study was, therefore, an overtly irenical document. Not before, perhaps, had a submission from the School for Independent Study so much appeared to be a submission from and with the rest of the institution rather than, covertly, against it. It was not long, however, before the BA/BSc and the MA/MSc, in alliance, appeared to be against the rest of the School.

In November 1984, the panel which conducted the polytechnic's internal review of the BA/BSc by Independent Study had noted that

> the balance of registered proposals in June 1984 was such that NELP DipHE holders would be slightly in the minority on the course.[27]

Equally, the first small intake to the Master's degree course in January 1985 comprised only two graduates from the BA/BSc by Independent Study out of a total of 12 students. As the staff associated with the post-diploma courses began to insist more aggressively on the need for the Registration Boards to satisfy public criteria of level, the staff associated with the DipHE were at the same time inclined to wish to celebrate the values of student self-development without reference to the public recognition of qualifications. In June 1985, the Course Committees for the BA/BSc and the MA/MSc both agreed a paper which argued that there should be established an autonomous Independent Studies Unit which would operate their two courses in separation from the School for Independent Study. It was suggested that there should be a probationary period of operation for this arrangement to last from October 1985 to July 1987. The rationale for this development was clear:

> In recent years, an ideological tension between the School's DipHE and the post-DipHE and associated planning courses has developed.

Whereas the BA/BSc and the MA/MSc have both concentrated upon the issues involved in the engagement of independent study with the rest of the higher education system, the DipHE has tended to concentrate upon the value of its 'independent study' practice in itself. Moreover there are clear conflicts of interest. For example, it is vital for the degree operation to maintain and extend the constituency of its potential students so that the DipHE by Independent Study is but one of several sources of recruitment.[28]

Just as, in 1979, the separatist tendencies of the part-time DipHE course committee were arrested by the imposition of a Joint Programme Management Group to run both the full-time and the part-time DipHE, so, in 1985, the bid for formal secession made by the BA/BSc and MA/MSc course committees was defeated by the majority vote in the School Board of the School for Independent Study. Analysis of the DipHE revised submission documentation of 1982 has suggested that the 1979 victory of the full-time DipHE over the part-time was Pyrrhic. As both the DipHE and the BA/BSc by Independent Study approach CNAA reapproval in November 1987 – a process which, for this account, should now be deemed to be sub judice – it remains to be seen whether the victory of 1985 of the DipHE over the post-DipHE courses will turn out to have been equally Pyrrhic.

Notes

1 J. Stephenson, *Possibilities for the Development of Independent Study with implications for student placements*, Internal paper, Autumn 1983, p. 1.
2 ibid. p. 10.
3 *The Diploma of Higher Education 'red book'*, NELP, 1977, par. 56.
4 A. Merry, *First Year Central Studies Project Work. Spring Term 1980*, January 1980, p. 1.
5 ibid. p. 1.
6 *Diploma of Higher Education by Independent Study (full-time and part-time) Part I. Renewal Proposal*, February 1982, p. 21.
7 ibid. p. 21.
8 ibid. p. 21.
9 ibid. p. 21.
10 ibid. p. 21.
11 ibid. p. 12.
12 ibid. p. 13.
13 ibid. p. 16.
14 ibid. p. 15.
15 *The Diploma of Higher Education 'red book'*, op. cit. par. 28.
16 *Renewal Proposal*, op. cit. p. 25.
17 Minutes of CNAA Inter-Faculty Studies Board visit to NELP on 6 and 7 May 1982, par. 1.4.
18 ibid. Summary.
19 ibid. par. 4.4.

20 Minutes of CNAA Inter-Faculty Studies Board meeting held on 12 July 1982, par. 2.2.
21 ibid. par. 5.
22 Minutes of CNAA Inter-Faculty Studies Board visit to NELP on 13 December 1984, Summary.
23 ibid. par. 21.
24 *Proposal for a Course to Provide Opportunities for Programmes of Study leading to the awards of MA/MSc by Independent Study and Post-graduate Diploma by Independent Study*, 1984, par. 2.3, p.5.
25 ibid. par. 1. p. 1.
26 ibid. par. 1.3. p. 2.
27 NELP Academic Programme Committee, *Report of the Triennial Review of BA/BSc by Independent Study held at the Barking Precinct, on Thursday, November 15th, 1984*, p. 2.
28 D. M. Robbins, *Planning and Development: A paper for the consideration of the course committees*, Internal paper, 31.5.85, par. 3.

Part 3

The Movements

Part 2 has shown that the goals of the original DipHE working party were consistent with those intended for NELP and for the public sector of higher education. It has shown that staff involved with the development of the new course shared the political commitment embodied in the new institution, but that differences emerged within a few years. Part 2 has described the ways in which three different emphases crystallized in association with the three courses – the full-time DipHE, the part-time DipHE, and the BA/BSc by Independent Study. It would be false, however, to suggest that three ideological positions have been involved historically in an equal contest for supremacy within the School for Independent Study. It has always been the case that there has been one fundamental position which has wanted to regard the other two as revisionist tendencies. In the early 1970s all of those involved with the development of the School for Independent Study were reformers or, at the very least, were prepared to subscribe to a common reformist platform. Broadly, this implied a commitment to equal opportunities for all and to the attempt to realize an equal society. The values and the goals of post-World War II socialism were assumed. The differences of emphasis seemed, at first, to be only differences in relation to means rather than to ends. The originators of the NELP DipHE believed that the reform of the educational system would be a significant advance towards an equal society. Educational reformism was, therefore, the primary strand in the development of the School. Since the other two strands which, for convenience, I call the 'personalist' and the 'intellectualist' positions, seemed to evolve within the educational context, it is understandable that they should appear simply to be off-shoots of educational reform. During the 1970s, however, the logic of both the 'personalist' and the 'intellectualist' positions meant that neither could be confined within an education context alone. Both offered reforming emphases in their own right. 'Personalism' believed in the potential for social change of encounters between people across all barriers while 'intellectualism' believed that the impetus towards social equality which might be made by the redistribution of knowledge within society would be constricted by an identification of knowledge with school or educational knowledge. One phenomenon of the period has been, therefore, that the educational reformers have lost the monopoly of reformist thought and endeavour which they confidently possessed at the outset.

The following pages attempt to differentiate between 'personalism', 'intellectualism' and what I would prefer to call 'Educationism'. What emerges from the three accounts is that the one strand which has diminished to an 'educationist' stance in wishing to bring about social change by tinkering with some of the elements of the educational system – such as access and assessment – still attempts, nevertheless, to assert its ideological comprehensiveness and to appropriate or assimilate the other two strands. It is my contention, however, that attempts to assimilate become attempts to neutralize. 'Personalism' and 'intellectualism' cannot be subsumed under educational reformism. They are both products of a disenchantment with educational reformism and they both defy and oppose the limited reformist perspective of educationists.

It follows that the next three chapters are not simply meant to differentiate between three orientations. They are meant to disengage and disentangle. They are meant to offer a basis for resisting the incorporation of discrete approaches into an educational reformist attitude which still possesses some nostalgic, emotional attraction but which no longer engages with our real social and political difficulties. In particular, these chapters are meant to identify and liberate the 'intellectualist' strand, so that I can indicate its distinctive importance in my Conclusion.

These chapters are also characterized by an attempt to oscillate backwards and forwards between the 'private' world of the School's courses – detailed in Part 2 – and the public sphere of British social, political, and intellectual history, certainly of the last 20 years and, sometimes, of the post-World War II period. What has to be remembered is that this book itself is casting into a public sphere an interpretation of events which I have constructed in the year of writing – 1987. I am both analysing connections which were articulated and projecting some which were not. The significance of the temporal dimension has to be acknowledged and allowed for. There is undoubtedly, and unashamedly, a sense in which I am now projecting vicariously in the present some interpretations which were not projected in the past. Equally, my present interpretation of events does not emanate only from these events themselves, but from my present retrospective reflection on the ways in which ideas and occurrences were historically interconnected. I can illustrate these general comments by making some introductory remarks about the three chapters which make up Part 3.

The first chapter examines the movement which sought to promote social change through educational reform. It begins with an analysis of a book – *Dear Lord James* – in which one of the main protagonists in the development of the NELP DipHE – Tyrrell Burgess – had already advanced a political and philosophical position in the public sphere before the establishment of the original working party at the polytechnic. The stance presented in that book tacitly had ruling authority in the deliberations of the DipHE working party. The essential feature of the educational reformist position was the conviction that the education system militated against equality because the middle class training of middle class teachers inevitably resulted in the failure of working class pupils. The programme of the educational reformers was about empowerment. It was about engineering ways in which working class people might become accredited as teachers so as, in their turn, to accredit the achievement of pupils. The beauty of the DipHE was that it was a new award which constituted the 'first cycle' of a new pattern of teacher training. The beauty of the NELP DipHE was that the course offered a mechanism by which it undertook to accredit the achievement of students in meeting the needs which they had identified for themselves. The purpose of the exercise was to process people out of positions of impotence into positions of power, out of situations in which they were branded as failures into ones in which they could have confidence derived from educational success. The purpose was to increase people's self-fulfilment and to enhance their life-chances. There was little overt concern about the level of attainment of students, either at the point of entry or at the point of assessment. The process could, therefore, engender confidence in students, but it could not guarantee that the confidence was not, objectively, misplaced. The educational reformers wanted to secure professional recognition for the DipHE award so as to continue the process of empowerment of the underprivileged through education and into occupations and professions. The political platform of the educational reformers did not involve the de-construction of the professions but it did involve attempting to insert the underprivileged into professions on the strength of the credit of the DipHE. Because the diploma neglected to secure objective levels of attainment, professional bodies were normally unimpressed by the confident assertions of standing made either by diplomates or by the course on their behalf.

The essence of the practice of the course was, I believe, to secure empowerment for people who had hitherto been marginalized in our society. Additionally, however, the educational reformers produced an elaborate rationale for the course's practice which was designed to secure credibility for the process. This rationale argued that 'competence' rather than 'knowledge' should be the goal of higher education courses and, in turn, the prerequisite for flexible employment. This might have carried weight had the course been able to devise methods for assessing the attainment of levels of competence. It did not do so, and the chapter documents the way in which 'competence' came to mean 'personal competence'. The practice of the DipHE became steadily more 'personalist' while, in the public sphere, Tyrrell Burgess himself continued to advance the claims of independent study as an example of student-centred and problem-based learning. The course continued to represent in public what it no longer was in private. The first chapter then tries to show that in the sphere of publications and public affairs, the rationale for the course – which was now a disembodied rhetoric – became appropriated by positions which were hostile to the traditional sympathies of the educational reformers. Government policies have made capital out of the weak link of educational reformism – its neglect of the development of a critical intellect. There is now little to choose between the platforms of the Government and the educational reformers. Both now are educationists who seek to use schools to engineer social change and both seek to minimize intellectual endeavour by encouraging 'competence' or 'capability' in course content and personality profiles in assessment.

Whereas the first chapter follows the relationship – mediated by Tyrrell Burgess and, latterly, also by John Stephenson – between the private practice of the School and the public representation of it from 1970 until the present, the second chapter begins the consideration of 'personalism' by analysing the progression in the thinking though the period of an influential social psychologist – Paul Halmos. I wanted to understand the rise of counselling historically and sociologically and Halmos's *The Faith of the Counsellors* (1965) was an obvious introduction. A great deal followed from this point of reference and the chapter uses Halmos's subsequent work as an indicator of changes which were occurring in parallel with the endeavours of the educational reformers. Halmos argued in 1965 that political mechanisms for securing social change were discredited and his blueprint for the 1970s was that society would be transformed by the steady growth of the caring professions. Training for these professions would involve preparing people to be personally affective and also encouraging them to test the relevance of sociological or psychological theory in their case-work practice and to modify it accordingly. Halmos's ideal for social work training was not unlike that of the educational reformers for teacher training, but he insisted more forcibly on the need to sustain an attitude of critical intelligence. By 1978, Halmos felt that an upsurge of political activism had discredited his personalist hopes. The second chapter tries to show, however, that a movement was growing simultaneously which advocated a form of 'personalism' with which Halmos would not have been at all happy. The 'personal growth movement' can either be seen to be totally a-political in its concern with the self-development of individuals or it can be considered to be politically utopian in supposing that social change will follow automatically from the personal transformation of all. In either case, the 'personal growth movement' is not political in the sense so far used of the movement for educational reform. It does not propose procedures for securing social and political change. The chapter considers the development of the personal growth movement in the period by particular reference to the work of John Rowan. Against this back-cloth in the recent history of ideas, the chapter examines the nature of the 'personalist' influence on the practice of the School. The main source for this interpretation is an article written by Ian Cunningham which was included as a case-study of experiential learning by Boydell and Pedler in their *Management Self-development. Concepts and Practices* (1981). The use of this article deliberately links Cunningham's contribution to the development of the School both to the historical account of 'personalism' contained in this chapter and to the accounts of varieties of 'personalism' assessed in Part 1.

The second chapter ends by re-affirming the suggestion made in Part 2 that an alliance has now developed between the 'educationist' and the 'personalist' strands. The remainder of the book tries to argue that this alliance has forfeited the conditions for possible, continuing reformism. In short, the book now argues that 'intellectualism' must take the initiative as a hopeful successor to the educational reformism which first inspired the DipHE in the early 1970s. Chapter 3 of this Part analyses the movement of ideas in the 'new directions in the sociology of education' which I adapted to the context of the School for Independent Study in the 1970s and which found expression in the submission for the BA/BSc by Independent Study and in the operation of the course itself. The crucial book in the public sphere was *Knowledge and Control* (1971), edited by Michael Young. The chapter argues that there were several conflicting positions contained within that collection of essays. It follows one intellectual route from phenomenology to Marxist political activism, and it suggests that the aspect of the book devoted to classroom inter-action was congenial to the personalist/educationalist alliance. The chapter agrees with the generally held judgement that this movement foundered at around 1977, but it tries to salvage two positive conclusions. Firstly, it claims that the element of *Knowledge and Control* supplied by Bourdieu – emphasizing the inter-relationship between the subjective construction of knowledge and the reception of past subjective knowledge which has become objectified – has come to the fore in the period since 1977 and remains a tenable position. Secondly, it shares Bernbaum's explanation for the failure of 'new directions'. Bernbaum argued in 1977 that the movement had intellectual aspirations which were contaminated by the fact that they were generated and then disseminated in contexts which were dominated by the affective norms of educationists. This chapter applies this critique of 'new directions' to the BA/BSc by Independent Study which had been modelled on its thinking. The conclusion here is that the 'intellectualist' revision of educational reformism must shake off the 'educationist' norms – now reinforced by 'personalist' values – if it is still to offer a reformist stance.

For too long educational reformism has branded intellectual rigour and integrity as elitist along with academicism. In no sense is this book a defence of academicism. I have not deviated from the view I shared with the educational reformers in the early 1970s that the opportunity to think and reflect should not be the preserve of a sponsored minority group of 'academics'. The campaign for academic freedom has been a campaign for the freedom of academics when, instead, we need to strive to create the conditions which allow everyone the opportunity freely to develop and exercise their intellectual powers. If we are undergoing a Knowledge Revolution and if, therefore, knowledge is power, a renewed commitment to the advancement of the democratic intellect might offer the hope that the empowerment of the deprived might become real rather than illusory.

8

The Promotion of Social Change through Educational Reform

Eric Robinson's *The New Polytechnics* (1968) acknowledges the advice and encouragement given by Tyrrell Burgess.[1] Since 1965 Burgess had been a senior research officer and, later, a research fellow in the Higher Education Research Unit at the London School of Economics. Earlier he had first made his reputation by editing *After the Sixth Where?* for the Advisory Centre for Education in 1962[2] and with his *Guide to English Schools* (1964).[3] He joined the staff of North-East London Polytechnic in 1970, the same year he published his report on comprehensive schools – *Inside Comprehensive Schools*.[4] He became Head of a unit which was created at the beginning of the polytechnic's existence – the Centre for Institutional Studies. Whereas the Course Development Unit was established to control the kinds of courses which the polytechnic might develop for CNAA approval, the function of C.I.S. was to monitor the progress of the institution in fulfilling its policy intentions. With John Pratt, Burgess produced *Innovation in Higher Education: technical education in the UK* (1971)[5] and *Polytechnics: a report* (1974)[6] in both of which they observed a process of 'academic drift', by which they meant that they detected a tendency for technical institutions or polytechnics to adopt academic norms – to reproduce academic courses and to be compromised by reducing the attention given to sandwich and part-time students. It was not only the substance of Burgess and Pratt's findings that was important. Their researches gained their coherence and conviction from a firm attempt to adhere to Popperian procedures. They made a concerted effort to regard social policies as equivalent in status to natural science hypotheses and, with Popper, to treat them as subject to falsification rather than verification. To what problem might a social policy be thought to be or be intended to be a solution, and what would tell us, not that the policy has succeeded – since no such evidence could ever provide absolute validation of the policy – but that it had failed and was in need of a further hypothetical reformulation? It was the rigour with which this approach was carried through at the Centre for Institutional Studies which caused Bryan Magee to indicate in his introduction to Popper in the Fontana Modern Masters series that it was only in this unit at NELP that there had yet been any serious attempt to apply Popperian principles in the analysis of social issues.[7]

But Burgess was not only a researcher. He was – and is – supremely a campaigner. In the late 1960s he was involved in founding a Society for the Promotion of Educational Reform through Teacher Training (SPERTTT), and out of the discussions of members grew *Dear Lord James. A critique of Teacher Education*, edited by Burgess in 1971. It was published as advice to the committee of enquiry under the chairmanship of Lord James of Rusholme which had been established by the then Secretary of State for Education and Science – Mrs Thatcher. Although Burgess's introduction is anxious to state that the book is not a manifesto, he is eager to insist that it is representative of the thoughts and feelings of a diverse group of people who initially came together in protest:

> SPERTTT began as a protest, a protest first against the inadequate experience, despite improvement, of most children in our schools. We believed reform was vital – but however much the Inspectorate may advise, the Schools Council publish, the DES suggest, or the LEAs withhold or dispense, none of these seemed likely to enrich the provision in schools or the experience of children unless the classroom teachers were adequately trained and prepared.
>
> So our protest was directed at this most sensitive area of the educational cycle – at the point where teachers are made. . . .
>
> We haven't ourselves had the resources to mount a full-scale inquiry. Most of us believed this was necessary and have urged successive Governments to establish one. But even without such an inquiry there was much evidence we could rely upon, much that could be collected by volunteers. We appealed, therefore, for members – and we were joined by a host of supporters from all over the country – to mount local study groups, arrange conferences, examine special facets of teacher preparation, with a view to publicizing and disseminating good practices, and in order to incite those responsible for preparing teachers to think critically, and to act radically in pursuit of improvement.[8]

According to Burgess's summary this swell of protest originated in three grounds for complaint. The first was, in essence, that the egalitarian potential of comprehensive schools was being undermined by the provision of dominantly middle-class teachers by the teacher training establishment:

> We know that the students in colleges of education, like students in universities, are socially homogeneous. They come, on the whole, from middle-class families – at least very few of their parents are manual workers, skilled or unskilled (and those who have such parents soon adopt an attitude and style indistinguishable from the rest). Their experience of education has been typically success at 11-plus and grammar school. In other words, their background and education are quite different from those of most children, indeed from those of the children they themselves will be teaching.[9]

The corollary of this observation was that working-class children were being failed in schools by their middle-class teachers. In consequence, the actual complaint brought to the attention of the James Committee was that too little was currently being done in teacher training to acquaint potential teachers with the social context in which they and their pupils would be working. Training was needed which would 'free teachers from the presuppositions of their background' and 'help them positively to understand' the social context from which they were alienated by their background.

The second complaint about teacher education was 'that it is academic and remote from reality'. Burgess is cautious in representing this position because he acknowledges that a training which derives too closely from real experience forfeits the possibility of becoming critical, but he insists that existing training does not help the potential teacher to cope with some of his or her likely real professional problems – typically represented here as difficulties of control rather than of communication:

> Many young teachers find, not that their ideas are inappropriate but that their training has ignored some of the most obvious practical skills which a teacher needs – like how to achieve order in a difficult school.[10]

College of education courses had failed to 'evolve a properly understood vocational education at a high intellectual level' and the committee was urged to attend seriously to this problem. The third complaint was related. The first two chapters of *Dear Lord James* – one written by a student – provide evidence to suggest that the typical teacher training course 'offers too little intellectual challenge'. Burgess's summary suggests that this news would surprise nobody in education and hints that failure rates were notoriously and suspiciously low and that student teachers often found themselves 'covering similar ground to that which they tramped over at A-level' and involved in practical work which was 'appropriate for seven year olds'.

Dear Lord James substantiates these grounds for complaint but, more importantly, it recommends solutions. These are mainly contained in Part Three – 'New Structures' which is dominated by the contributions made by Robinson – 'Degrees for Teachers' and by Burgess himself – 'Teacher Training within Higher Education'. Together, these articles constitute a bid for the inclusion of degrees for teachers as an intrinsic part of the provision of the new polytechnics. Burgess's summary of aims in his Introduction is a clear statement which approaches a manifesto:

> We believe that the structure and content of courses should be based on clear objectives. The curriculum needs to be conceived in relation to a knowledge-based, rationally constituted teaching profession, in which unity arises through diversity of function. The general principle underlying it is that all academic study should be viewed within the professional frame of reference. We are quite clear in wishing to reduce the academic and social isolation of the colleges. The recommendations for the detailed curriculum are rooted in what we take to be the future needs of the schools, and they imply a much closer relationship than

hitherto between educational theory, subject specialization and educational practice. Our suggestions for doing this centre round a strengthened relationship between schools and colleges. We accept the need for a well-considered teacher-tutor system based on schools, and we seek a coherent system involving schools, teacher centres and colleges, in which initial training, the probationary year and in-service education offer a total and continuing form of teacher education.[11]

This general approach was the thrust behind the particular developments in the Department of Education at NELP in the first year of its existence – before there was any suggestion of a proposed Diploma of Higher Education. Burgess and Pratt – with the support of Deputy Director Robinson – were active in injecting Popperian principles into the submissions for the initial B.Ed and the in-service B.Ed as well as, later, for the M.Ed. These courses either developed the students' capacities to become 'teacher researchers' within their subsequent professional positions or encouraged practising teachers to formulate problems and propose solutions which were rooted in their real experiences in schools. The NELP In-Service B.Ed Degree (submitted to the CNAA in 1972 and re-submitted in 1978) was one of the six evaluated by Norman Evans between 1977 and 1980 in preparing his report for the DES on In-Service B.Ed Degrees. He clearly describes its characteristics in finding the causes of the sharp differentiation of the NELP case-study from the other five under his consideration:

> One of the vital reasons comes from the decision to have a 'bottom to top' design for the degree rather than a 'top to bottom'. This is vital because it means a decision to start from where the teachers are when they begin the programme, rather than making assumptions about where they are. And that means finding out where they are. As that is done as part of the programme rather than before it then one reason for this degree being different is clearly established. . . .
> This means that, as well as studying theory, teacher/students find that they are required to pay just as much attention to what is called 'course process'; the overall experience of working over the three years of the programme. 'Process' and theory are two complementary kinds of knowledge. At the same time, considerable emphasis appears to be given to the development of teaching competence. The authority of experts is accepted, but the value of experience has its own authority and both are subject to the same kinds of critical appraisal. The content of the programme is important, but no more so than the structure which organizes it. The emphasis is on inductive learning and teaching, though a didactic approach may be appropriate in some instances.[12]

So much of this might have been written about the Diploma of Higher Education course which was developed at NELP between 1972 and 1974 as a 'first-cycle' proposal in accordance with the James committee recommendations for a three-cycle process of teacher training. Why was NELP's DipHE not developed within its Department of Education? What happened between 1972 and 1974 which caused the pioneering DipHE to be situated within a new unit – the School for Independent Study?

The internal working party which met in 1972 and which prepared the blueprint for the NELP DipHE during the autumn of that year was dominated by educationists. Apart from Robinson and Burgess themselves, it also included David Gorbutt[13] who was Head of the Education department and John Stephenson who was at that time a member of that department. Additionally, there was one member from each of the departments of Biology, Humanities, and Art and Design. The educationists were determined to use the possibilities which had opened up as a result of the James committee's recommendation of a generalist first cycle to move a step beyond the goals of the Society for the Promotion of Educational Reform Through Teacher Training. The incorporation of the professional training of teachers into higher education had been achieved with the development of the B.Ed degree within the polytechnic, and the influence of this course would have the repercussions within schools desired by SPERTTT. But there now existed the possibility of infiltrating all professional training with the same ideology that had been developed specifically within the context of the teaching profession. Rather than the slow process of changing society by changing schools by changing teachers, there now existed the possibility of using a new two-year award within the system to promote directly social change through the educational reform of higher education.

While the B.Ed submission sought to combine a 'bottom to top' approach with the transmission of the bases for acquiring specific teaching competence, the DipHE working party sought to adapt the same approach to enable students to become generally competent – equipped with 'transferable skills' which would enable them to become competent in a range of professional situations. The working party advanced cautiously with a common purpose. It singled out for attention a restricted range of professions – teaching, social work, administration, and communications – within which the necessary competences could, with some justice, be thought to be comparable. In essence, the notions of 'general competence, and 'transferability of skills' were defensible because the targeted professions were all ones which involved the common capacity to relate with other people, or to communicate with them, or to manage them. The skills which were to be transferred between professional contexts were, primarily, personal skills. The working party's report tentatively suggested that general competence might also involve the capacity to formulate problems and to test solutions, but this Popperian emphasis was not yet dominant.

The crucial change occurred at the beginning of 1973 with the establishment of the 'extended working party' and, simultaneously, with the news that Eric Robinson was to leave NELP at the end of that academic year. The solidarity of the original working party in supporting the pursuit of reformist educational goals was disrupted by the extension of the group to comprise, additionally, formal representatives of each of the faculties of the polytechnic. These representatives were scrutinized carefully (so that, for instance, the representative suggested by the faculty of Environmental Studies was never thought to be acceptable and never attended), but there was no altering the fact that the scope and balance of the group were inevitably different as, for the first time, it included engineers, economists, and sociologists, and was augmented by staff who saw their prime allegiance to their intellectual specialism rather than to the process of educational change. The extended working party and, subsequently, the DipHE Development Unit which sustained its more fully representative character both inherited the blueprint for the DipHE of the orignal working party and also found themselves caught up in an attempted process of initiation into the ideological perspective which had generated that blueprint. The success of that process was apparent in the mainly unchanged adoption of the basic structure for the course recommended by the original working party in the documentation submitted to the CNAA in December 1973. The differences of approach deriving from some of the new members of staff which began to emerge during the year of the DipHE Development Unit did not affect the writing of the main text. These differences were, however, embedded in the appendices submitted to the CNAA in May 1974. Appendix 5.5 offered 'specimen profiles of special interest study' which hypothesized in great detail several individual programmes of study, while Appendix 5.4 outlined the nature of the Central Studies Activity Programme and included 'specimen profiles of student activity' for that part of the course. Here were foreshadowed, respectively, the assumptions of the BA/BSc by Independent Study and of the part-time DipHE, both of which were approved in 1976. Those differences which had been contained in 1974 emerged, therefore, within two years, and the divergent versions of 'independent study' are discussed in the next two chapters. It was not, however, only the latent divergences which were relegated to appendices to the submission. These appendices also extended the argument of the educational reformists on two fronts – the practical and the philosophical.

Appendix 3 was devoted to a 'justification of the entry requirements: a review of the research'. It was a clear view of SPERTTT, as represented in *Dear Lord James*, that the exclusion of working-class students from places in teacher training institutions created and reinforced the detachment of many teachers from their pupils. Since working-class students were excluded because they lacked the formal qualifications for admission required by middle-class institutions, the inherently self-fulfilling cycle could only be destroyed if other criteria for admission could be shown to be legitimate. It was the intention of Appendix 3 to the DipHE submission to draw upon research evidence to show that there was 'no clear relationship between student achievement at entry and performance at the end of courses'. Part One of the appendix summarized, in particular, the work of Stock and Pratzner,[14] Scott,[15] and Petty,[16] which led to the conclusion that

We are therefore encouraged in our view that entry to our programme should not be determined solely on academic grounds, and are willing to waive the formal entry requirements in the case of applicants who demonstrate a high level of interest and motivation.[17]

Part Two illustrated the low take up rate of higher education in the polytechnic's three parent authorities – showing that Newham, Barking, and Waltham Forest had the lowest take-up rates of university places in the Greater London area, with two of them having less than a third of the GLC average. The evidence was overwhelming that the constituency of the polytechnic was precisely one in which exclusion from higher education was self-fulfilling. Part Three presented an analysis of the performance of students studying for the University of London teacher's certificate within the polytechnic's department of Education in relation to their prior academic qualifications. Based on the analysis of one intake of students, the report from the department of Education staff suggested that

> high academic entrance qualifications do not necessarily lead to marked success on our course.[18]

This concentration on evidence provided by the department of Education in respect of performance within a teacher training course indicates that the appendix was primarily the product of the educational reformists. The appendix regards the DipHE as cycle one of a reformed teacher training package. When, therefore, the appendix summarizes the findings of G.A. Cortis in 'Predicting Student Performance in Colleges of Education' (1968),[19] in which he demonstrated that the academic performance of students was dependent on prior academic qualification while their practical teaching success was related to previous experience, the conclusion is quickly drawn that the indicator of practical success is the relevant one for the DipHE:

> This type of investigation is more relevant to the DipHE programme because of its dependence upon practical and personal relationship elements.[20]

The logic of this case would have been strong had the DipHE still been oriented towards people-centred professions. But from January 1973 onwards this was no longer the situation. The course's willingness to respond to the 'special interests' of all students meant that students might come into contact with specialist staff and departments within the polytechnic where personal qualities were less highly esteemed than knowledge or understanding. It was here that Burgess's Popperianism offered a solution. The essence of the DipHE programme was not just that it was 'student-centred' but also that it was 'problem-centred'. For Burgess, the proposed DipHE course was itself a trial solution to the formulated problems of higher education and, as such, subject to testing and falsification. Even more, however, was this framework of thinking to be seen as the key constitutive focus of the course. Students were to be asked to propose programmes of study for themselves which would be solutions to the problems which they had identified. The purpose of monitoring assessment was to provide a formal context for falsification and, therefore, for the reformulation of problems and the redesigning of proposed solutions. If Popperian principles informed the course's process, it was also assumed that the content of the students' proposed solutions should have a problem-orientation. The group activities which were to be part of the Central Studies programme were to involve an enactment of the problem-solving process. This central concentration on methods of acting and learning would provide support to students in their confrontation with the subject specialists throughout the polytechnic with whom they would work in their special interest studies. By identifying a problem in the 'real world' for which existing knowledge – organized in traditional compartments of subject specialism – offered only a provisional solution, the students were to be the instruments of the course in issuing an epistemological challenge to the institution's discipline-based expertise and, at the same time, instruments of their own self-determination since the solution of the 'objective' problem which they identified would enable them to solve the personal or educational problem which had generated their total proposed curriculum. It was in this way that the Popperian rationale for the course accommodated the 'people-orientation' of the original working party as well as the new orientation which had grown stronger as the course planning of the extended working party had inevitably come to recognize the intellectual characteristics of the whole institution.

The logic of discovery dispenses with the need for the prior accumulation of knowledge to secure knowledge's further advancement. Appendix 3 of the DipHE submission did not apply Popperian principles in its justification of non-standard entry, but other appendices offer an outline of Burgess's view of the proposed course in relation to his larger, social vision. *Education After School* which Burgess published in 1977 builds substantially on material which had been used in those parts of the appendices which were devoted to the 'substantiation of the philosophy of the programme'. The effect of this publication, therefore, was to represent in a public sphere a philosophical rationale for the course which might otherwise have been confined to the pages of a CNAA submission. As Burgess admits in his first chapter:

This book began as a survey and has ended as a manifesto.[21]

The introduction of the DipHE course at NELP had been an attempt actually to insert the aims of SPERTTT into the practice of British higher education, while *Education After School* uses the thinking which developed in preparing that one course to confront ideologically the structure and organization of the whole of the world's post-school education systems. The second chapter of the book asks what education after school is for. Drawing on material used in Appendix 2.3 of the DipHE submission, Burgess elaborates, with international examples, his distinction between the 'autonomous' and the 'service' traditions of higher education, and he concludes:

My own view is that the balance of post-school education in a democratic society should be heavily in favour of the service tradition. Its
object must be explicitly to serve the needs of individuals and of society
at large, rather than the needs either of the academic community or of
individual disciplines. There is a place for the autonomous tradition,
but it is a limited one. A society might well decide to support it: indeed
many societies do support museums, concert halls, opera houses, art
galleries and even authors. There is a case to be made for the university
as a work of art.[22]

The third chapter asks 'Whom is it for?' and considers distinctions between
'elitist' and 'mass' provision through a discussion of the Robbins Report and
the 'binary policy' introduced by Anthony Crosland. Burgess's position is
that the slight and gradual extension of 'elite' provision cannot be accepted
as a substitute for a 'mass' provision which must genuinely respond to the
needs of all. The lesson is that

in the future it will not be enough to expand higher education as
hitherto.[23]

The fourth chapter describes existing world provision of education after
school. In spite of an apparent diversity of forms, Burgess contends that
there are underlying features of conformity. One of these is 'The "structure"
of knowledge' which manifests itself in common academic organizations,
particularly in the form of 'subject departments'. Burgess argues:

The department presupposes an organized body of knowledge, which is
understood by some people (professors, and to a decreasing extent
assistant professors and lecturers of various grades) and passed on to
others. The teachers possess something which it is their duty to impart:
their job is to initiate the young into the mysteries of a craft.[24]

This domination of the subject department is a recent phenomenon and it
is one which would appear to have been challenged by the 'interdisciplinary'
innovations of the new universities in Britain in the 1960s. Elaborating on
points made in Appendix 2.4 – devoted to 'Reasons for Rejecting a "Modular" Solution' – Burgess suggests that 'innovative' inter-disciplinary or modular approaches to course design simply reinforce the 'top-down' attitudes to
which higher education generally conforms. Burgess's discussion of 'levels',
'standards', and 'excellence' and his consideration of the prevailing theories
of teaching and learning lead him to conclude that the conformity in higher
education practice which he perceives derives from the need of some people
to use knowledge as a way of maintaining power over others:

The teachers possess the power, and the students do not. The teachers
determine what the subject is and how it shall be presented. They
arrange, before the students arrive, the course, curriculum, syllabuses,
and the detail of timetables. The students must take it or leave it.[25]

At this point *Education After School* shifts from a diagnosis of the problem towards the proposal of a solution – from 'survey' to manifesto. In a section of the book devoted to 'The Logic of Learning' the implications of Popperianism are detailed more comprehensively than they had been in Appendix 2.5, which had explored the 'Implications of the Logic of Discovery for Educational Theory and Practice', but the fundamental point remains the same:

> what is important is not a particular fact or even a particular ordered collection of facts, but *method*. It is method rather than information which gives mastery, and it is method which must be the chief business of education.[26]

The acquisition of this mastery will enable people to gain control over their own situations. In a passage which potentially destroys the separation of adult education from higher education, Burgess comments:

> Education after school, then, is education for adults, all adults. And the job of the education service can be briefly stated. It is to go to adults, and help them to formulate their problems, to try solutions, to test them – and thus to build up a mastery of their circumstances. The accumulated wisdom of the ages is little use to an idle man with a depressed wife and two small ricketty children contemplating the damp pouring down the wall of their one room. But education need not be so impotent.[27]

It is not just that education after school must assist people with their practical problems. Burgess is explicit in relating his notion of competence to the grander needs of a social democracy:

> Democracy requires political competence of a high order. . . . if democracy is not to be merely oligarchy tempered by electoral defeat, people need to know how to run democratic institutions. If power is to be shared, people need to know how to use it. They need to know how social institutions work and how they can be changed.[28]

The necessary 'mastery' or 'competence' is to be acquired by allowing students to take responsibility for their own learning, and Burgess proceeds to give a brief account of the development of the DipHE within the School for Independent Study at NELP. The purpose of this description is to show that the ideal form of education after school predicated by the first half of the book is actually possible, to suggest

> that it is possible to enable students to create their own programmes of higher education, to offer this opportunity to most people whether or not they have done well in the education service in the past, and to be, in short, a genuine service to the community. The programme differs from others in higher education in that it is based, not upon subject disciplines or upon combinations of subjects, but upon the logic of learning. It is this which gives the programme its coherence and the students an assurance of its value.[29]

It was this certainly which should have given the programme its coherence, but even as Burgess was writing these words in 1976 a widening gap was opening between the justificatory rhetoric of *Education After School* and the realities of the everyday dealings with students.

The divorce of the reforming activities of 'independent study' from the philosophical rationale which had been provided by Burgess's interpretation of Popper was dramatically consolidated when Burgess stood down as Head of the School for Independent Study in 1978. After taking a sabbatical year he has held the position of Reader in the Philosophy of Social Institutions at NELP – a position which has enabled him to undertake a range of social investigations and enquiries and simultaneously to sustain his more speculative interests in social philosophy. In the educational field he has been involved in the advancement of two movements which have their origins in the educational reformism of the late 1960s and early 1970s: the 'Education for Capability' campaign and the campaign in favour of educational 'profiles'. Burgess has maintained the theoretical connection between these two movements and the notion of 'independent study' described in *Education After School* while his successor as the Head of the School for Independent Study – John Stephenson – has sought both to retain internally in practice the School's allegiance to an emphasis of competence and to associate that practice publicly with the tradition of educational reform. Stephenson had been a member of the original DipHE working party in 1972 and had been largely responsible for the appendix to the CNAA submission which made the case for non-standard entry to the proposed course. It was his contribution to *Outcomes of Education* (1980), edited by Tyrrell Burgess and Elizabeth Adams, which specifically linked the practice of 'independent study' to the book's general consideration of

> one of the most serious educational problems of our time: that is, how to record and assess the outcomes of education at the end of compulsory schooling.[30]

Other contributors described their solutions to the problem of how to offer every young person

> something to show for the years spent in school.[31]

John Blanchard describes developments in English at Comberton Village College; Colin Fletcher the Sutton Centre Profile; Patricia Broadfoot the Scottish Pupil Profile System; and, amongst others, Don Stansbury describes the Record of Personal Experience which he has designed and used. Writing in 1979, the editors comment that they and the contributors all believe that

> a statement of pioneering practice together with feasible outline proposals for a new national system can make a particularly important contribution at this time. The present proposals for the reform of examining at 16 plus are for changes in form and organisation rather than of substance. After more than a decade of effort the reform of examina-

tions at this stage has been found to be a dead end. Already the new Chairman of the Schools Council can contemplate publicly the possibility that these examinations might cease.[32]

In other words, the practice of NELP's independent study is offered as an example of a possible alternative to the system of public examinations for schools. Whereas in the early to mid-1970s the developments at NELP of the B.Ed and then the DipHE were themselves consciously reformist activities, by the end of the decade it had become much more the case that representations of the practice of independent study were drawn upon in support of wider campaigns involving education at all levels. Whereas the practice of the School for Independent Study was offered in *Education After School* as a case-study in support of a philosophical position, the situation had altered significantly by the end of the 1970s. As the cohesive influence of Burgess's over-arching Popperianism steadily collapsed, the representation of the reformist practice which had seemed to be its logical consequence began to usurp its status and to take on the mantle of its functional or propagandist authority. Whereas there had been a counterpoint between philosophy and practice, there developed, instead, a counterpoint between an idealized practice in conformity with educational reformist principles and divergent actual practices. Nowhere has this been clearer than in relation to the 'Education for Capability' campaign.

'Education for Capability' was the title of a series of three lectures delivered at the Royal Society of Arts in November 1978. The message contained in these lectures (one of which was given by Tyrrell Burgess) was later summarized in a manifesto to which over 140 leading figures in British industry, commerce, public service and academic life appended their names in support when it was published in *The Times* in February 1980. An 'Education for Capability' committee of the Royal Society of Arts was established and quickly launched a Recognition Scheme which awarded prizes to courses in which the educational practice conformed with that advocated in the manifesto. NELP's DipHE was recognized under this scheme in 1982 and Tyrrell Burgess has subsequently edited an account of the campaign for the Royal Society of Arts under the title of *Education for Capability* (1986). These dates are all important in analysing the development of 'competence' and 'capability' in relation to 'independent study' since the early 1970s. With hindsight, it comes as no surprise that, as Minister of Education, Mrs Thatcher in 1972/3 wished to encourage the new Diploma of Higher Education course which Eric Robinson and SPERTTT so eagerly advocated. From opposite sides of the political fence both wanted to destroy the stranglehold of higher education exercised by academic institutions and an academic ideology. For both, the insertion of a new two-year course into the higher education system with non-academic goals and orientations might have just the effect which they held in common. Within the next five years, it became clear that the system had successfully resisted the skill-based infiltration of its ranks. The Thatcher government proceeded, instead, at first, simply to by-pass higher education in its attempts to make the country's training provision more responsive to its needs. The curriculum developments launched since 1979 by the Manpower Services Commission or advocated and analysed by the Further Education Unit have closely followed the thinking which under-pinned the original proposals for the NELP DipHE. The 1979 FEU publica-tion, *A Basis for Choice*, for instance, offered 12 key aims of a common core of training which have much in common with the skill objectives hypothetically produced both by the NELP DipHE working party and in the documentation to the CNAA for the approval of the DipHE. The FEU introduces these aims in the following way:

> The prescribed objectives are described in terms of a combination of observable performances to be expected of students and learning experiences which they should be offered. The commentary in italics following each objective is not prescriptive, but offers illustrations, examples and suggested methods.[33]

The emphasis is on the capacities to perform which the students should acquire, following the insistence of the planners of NELP's DipHE that the course should enable students to act more than to know. Similarly, FEU's commentary is illustrative within a general framework of purpose in the same way that NELP's DipHE submission was itself hypothetical rather than pre-scriptive. The 12 aims are summarized in a subsequent FEU document – *Basic Skills* (1982). They are to bring about:

(i) an informed perspective as to the role and status of a young person in an adult society and the world of work;

(ii) a basis from which the young person can make an informed and realistic decision with respect to his or her immediate future;

(iii) a continuing development of physical and manipulative skills, in both vocational and leisure contexts, and an appreciation of those skills in others;

(iv) an ability to develop satisfactory personal relationships with others;

(v) a basis on which the young person acquires a set of moral values applicable to issues in contemporary society;

(vi) a level of achievement in literacy and numeracy appropriate to ability and adequate to meet the basic demands of contemporary society;

(vii) competence in a variety of study skills likely to be demanded of the young person;

(viii) a capacity to approach various kinds of problems methodically and effectively, and to plan and evaluate courses of action;

(ix) sufficient political and economic literacy to understand the social environment and participate in it;

(x) an appreciation of the physical and technological environments, and the relationship between these and the needs of man in general and working life in particular;

(xi) a development of the everyday coping skills necessary to promote self-sufficiency in the young people;

(xii) a flexibility of attitude and willingness to learn sufficient to cope with future changes in technology and career.[34]

This is not the place to analyse in detail the developments in training in the United Kingdom since 1979. My point is simply that there is a marked affinity between the language and concepts associated with these developments and those associated with the planning of the NELP DipHE. The affinity has remained from the beginning of this period through to the present. The R.S.A Practical Communication Skills syllabus proposed in April 1980, for instance, is closely related to the FEU 'Basis for Choice' document and it comments:

> The range of skills included in the Practical Communication Skills syllabus corresponds closely to the objectives and experiences listed under Aims 4, 6, 7, 8, 11 and 12 in Appendix 1 of 'Basis for Choice'.

> *Transferability of Skills*
> Because of the high transferability of all the communication skills mentioned in the syllabus it is likely that they will also be used in and developed by the learning done in connection with Aims 1, 2, 3, 5, 9 and 10. All the skills, in fact, can be used in a variety of social and/or vocational contexts other than those in which they were learned.[35]

The belief in the 'transferability of skills' was a cornerstone of the NELP DipHE submission, but it was always only a belief and it was one which was soon shaken by the experiences of attempted implementation. Nevertheless, the same belief remains an important component of the rhetoric of recent training initiatives. It is present, to take another example, in the *Guide to Content and Quality on YTS/Approved Training Organisations* (1986), published by the Manpower Services Commission to bring together guidance issued by the Commission about the principles which should be applied to the design and delivery of YTS training programmes and the requirements an organization must meet to gain approval as an Approved Training Organization. In describing the recommended 'training plan with competence objectives', the Guide states:

> It is important that trainees, tutors and supervisors are clear about the competences that are expected to be achieved by the end of the programme. For this reason, the training plan should contain a range of competence objectives. Competence objectives say what a young person might be expected to be able to do by the end of the two-year period. They must be written in terms that trainees and their supervisors will understand, and should normally be couched in occupational terms. The set of competence objectives for a programme should encompass a broad occupational area. The achievement of these objectives taken together will require trainees to exercise occupational and

core skills, to demonstrate their ability to transfer skills and to show personal effectiveness (i.e. covering all four outcomes.)[36]

What is described here is a two-year course to enable young people to acquire general vocational competence through the learning of transferable skills. The brief for the 1986 YTS scheme very closely replicates the brief which the original DipHE working party set itself at NELP in 1972. Just at the moment in 1979 when this ideological orientation was set to engulf the world of training for the next decade[37] and when the experience of the School for Independent Study in operating the DipHE between 1974 and 1979 might have been in demand, there was, instead, a re-alignment of the public representation of independent study. The launching of the 'Education for Capability' campaign at this time represents the conclusive public differentiation of Burgess's notion of general competence from Robinson's more restricted notion of general vocational competence. The adoption of the DipHE ideology by the Manpower Services Commission reinforced the separation of 'training' from 'education' which the DipHE had sought to destroy. Having been rebuffed by academicism, the DipHE was now to be appropriated by training. The RSA manifesto of 1980 insists, therefore, that 'education' rather than simply MSC training schemes must be 'for capability'. In short, Burgess's endeavour to associate independent study practically and philosophically with the RSA campaign has been an attempt to sustain the challenge to the whole education system which the educational reformers had originally sought to make through the introduction of the DipHE. Elements of the manifesto reflect the wider vision of Burgess's *Education After School*. It reads:

> We, the undernamed, believe that there is a serious imbalance in Britain today in the full process which is described by the two words 'education' and 'training'. Thus, the idea of the 'educated man' is that of a scholarly, leisured individual who has been neither educated nor trained to exercise useful skills. Those who study in secondary schools or higher education increasingly specialize; and normally in a way which means that they are taught to practise only the skills of scholarship and science; to understand but not to act. They gain knowledge of a particular area of study, but not ways of thinking and working which are appropriate for use outside the education system.
>
> We believe that this imbalance is harmful to individuals, to industry and to society. Individual satisfaction stems from doing a job well through the exercise of personal capability. Acquisition of this capability is inhibited by the present system of education which stresses the importance of analysis, criticism and the acquisition of knowledge and generally neglects the formulation and solution of problems, doing, making and organizing; in fact, constructive and creative activity of all sorts.[38]

The hostility of the educational reformers to the acquisition and transmission of knowledge as expressed in *Dear Lord James* is here re-stated but there are new allies against academicism. The manifesto indicates its belief that there should be a culture of 'doing, making and organizing'. Burgess's distinctive emphasis of the exercise of reason in formulating and solving problems is united with those of designers, manufacturers, engineers, and managers in down-grading knowledge. The statement of 1980 anticipates the findings of Martin Wiener's *English Culture and the Decline of the Industrial Spirit, 1850-1980* which was published in 1981. Purporting to offer an historical account of Britain's ambivalent response to the industrial revolution which it had inaugurated, Wiener's book engages polemically with the political debates of the 1970s, and its partisan position rapidly acquired a 'factual' authority. Having argued that both Harold Wilson and James Callaghan retreated, after 1974, from the consequences of technological change back to the traditional, conservative, and moribund counter-culture which had stultified Britain's growth for a century, Wiener concludes:

> At the end of the day, it may be that Margaret Thatcher will find her most fundamental challenge not in holding down the money supply or inhibiting government spending, or even in fighting the shop stewards, but in changing this frame of mind. English history in the eighties may turn less on traditional political struggles than on a cultural contest between the two faces of the middle class.[39]

This cultural explanation of British economic decline has been one factor influencing the policy of the Conservative governments for higher education since 1979. The 'Education for Capability' campaign found itself caught up in that trend and it has offered a forum through which British Business and Industry have been able to express their discontent with the provision of the educational system. Through its influence in the University Grants Committee and the National Advisory Body the Government has been able to translate this discontent into tangible cultural change within higher education institutions. The ideological emphasis of the DipHE development of 1974 and of the MSC training schemes since 1979 has manifested itself in higher education in the 1980s as abrasive entrepreneurialism. In mitigation, however, there has been a further strand in the progression of 'competence' or 'capability'. 1981 was not only the year of the publication of Wiener's book but also Shirley Williams's *Politics is for People* in which she concludes:

> the old politics is dying. The battle to decide what the new politics will be like is just beginning. It is possible, just possible, that it will be a politics for people.[40]

The RSA manifesto of 1980 had wanted to generate a new cultural atmosphere which would enable greater national productivity, but it had also emphasized the importance of enhanced 'personal capability' for people within society. Burgess joined the Social Democratic Party as a founder member in 1982 and he has increasingly presented the notion of 'personal competence' as a means to the achievement of participatory democracy in opposition to a vocational competence which has become a means to occupational and economic success. The contributions which he has collected in *Education for Capability* (1986) highlight the need to bring about social change through educational reforms which recognize the efforts of individual people or projects. In describing the RSA Education for Capability Recognition Scheme in his Introduction, Burgess remarks:

> Whatever the general state of education, there are, buried away in the system at all stages, often unknown and unacknowledged, the projects and programmes which offer hope for the future. Throughout the system, people have found it possible to use to good advantage the circumstances in which they find themselves. Our Recognition Scheme rests on the belief that it is from the energy, imagination and ability of individuals that desirable change must come.[41]

In contrast to the centralizing tendencies of recent moves by the Government – the recommendations for a 'core' curriculum, the reform of external examinations at sixteen-plus and the use of the MSC to direct vocational education – the initiatives which show signs of hope are those which allow people to take responsibility for their own lives. Included amongst these hopeful initiatives are several which have already been celebrated in *Outcomes of Education* – notably Don Stansbury's techniques for recording Personal Experience and the practice of the NELP DipHE which is described specifically by Ginny Eley and referred to by Elizabeth Adams and Sir Toby Weaver.[42] It is not now simply that the practice of independent study at NELP respects individuals but also that the course development itself constitutes an example of hopeful 'bottom-up' initiating possibilities. In the post-1982 period, therefore, Burgess has articulated a new approach to the possibility of effecting social change. The educational reformism of the late 1960s assumed that social change would be secured by introducing changes into the educational system – whether by changing the training of teachers or by demolishing the academic orientation of most existing higher education. Paradoxically the success of these reforming activities has led to changes in society which in many respects the reformers have found unacceptable or undesirable. Instead of adopting student-centred practices in order to transform the nature of higher education, the educational reformers are now forced to embrace person-centredness itself as a direct means of social change. In the last decade, the educational reformism which considered itself to be radical has been appropriated by the ideological innovations and financial management of the Conservatives. The reformists have retained an apparent attachment to educational change but, increasingly, the real commitment is to the view that social change may be secured by changing people. Educational reformism has entered into a tacit alliance with the personal growth movement.

Notes

1 E. Robinson, *The New Polytechnics. The People's Universities*, Penguin Books, 1968, Acknowledgements.
2 T. Burgess (ed.), *After the Sixth Where?* Advisory Centre for Education, 1962.
3 T. Burgess, *Guide to English Schools*, Penguin Books, 1964.
4 T. Burgess, *Inside Comprehensive Schools*, HMSO, 1970.
5 T. Burgess and J. Pratt, *Innovation in Higher Education: technical education in the UK*, OECD, 1971.
6 T. Burgess and J. Pratt, *Polytechnics: a report*, Pitman, 1974.
7 B. Magee, *Popper*, Fontana Modern Masters, 1973, p. 77.
8 T. Burgess (ed.), *Dear Lord James. A Critique of Teacher Education*, Penguin Books, 1971, p. 8.
9 ibid. p. 9.
10 ibid. p. 10.
11 ibid. p. 11.
12 N. Evans, *Preliminary Evaluation: In-Service B.Ed Degrees. Six Case Studies*, 1980, p. 8.
13 Author of D. Gorbutt, 'The New Sociology of Education' in *Education for Teaching*, 1972.
14 W. E. Stock and F. C. Pratzner, 'Review of Research on Student Selection and the prediction of Success in Occupational Education.' Aug. 1969, Minnesota Research Co-ordination Unit in Occupational Education.
15 R. A. Scott, *Challenges Presented by Open Enrolment*, Cornell University, Ithaca, N.Y. 1971.
16 W. H. Petty, 'Entry Standards and Student Quality', *Times Educational Supplement*. 26.3.71.
17 Diploma of Higher Education, Submission to the CNAA, NELP, 1974. Appendix 3. Introduction. p. 1.
18 Diploma of Higher Education, Submission to the CNAA, op. cit. Appendix 3. Part 3. p. 1.
19 G. A. Cortis, 'Predicting Student Performance in Colleges of Education', *British Journal of Educational Psychology*, 1968.
20 Diploma of Higher Education, Submission to the CNAA, op. cit. Appendix 3. Part 1. p. 5.
21 T. Burgess, *Education After School*, London, 1977, p. 11.
22 ibid. p. 46.
23 ibid. p. 88.
24 ibid. p. 96.
25 ibid. p. 126.
26 ibid. p. 134.
27 ibid. p. 137.
28 ibid. p. 142.
29 ibid. p. 159.
30 T. Burgess and E. Adams, *Outcomes of Education*, London, Macmillan, 1980, p. xv.
31 ibid. p. xv.
32 ibid. p. xvi.
33 *A Basis for Choice*, Further Education Unit, 1979, p. 21.
34 *Basic Skills*, Further Education Curriculum Review and Development Unit, November 1982, p. 1.

35 E. P. Clark, 'The R.S.A. Practical Communication Skills Syllabus and the Common Core Curriculum for 16-year-old School Leavers', 14.4.1980.

36 *Guide to Content and Quality on YTS/Approved Training Organisations*, Manpower Services Commission, February 1986, p. 3.

37 For a sample of other works, see:

Towards a Competence-Based System, An FEU View, FEU, August 1984.

Development of the Youth Training Scheme. A Report, Manpower Services Commission, July 1985.

Core Competences in Engineering, An FEU View, FEU, November 1985.

Implementing Open Learning in Local Authority Institutions, FEU & Open Tech Unit of the Manpower Services Commission, 1986.

Continuing Professional Development: A Learner-Centred Strategy, FEU/PICKUP, Project Report, March 1986.

Staff Development for Open Learning Tutors. A summary, FEU/PICKUP, Project Report, 1986.

Training for Skills, Manpower Services Commission, May 1986.

Retraining Adults, FEU/REPLAN, Project Report, August 1986.

38 This is an extract from the text as it was issued by the RSA at the time of its advertisement of the second Recognition Scheme in 1981. The text which is reproduced at the beginning of T. Burgess (ed.), *Education for Capability* (1986) is modified interestingly. In particular, the 1986 version explicitly emphasizes the assumed value of the acquisition of knowledge in its rendering of the second paragraph:

> This imbalance is harmful to individuals, to industry and to society. A well-balanced education should, of course, embrace analysis and the acquisition of knowledge. But it must also include the exercise of creative skills, the competence to undertake and complete tasks, and the ability to cope with everyday life; and also doing all these things in co-operation with others.

39 M. J. Wiener, *English Culture and the Decline of the Industrial Spirit, 1850-1980*, Cambridge University Press, 1981, p. 166.

40 S. Williams, *Politics is for People*, Penguin, 1981, p. 209.

41 T. Burgess (ed.), *Education for Capability*, NFER-Nelson, p. 4.

42 See Burgess, op. cit. pp. 146-50; p. 77; and p. 57.

9

The Promotion of Social Change
through Personal Growth

In his posthumously published *The Personal and the Political. Social Work and Political Action* (1978) Paul Halmos clearly articulated the distinction which he was making in his title:

> Today, a seemingly simple polarization emerges. *On the one hand*, one can work for the betterment of human relations by working chiefly politically, that is to say, by advocating, prompting, and actively effecting 'the authoritative allocation of resources'. Acting politically means working so as to affect the very scaffolding of the rules whereby society's edifice is erected. *On the other hand*, one can work for the betterment of human relations at an individual level, working as a 'personal service professional' or paraprofessional or voluntary worker. Here one's own personality, as well as one's knowledge and skills are made to serve other single individuals or families so that they can review their own ways of conducting themselves in human relationships.[1]

The whole point of his book is to argue against this polarization in favour of a constant process of 'equilibration' between the two modes of social change, but the differentiation helps to clarify the argument I was presenting at the end of the last chapter. The movement for educational reform, which was an important influence on the development of independent study at NELP, began as a political movement which harnessed person-centredness as a means towards the achievement of system-reforming ends, but it has almost become buried in a personal movement in which the means have become the ends. To continue with Halmos's distinction, the staff who were once 'reformers' have become 'therapists':

> Both types are 'betterers' of the condition of man according to their criteria of what constitutes 'betterment'. The first, the *reformers*, take recourse to advocacy or action on behalf of a group or a whole society; their objective is the changing of the system of society or, at least, of part of the system. Sometimes the urgency, the radicalness and total ambition to change things ranks the reformist as a 'revolutionary', who is only a reformist in a hurry. The social change-agent in the second

category aims at relating himself personally to another, enabling the other to make use of certain aspects of the change-agent's personality, or of the change-agent's knowledge and skill, or of the relationship between the change-agent and the other, to bring about a change in his relationship to his environment. I call this betterer – this change-agent – the *therapist*, or the *counsellor*.[2]

Much of Halmos's published work throughout his career was devoted to an exploration of the tensions between the political and the personal, reform and therapy. His work both analyses the oscillations between the two poles and also registers them historically. The first chapter of *The Faith of the Counsellors* (1965) was entitled 'The Discrediting of Political Solutions', but in the opening paragraph of that chapter in the 1978 edition Halmos comments:

This historical account was written in 1965, for the first edition of this book, and the same account would have to be given today for the second edition if we were to describe what had happened to the faith in political initiatives during the middle decades of this century. Since the end of the 'Sixties there has been a strong political revival in the west and a corresponding disillusionment with personalist or personal counselling solutions. And now, by the end of the 'Seventies it would be appropriate to study the 'discrediting of personalist solutions' by political radicalism.[3]

It is now almost 10 years since Halmos made this observation. Consideration of the ways in which the personal growth orientation has permeated the practice and ideology of independent study since 1972 will offer a basis for reflecting on the accuracy of Halmos's historical perceptions as well as on the present situation.

In *The Faith of the Counsellors* Halmos listed seven factors which he thought had contributed to the discrediting of political solutions in the middle of the twentieth century. Two of these can be located with some historical precision. Halmos's second factor was that

having been repelled by the mendacity of grand generalizations, by the deceptions of ideological doctrines, by the lures of utopias, and by the political expediencies, scientific man tried to impose his rigour of truthfulness on his thinking about society and hoped to derive some satisfaction from thereby retrieving his intellectual integrity and honesty.[4]

This is clearly an attempt to establish a general principle from the Western European revulsion from the ideological antagonisms of the 1930s and the years of the Second World War towards rational post-war social reconstruction. The war discredited political ideology, but it was the discrediting of the subsequent political action for social reform which generated the personalist moment. Halmos's fourth factor represents, in other words, a second stage discrediting of political solutions. Again it expresses a general principle which reflects an actual historical disenchantment with the potential for 'betterment' of the creation of a Welfare State:

> political action is wasteful of human sympathy; it either fails to reach those one wants to help or it hardens and depersonalizes the character of one's care at its source as well as in its results by the time it is distributed among the many.[5]

Halmos argued rather loosely that there had been a change in the preoccupations of 'mid-century social science' which was self-fulfilling. The decline in confidence in the capacity of sociology to offer societal explanations had been mirrored by a decline in confidence in grand social solutions and social policies to relieve suffering. The development of a micro-sociology and the growth of small groups in society were mutually reinforcing processes. This analysis is not referenced or substantiated but the assumption must be that Halmos was offering this view as an account of the late 1940s. The second chapter of *The Faith of the Counsellors* gives an account of the 'coming of the counsellors' which characterizes, instead, the period from the 1950s until the point in the early 1960s when the book was written. Halmos argues that post-war personalism could not completely dispense with politics. 'Post-political man'

> would wave aside suggestions that by legislative acts or by changes in social institutions one could dispense with personal ministrations, but he has not altogether abandoned the idea that these ministrations could be made more readily available to people, and their effectiveness possibly also increased by large-scale measures and provisions.[6]

For Halmos, it is this post-war personalist reluctance to relinquish political solutions absolutely which offers an explanation for the surge in professional counselling in the early 1960s:

> subsidized by state and local government, more and more of these counselling positions have been created for professionally specialized practitioners mainly in social work, social casework, clinical psychology and psychiatry.[7]

Halmos proceeded to analyse the growth of the counselling professions sociologically and statistically, and this analysis was updated for the second edition. The important point to stress, however, is that Halmos was interested in documenting the expansion of a profession. The third chapter, which contains the crux of his philosophical argument, tried to assess the ethical implications of the professionalization of care. Similarly, the final chapter was concerned to explore the transforming effects on society generally of the existence of the new caring professions. This was the theme to which he devoted the whole of his next book – *The Personal Service Society* (1970).

It was a deliberately optimistic book. Halmos sought to extrapolate from the social processes of the recent past towards a future in which a Personal Service Society was in the making. He sought to counter pessimistic cynicism about the human condition and to welcome the developments which he perceived:

> Science, technology, and economic growth have profoundly changed the division of labour in society and the changes will continue along lines which are not altogether unpredictable. One line, the direction of which appears to be set for some time to come points towards a continuing growth in the proportion of those of the total working population whose work is done in the personal services of health, welfare, and education.[8]

The likelihood of the continuing growth of these professions was the first hypothesis which Halmos advanced in his first chapter. The second was that

> I also believe that the pedagogical regime of these personal service professionals as well as their professional ethics are influencing the self-image of other professional workers whose calling is not in the area of the personal services. Engineers, architects, lawyers, and others like them are trained in higher education institutions, which now include in these courses of impersonal technologies the sociological and social psychological tuition originally reserved for students of the personal service professions.[9]

It is no accident that Halmos had been Professor at the University of Keele which had implemented A. D. Lindsay's social ideals in the form of a generalist, first year Foundation year for all undergraduates. Equally, it is important to remember that *The Personal Service Society* was published in 1970 at a time when polytechnics, in particular, were introducing new courses in which 'Science in Society' or 'Technology and Society' components were often incorporated into Science or Engineering degree proposals, and also at a time only shortly in advance of the post-James integration of teacher training with higher education. Halmos's prediction of an increasing pedagogical influence of personal training upon impersonal technology seemed, therefore, to be well founded and to offer a sound base for his third hypothesis that the general transformation of professional ethics would filter through to all social and political attitudes and alter the assumptions of government itself. Since, for Halmos, the spread of the professionalism of the personal services was the mechanism for social change, it was natural that he should concentrate on the elements of training for the personal services. These were essentially two and they were the products of two distinct intellectual traditions:

> Social science in general is manipulative, positivistic and impersonal; the social psychological science of the helping professions is lured away in the direction of the personal and the phenomenological.[10]

Nevertheless, Halmos was immediately eager to counter the suggestion that these traditions might be firmly fixed in unalterable separation. *The Personal*

Service Society was, intellectually, a book of 1970 in that Halmos made it clear that his sympathies lay with the 'new directions in sociology' in opposing the positivism of traditional social science. The first section of the second chapter of the book explains why

> the cultivation of social science can never be a 'pure science' activity, and why it is impossible to 'explain' without changing it through the rendering of explanations.[11]

In practice this means that the positivist analyses into which professionals are initiated in their training need constantly to be checked against everyday working experiences. As Halmos puts it in more detail:

> Psychology and sociology still provide the base-lines of the practitioners' thinking. All accretion of knowledge in the positive social sciences is put at the disposal of the novice practitioners, and they have to assimilate social science intelligence in the mode and techniques of their day-to-day practice.[12]

But the personal service professional must simultaneously blend this perspective with its critique:

> The personal service professionals, as agents of social change, will for ever be receptive to the propositions of social science but they will for ever be reappraising these propositions in terms of what their subjective self-awareness does to them in the course of practice.[13]

It is this notion of continuous and creative counter-point between initiation and criticism that underpins Halmos's view of the personal services professional. As he proceeds to test his three hypotheses, Halmos welcomes the extent to which the counselling ideology has become 'ubiquitous, prominent, and deeply embedded'[14] in teacher training institutions and he further observes that it is now

> rapidly coming into view . . . that there is also a generic factor in all the personal service professions of teaching, social work, nursing, doctoring, and so on.[15]

That 'generic factor' was precisely the people-centred dimension which informed the idea of 'transferability' as employed by the original working-party of the NELP DipHE. There is no evidence that the educational reformers of that group had related their thoughts to those of Halmos about the potential influence of personal services professionalism, but there are clear affinities. The working party was committed to the integration of teacher training into higher education institutions and was involved in exploring the ways in which the generic factors common to the practices of the people-professions might be extrapolated and taught as 'transferable skills'. From the outset, however, it can now be seen that there was a crucial difference which separated the working party from the views expressed by Halmos. Just as the SPERTTT critique of teacher training argued that the intellectual content of that training acquiesced in a process of discrimination against the admission of working-class students, so the NELP working party adopted the view that an insistence upon the acquisition of social science knowledge in social work training acted as a similar deterrent. The orientation of the working party was to disengage practice from theory. Whereas Halmos assumed that practice would constantly modify social science knowledge, the working party argued that knowledge was only necessary at all in as much as it assisted in the solution of practical problems.

The original working party for the DipHE did not have a social scientist, and only one member of staff from the Sociology Department joined when it was extended at the beginning of 1973. He retained his association with the DipHE until leaving the polytechnic in July 1975,[16] but it is clear that the unit's attempted onslaught on the professions was still concentrated on the teaching profession. The incursions into the territory of other professions were less well organized and mainly regarded simply as extensions of the movement for educational reform. Some attempts were made, for instance, to negotiate the acceptance by the Central Council for the Education and Training of Social Workers (CCETSW) of the DipHE as an entry qualification for its CQSW qualification. Similarly, attempts were made to design a new post-DipHE cycle two course in Social Work which would establish a completely new route through to professional qualification.[17] Or again, attempts were made to interest the CCETSW in the possibility that it might cooperate in validating proposals from students for the BA/BSc by Independent Study which would enable the validated programmes to secure professional recognition as well as graduate status. Or again, finally, attempts were made to foster 'new' professions, such as Community Work,[18] for which new competences, independent of social science knowledge, might be required in order to gain professional recognition. In short, the movement for educational reform was committed to the destruction or, at the least, the re-definition of credentialism. Whereas Halmos saw the personal services professions as the instruments of gradual social change, the educational reformers saw them as inhibiting institutions which were slowing down the direct political momentum of personalism. By the time of his death, Halmos could identify this politicization of the personal as the dominant mood of the day and the chief threat to his earlier ideals:

> Today, the politicized view of the formal and institutional provisions for personal service sees them as fragmented and disjointed responses, chaotic guerrilla operations at most, which will never win any wars, though they will keep our energies occupied and even sapped for the convenience and benefit of vested interests in the *status quo*. The politicized view believes informal friendships and community supports are sure to be forthcoming in a social system which is by definition communitarian, comradely, fraternal, and necessarily socialist. According to this position there is no antithesis between the personal and the political: the latter comprises the former, and decisions on the 'micro-'

as well as the 'macro-level' are political. In this view the personal is a function of and dependent on the political, and a rational attitude must recognize this priority of the political. If we do not do this, so the argument continues, we only distract ourselves from what should come first.[19]

While Halmos was right in 1977/8 to believe that the political attack on the professions was undermining his vision of the introduction of the Personal Service Society, he seems, nevertheless, to have been unaware of the upsurge in personalism in the 1970s which might have been thought to have been marching towards his utopian future without any reference to the personal service professions. By 1976, John Rowan was already sufficiently assured about the arrival of 'humanistic psychology' that he was able to devote the first chapter of his *Ordinary Ecstasy* to an account of its 'Western Origins' and to offer a confident definition of the new movement:

> Humanistic psychology is not just a new brand of psychology, to set side by side on the shelves with all the old brands. It is a whole different way of looking at psychological science. It is a way of doing science which includes love, involvement and spontaneity, instead of systematically excluding them. And the object of this science is not the prediction and control of people's behaviour, but the liberation of people from the bonds of neurotic control, whether this comes from outside (in the structures of our society) or from inside.[20]

He identified three strands of thinking, going back to the late 1940s, which combined in the West to generate humanistic psychology. The ideas which converged in the early 1950s and led to the foundation of the Journal of Humanistic Psychology in the USA in 1961 were those of Lewin, Maslow, and Rogers. According to Rowan,

> one of the thoughts which all three approaches have in common . . . (is that) . . . people are all right as they are. There is nothing extra which they need in order to be whole – all that is necessary is for them to take down the shutters and the blinkers, and let the sun shine in.[21]

What was originally a development in post World War II American social psychology – the product, perhaps, in Halmos's terms, of the post-war personalist boom within a society which had not experienced the need for post-war political reconstruction – was also reinforced by an existentialist tradition running from Sartre to R. D. Laing. Expressed in existentialist terms, humanistic psychology can be presented as being devoted to

> a study of how to enable people to fight their alienation and become more authentic. The T-group developed into the encounter group; Rogerian therapy became an ally of Fritz Perl's Gestalt therapy and Lowen's bio-energetics; Maslow's emphasis on peak experiences became realized in psychosynthesis and meditation techniques . . . All these are ways of personal growth, which do produce people who are more like Rogers's 'fully functioning person'.[22]

Rowan devotes further interesting sections to the influence of the psycho-delic movement of the late 1960s and to the impact of the interest in Eastern philosophy and religion in the same period. Practical applications began to emerge in the United States from the late 1950s. Rowan traces the personal growth movement back to California at that date and refers to the establish-ment of growth centres, mainly following the model of the Esalen Institute, throughout the 1960s. He reports the following steady expansion of the movement:

> In 1968 the list compiled by the Association for Humanistic Psychology had 32 growth centres on it: in 1970 this had risen to 121 entries; and in 1973 to 265, in 9 different countries.[23]

Growth centres are institutions which have expert leaders. The importance of the personal growth movement, however, has been that the principles of humanistic psychology have been applied in de-institutionalized and de-professionalized contexts. As Rowan comments:

> One of the most powerful influences of recent years has been the rise of peer counselling networks quite outside the orbit of the growth centres. The basic idea of peer counselling is this: after proper training, which ensures the presence of shared assumptions and techniques, two people meet once a week (or as often as suits them) for two hours (or whatever time suits them). Then for one hour the first person is the client and the second the counsellor; and for the second hour they swap roles. Thus each person gets counselling and gives counselling equally.[24]

The co-counselling movement spread to Britain in the early 1970s, largely by the efforts of Tom Scheff. The British representative of the original Seattle-based parent organization was John Heron, who quickly seceded and estab-lished his own international organization which still flourishes. The Associa-tion for Humanistic Psychology started in Britain in 1969 and Rowan reports that

> the latest list shows more than 200 growth centres in thirteen different countries.[25]

The journal *Self and Society* was established in 1973 and it was there, in 1974, that the political argument was advanced against humanistic psychology that Halmos was experiencing in opposition to his ideals of professional personal service. The author, Barry Richards, argued that the activities based on humanistic psychology, such as co-counselling, were

> a means of drawing large numbers of intellectuals into active promo-tion of extreme individualism, hedonism, and psychotherapeutic ideology – the ideology of personal adjustment as opposed to political commitment and organization, of self-fulfilment as opposed to social change, and of serving self and not serving others.[26]

Rowan cites this accusation in *Ordinary Ecstacy* in a chapter devoted to a consideration of 'Social Action and Community Development'; in the third part of the book which explores 'The Future of Humanistic Psychology' he presents a response as he tries to outline directions for society which might follow from the increasing spread of personal growth activities. Rowan argues:

> What I believe is that if, by the kinds of methods and approaches outlined in this book, the sensitive imagination and the self-confident strength needed can be released in people, in groups, in organizations and communities, then social development will go in the direction of a more person-centred society. It needs a lot of work, but it is work we can actually start now. We can start where we are, in our own families, in our places of work. We can go to groups, we can learn co-counselling, we can acquire skills and start to use them. We can take seriously our own personal growth, and meet up with others who also care. We don't have to wait until everyone wants it.[27]

This 1976 articulation of a belief in the potential dynamism for social change of the grass-roots personalism of the personal growth movement helps to clarify the various categories of positions which were in tension in the mid-1970s. There was a continuum on which four positions can usefully be distinguished. There were, firstly, those people who were attracted to a post-hippie ideology of individual freedom for whom an ideal society might come about a-politically by the steady extension of shared personal experiences. The goal of the personal growth movement was a person-centred society. Halmos's goal, by contrast, was, significantly, of a personal *service* society which would come about as the political sphere gradually came under the control of trained personal service professionals. Whereas the personal growth movement envisaged a 'bottom-up' transformation of society as a means to the achievement of an unstructured, non-oppressive society as an end, Halmos's emphasis of professionalism implied the realization of a polis in which personal care would be expressed through institutions which would still reflect the hierarchical personal valuations of the society which had supposedly been superseded. These two positions, nevertheless, both gave primacy to the personal in opposition to the political. The other two identifiable positions favoured the primacy of the political. The third was prepared to use the personalist orientation for primarily political purposes. These were the reformers who recognized as much as the revolutionaries that the professional bodies as they existed were preventing social change towards an equal society, and who, therefore, sought to use personalism as a way of transforming the professions. The essence of the reformist position was that an emphasis on knowledge rather more than on personal competence was sustaining that exclusiveness of the professions which was inhibiting their effectiveness as instruments for social change. The reformists were prepared to accept the role assigned to the professions by Halmos as long as they could reject the one-sidedness of the reciprocity between social science knowledge and social work practice which, in his view, should characterize the foundation of all training for these professions. The 'revolutionaries' who, as Halmos suggested, were simply more extreme reformists, argued that the ideals held by those who adopted the positions at the other three points of the continuum could only be achieved by first altering the political structures of society. For them, an interest in personalism was a distraction from the prime political necessities which demanded political action rather than personal experience.

I have argued that the educational reformist approach of the original DipHE working party assimilated the slight sociological orientation of the subsequent DipHE Development Unit. There was, however, a personalist element which has gained in strength since 1973 in several waves of influence. The working party had suggested that students might acquire competence in the Central Studies component of the DipHE by attending interdisciplinary courses which would relate to that concept. It was one of the main achievements of the Development Unit that it completely changed the intentions which had originally been proposed for Central Studies. Although the unit did not use the term, in essence it argued that the acquisition of competence had to be an experiential process. The member of the unit who was mainly responsible for achieving this change was Ian Cunningham who had joined the extended working party in January 1973. Although Cunningham's first degree was in Chemistry, he had transferred in 1970 to a career in Training after spending two years (1968-70) as National Secretary of the National Union of Students. He had joined the Anglian Regional Management Centre – the polytechnic's Management Faculty – in 1972 where he had been made the Course Director for the Diploma in Management Studies (Local Government) course specializing in teaching areas such as corporate management, decision making, personnel management and organizational behaviour. He gained an MA in Occupational Psychology (Manpower Studies) in the same year, 1973, as he transferred to the DipHE Development Unit. These indications of Cunningham's background are important because they help to explain the ambivalence of his initial impact in relation to the personal/political continuum. The fact that he had held office in the N.U.S. at a time when student activism had been more politically significant in Western Europe than at any time since World War II ensured his acceptability to the educational reformers.

From the outset Cunningham was committed to the view that in the post-1968 world of higher education, student representation had to be transformed into student participation in the governance of institutions. It was Cunningham who eagerly insisted that the management structure of the newly established School for Independent Study, in 1974, should give equal power to students and staff so as to enable a process of self-managed learning. The experiential pedagogical implications of that term had not yet, however, become articulate. Cunningham's commitment to student involvement in course administration followed from an amalgamation of his political and his management training experiences. His pedagogical contributions to the Development Unit's planning for the operation of the DipHE stimulated resistance within the unit precisely because they were so clearly the products of a management culture. Where Burgess thought of a student planning statement which had a purely logical status analogous to a Popperian hypothesis, Cunningham thought of it as a life-planning exercise intimately related to the student's self-development and, as such, susceptible to continuous, temporary modification. Where Burgess thought of the projects which were to be undertaken by groups in the Central Studies of the DipHE as hypothetical social actions to be falsified – as task processes from which a transferable problem-solving method might be learned – Cunningham quickly came to see the groups as T-groups or Encounter groups in which the social psychological tasks of group maintenance had priority over the tasks of external performance. In the first two years of the DipHE (1974-76) these contrary views could be kept in balance because it was possible to argue that students should learn from projects that the efficient task performance of a group in solving external problems was dependent upon its collaborative competence in solving the internal interpersonal problems of group maintenance. Equally, differences of opinion were confirmed to the Central Studies component of the course. The Special Interest component was unaffected by the humanistic psychology orientation and the stability of the course structure was unshaken by student participation in management because the ideological link had not yet been successfully made between the student self-management of the course and the student self-management of activities within the course.

During 1975 there was an attempt to de-construct the DipHE course. This move came from the planners of what was to become the BA/BSc by Independent Study with a view to liberating students from the compulsion of competence-based objectives, and this de-construction would have assisted Cunningham in establishing also an independent ideology for Central Studies. But the de-construction attempt failed and, instead, Cunningham devoted himself, from 1976, to the planning and operation of the part-time DipHE. It was here that the two elements of his background came together. Whereas between 1974 and 1976 he had mainly seemed to be influenced by two of the social psychological founding fathers of humanistic psychology – Kurt Lewin and Abraham Maslow – there was, after 1976, increasing evidence of the influence of Carl Rogers, particularly of *Freedom to Learn* (1969) and then *On Personal Power* (1977). Within the School for Independent Study, therefore, 1976 marked the point at which the person-centred approach first moved outside the confines of a group dynamics interpretation of Central Studies group work to launch an educational attack on the inflexible course structures and processes of the whole DipHE. It is significant that 1976 was also the year in which Tom Boydell was trying to clarify the meaning of 'Experiential Learning,'[28] from the confused usage that he had encountered in a Management Training background which was similar to Cunningham's; and it was also the year in which John Rowan felt able to celebrate the arrival of the personal growth movement in *Ordinary Ecstasy*. As humanistic psychology shook off its management training associations and as, increasingly, it seemed to become a personal rather than a political movement, it became clear to the educational reformers who wished to sustain the competence emphasis of the DipHE that the a-political tendencies of the part-time DipHE would have to be resisted. The consequence of this resistance was that Cunningham withdrew from the School for Independent Study in 1978 to return to the Management Faculty in order to establish a Personal Development Division within which he established, in 1979, a Diploma in Self-Managed Learning.

Cunningham's own account of these developments was published in 1981 as a contribution to Boydell and Pedler's *Management Self-development: Concepts and Practices* under the title of 'Self-managed learning in independent study'. He describes some aspects of the full-time DipHE course between 1974 and 1976; the changes which he instituted in developing the part-time DipHE; and, finally, the developments which he found could only be made outside the constricting assumptions of the School for Independent Study. Cunningham describes the School's 'noble aim' in allowing students to do projects in groups, but his interpretation of events is that two kinds of project work emerged, one of which he calls 'investigative' and the other 'action'. For Cunningham,

> Investigative projects are those where a group investigates a situation and usually writes a report on it. There is no attempt to change the situation; to take action. At their worst they mirror third rate sociological research studies. At best groups write interesting impressionistic reports on 'social issues' like pollution or homelessness.[29]

whereas

> Action projects are closer to the best of the action learning kind of project, i.e. there is an expectation that there will be an attempt to do something about a problem.[30]

Investigative projects normally led to the production of written reports which quickly meant that the significance of project *activity* became subordinated to that of traditional literary expression. By contrast, groups doing action projects might not produce a report at all. Instead,

> By having to work together to get something done, the group is forced to face issues of personal relationships (and these have to be solved in order for the group to be effective).[31]

The irony here, however, was that the action projects gradually became so concerned with the inter-personal relationships within groups that the action dimension became secondary. There was a tendency for action project groups to become self-conscious support groups. Within the full-time DipHE there had developed a separation between 'tutor' groups and 'project' groups. All students were assigned to a tutor group with about 15 students and one member of staff. In these groups the students developed their statements and, throughout the two years of the course, shared their experiences of both Central studies and Special Interest work. But each term students might work in projects with randomly allocated project groups. This separation of tutor from project groups was rejected by Cunningham in planning the part-time DipHE. He argues that this provided inadequate peer group support and he explains the solution which he intended to offer in the part-time course in the following way:

> Prior to taking on the task of starting up the part time DipHE I have acted as a set adviser on the GEC action learning programme (see Casey and Pearce, 1977). I decided to transplant the 'set' concept from the action learning world into the part time DipHE.[32]

Not only did these 'sets' supplant both the tutor and project group of the full-time DipHE, but, most importantly, they had the power to influence the structure of the course of which they were parts. The development of the 'sets' was the key mechanism whereby Cunningham's commitments to person-centred pedagogy and participatory managerial style became integrated. He describes how the part-time course committee was constituted with three students and three members of staff and how it was deliberate policy that a student should be its chair person. Nevertheless, these actions were, in the event, mainly symbolic. As Cunningham admits, the liberalism of these policy decisions was overtaken by a more consensual practice:

> As the course evolved we tended to use the course committee mainly as the formal 'rubber stamp' to decisions that evolved through sets or through meetings of all students.
>
> These meetings were held on what we called a 'core evening' when all students were asked to attend so that we could deal with general problems affecting everyone . . . These meetings evolved as a forum to work out policy matters and by and large were more effective than the 'representative' system.[33]

As a result of his experiences between 1974 and 1978 Cunningham identifies four categories of course, and he distinguishes between them. Traditional courses offer students no control over either their learning or over course management. 'Summerhill-style schools' offer students a high level of involvement in general policy and structural decisions but still operate within the context of 'fairly traditional approaches to teaching'. The full-time DipHE, in common with many self-development programmes, offers the learner

> a high level of control over his own personal learning, but it is within a structure imposed on him (over which he has little or no influence).[34]

Significantly placing the part-time DipHE in the same category as 'Carl Rogers' person-centred workshops (Rogers, 1977)' and 'some learning community events', Cunningham concludes that

Here learners have a high level of involvement in decisions affecting their own personal learning and affecting the overall structure of the event. Clearly it is not possible to separate control of one's own learning from the level of one's influence on structures and policies. To that extent the other three situations must provide less opportunity for genuine self-development.[35]

Clearly the view of the educational reformers that a competence-based higher education course might transform the educational system and clear the way towards greater social equality was challenged by the possibility that students might acquire the power to reject and to overcome that view of their course. The development of both the part-time DipHE and the BA/BSc by Independent Study exposed, in different ways, the extent to which the educational reformers were using 'student-centredness' for political purposes. The development of the part-time DipHE exposed the dogmatically political stance of the full-time DipHE from a personalist perspective. Cunningham argues that he was forced to withdraw from the School for Independent Study because it was intractable on four points. He argues, firstly, that the School was committed to Group projects and that

it was impossible to engineer any appropriate changes in the way group projects were organised (or alternatively to get them scrapped).[36]

Secondly, he found that the School's effort was excessively geared to assisting people who wanted to do qualification courses and, related to this, thirdly, that the School was not prepared to give students enough involvement in their own assessment. As a consequence of these divergent views, the Personal Development Division was established within the Faculty of Management in January 1979. Initially, this division provided a focus for independent study programmes – accommodating 'independent study' students who were undertaking their specialist studies in the field of management, but, as Cunningham states,

it soon became apparent that we would be diverging quite a bit from the SIS view of independent study. Hence we coined the term 'Self-Managed Learning' to describe the kinds of activity we would be promoting.[37]

In essence, the self-managed learning approach has involved dropping the idea of encouraging group projects:

Our experience of using 'sets' is that they provide much the best way to facilitate collaborative activity. Hence we see the use of sets as an important corner-stone of most of our programme.[38]

It has also insisted on an approach to assessment which is itself person-centred:

We believe that final assessment to award a diploma or not should be made on the basis of a consensual agreement between the learner, his peers, his tutors and his external assessor. The person's self assessment should be the starting point and external judgements are best used to help the learner reach his own conclusions about his competence.[39]

In 1979 these features of self-managed learning distinguished the developments within the Management Faculty from the practice of the School for Independent Study. Cunningham had been supported within the School by a handful of staff who were committed to the advancement of the personal growth movement and to the implementation of its educational implications for independent study. These few staff retained their main involvement with the part-time DipHE which was brought under the control of a Joint Management committee responsible for both the full-time and the part-time DipHEs. Since 1980, however, staff allegiance to person-centredness has steadily increased until the present time when perhaps 10 staff have undergone various kinds of counselling training and endeavour to apply what they have learnt to their situation within the School for Independent Study. Some, indeed, have themselves been students on the Diploma in Management Studies by Self-Managed Learning which Cunningham established. Others have been more specifically introduced to Rogerian counselling – following the lead of one of the original members of the part-time DipHE group, Tony Merry, who, in 1980, secured formal agreement within the School for the establishment of a centre devoted to person-centredness. The penetration of the full-time DipHE by the ideology of Cunningham's part-time DipHE – manifested in the adoption of 'sets', 'learning communities', and of initiatives tending towards self and peer assessment – was consolidated by the appointment in 1982 to the post of full-time DipHE Course Tutor of one of the earlier staff members of the part-time DipHE course committee.

For a large proportion of the staff of the School for Independent Study, 'independent study' and 'self-managed learning' have now become synonymous. The practice of the School in the DipHE has become heavily personalist and a-political precisely at the time, in the post-1979 period, when, as I have already argued in the previous chapter, the educational reformers were experiencing a crisis of confidence in their political stance which was causing them to redefine competence in terms of personal qualities rather than vocational skills. The dominant operational ideology of the DipHE practitioners has become personalist and Merry's review of 1983 of Rogers's *Freedom to Learn for the 80's* is typical in welcoming that book's contribution to the progress of psychological rather than sociological reflection on educational practice. Rogers, he concludes,

> is the latest in a long line of distinguished progressive thinkers and *Freedom to Learn for the 80's* is an articulate, persuasive re-affirmation of the creativity inherent in every individual.[40]

Whereas in the mid-1970s educational reformism sought to appropriate Halmos's vision of a personal service society by modifying his conception of professionalism, it now seems to be endeavouring to appropriate the grass-roots personalism of the personal growth movement. Increasingly, the old political rhetoric of 'competence' is implying an attachment to notions of personal liberation rather than to notions of systemic change. In a recent paper on Independent Study and the Development of Capability, for instance, John Stephenson[41] has proposed a new definition of capability based on the development of the Rogerian notion of 'personal power'. This tendency has been underwritten by Rowan's liberationist interpretation of the personal growth movement. At the time that Halmos was fearing the discrediting of personalist solutions by aggressive political activists, Rowan was beginning to represent humanistic psychology as a politics of the personal which alone could counteract the forces of oppression in our society which could all be seen to follow from the phenomenon of 'patriarchy'. In *The Structured Crowd* (1978), Rowan claimed that

> It may be that the essence of patriarchy is the assigning of fixed roles, of a superior/inferior kind. And social scientists are no different from anyone else in playing such roles, and taking such a role system for granted in all that they write . . . I believe it is to humanistic psychology that we must look for the theory and the methods which will be most useful in understanding the fight to question patriarchy on a wide scale. The really important things we can do in relation to other people are to open doors for them, reveal new possibilities for their lives, break down the barriers of roles and the groups fears that often maintain them, encourage them to be who they really are: and in doing so, to make genuine social change easier and more likely[42]

In aligning itself with this view that personal change will bring about social change, the movement for educational reform has found that liberationism offers a new rationale for its traditional anti-academicism. The acquisition of positivistic scientific knowledge can now be seen to be oppressive and inhibitive of the liberating personal growth which may lead to social change. Rowan has led the personal growth movement towards the development of 'new paradigm research', as defined in *Human Inquiry. A Sourcebook of New Paradigm Research* (1981). Whereas in the 1970s the educational reformers were so preoccupied in resisting the apparently subversive influences of personalism which were emerging in the practices of the part-time DipHE that they tolerated the divergence of the BA/BSc by Independent Study, the alliance between educational reform and personal growth in the 1980s has found support in new paradigm research in challenging the third movement which has co-existed within the School since the early 1970s – the movement which has sought to effect social change by developing mechanisms that might enable the intellectual content of curricula to become a matter of negotiation between social equals.

Notes

1 P. Halmos, *The Personal and the Political. Social Work and Political Action*, Hutchinson, London, 1978, p. 32.
2 ibid. p. 34.
3 P. Halmos, *The Faith of the Counsellors*, Constable, London, Second revised edition, 1978, p. 11.
4 ibid. p. 25.
5 ibid. p. 26.
6 ibid. p. 28.
7 ibid. p. 31.
8 P. Halmos, *The Personal Service Society*, Constable, London, 1970, p. 1.
9 ibid. p. 25.
10 ibid. p. 2.
11 ibid. p. 2.
12 ibid. p. 90.
13 ibid. p. 90.
14 ibid. p. 104.
15 ibid. p. 112.
16 This was Andrew Cornwell who took a post at the Central Council for the Education and Training of Social Workers.
17 The NELP Sociology department had itself already pioneered a four-year CNAA Sociology degree which incorporated one year (the third year) of professional training and enabled students to obtain an award which was both an Honours degree and a professional qualification. The negotiations of the School for Independent Study were thought to be designed to subvert that existing package by reducing the sociological initiation and by consequently abbreviating the period of academic and professional training to three years.
18 One member of polytechnic staff who subsequently transferred to the School for Independent Study – Jo Benjamin – was particularly involved in this initiative.
19 Halmos, *The Personal and the Political*, op. cit. p. 66.
20 J. Rowan, *Ordinary Ecstasy. Humanistic Psychology in action*, RKP, 1976, p. 3.
21 ibid. p. 7.
22 ibid. p. 11.
23 ibid. p. 39.
24 ibid. p. 46.
25 ibid. p. 145.
26 B. Richards, 'Against humanistic psychology', *Self and Society*, 2, 1974. quoted in Rowan, op. cit. p. 123.
27 Rowan, op. cit. p. 169.
28 See Part I. Chapter 1.
29 T. Boydell and M. Pedler (eds), *Management Self-development: Concepts and Practices*, Gower, 1981, p. 194.
30 ibid. p. 194.
31 ibid. p. 195.
32 ibid. p. 197.
33 ibid. p. 198.
34 ibid. p. 199.
35 ibid. p. 199.
36 ibid. p. 199.

37 ibid. p. 201.

38 ibid. p. 201.

39 ibid. p. 202.

40 A. Merry, review of Carl Rogers *Freedom to Learn for the 80's*, Charles Merrill, 1983, in *International Newsletter for Independent Study*, no. 7., issued from the School for Independent Study, 1983.

41 Paper given at a Conference of the Standing Conference of Educational Development Services in Polytechnics held at Napier College, Edinburgh, 21-22 May, 1987.

42 J. Rowan. Psychological Aspects of Society. Volume IV: *The Structured Crowd*. Davis-Poynter, London, 1978, p. 151.

10

The Promotion of Social Change through the Redistribution of Knowledge

In the year in which North-East London Polytechnic was established – 1970 – an important article on educational research appeared in the European Journal of Sociology. Entitled 'Egalitarianism in English and French Educational Sociology', the writer Margaret Scotford Archer offered some general observations on the tendencies in educational sociology in the two countries arising, particularly, from her reflections on the events of May 1968 in Paris and on some attempted sociological interpretations of the factors which had generated those events. She concluded from the different analyses offered by Alain Touraine and Pierre Bourdieu that

> These two studies have only been dwelt upon to illustrate the ways in which weakness in the macrosociological understanding of education leads to overemphasis of either internal or external determination of University goals and how over-preoccupation with social stratification leads to an exaggerated view of students as either future elites or sub-elites. In other words, they are studies which find their place in a distinctive sociological tradition and share with it the overriding preoccupation with egalitarianism.[1]

In spite of the fact that Touraine welcomed the possible production of new class relations while Bourdieu feared that the concealed structures which reproduced the old class system remained unaffected, Archer argued that both analyses were the products of the same tradition of educational research which concentrated excessively upon the differential chances of students according to social class. She claimed that within this tradition two types of investigation had tended to predominate throughout the 1950s:

> the first confirmed the influence of social class origins upon various levels and types of educational achievement, while the second indicated that a variety of factors related to attainment were also associated with social background.[2]

It was Archer's contention that the work of the 'levellers' in this tradition ignored issues about educational content. Her solution was to propose the development of comparative, macro-sociological studies in which the functions of educational systems might be taken as socially problematic.

Similar views were being expressed at very much the same time at the Durham conference of the British Sociological Association of April 1970, which was devoted to education. It was in discussion after this conference between Michael F. D. Young, Basil Bernstein, and Pierre Bourdieu, that the idea was conceived for *Knowledge and Control. New Directions for the Sociology of Education* which was published in 1971. In his introductory chapter – 'Knowledge and Control' – Young makes the point that sociologists had hitherto accepted for analysis the educational problems which had been provided by the educators. In particular, Young was in agreement implicitly with Archer that the concentration on equalizing processes within the educational system had been at the expense of a consideration of content. The work of the early 1960s on the class determinants of educational opportunity had re-made the problems as they had then been perceived by the educational administrators, but the time was now ripe for a further re-making. He says of the earlier research that

> by treating as unproblematic 'what it is to be educated', such enquiries do little more than provide what is often a somewhat questionable legitimacy to the various pressures for administrative and curricular 'reform'.[3]

Young believed that the only way in which alternative problems and explanations might be developed would be to examine the ways in which pupils, teachers and knowledge are organized, and this, in turn, would mean that

> existing categories that for parents, teachers, children and many researchers distinguish home from school, learning from play, academic from non-academic, and 'able' or 'bright' from 'dull' or 'stupid', must be conceived of as socially constructed, with some in a position to impose their constructions or meanings on others.[4]

Previous educational research – notably that of A. H. Halsey and Jean Floud in the late 1950s and the 1960s had operated with structural-functionalist assumptions about society in which the relations between educational institutions, occupations and mobility were taken for granted. Clearly influenced by the publication in the United Kingdom of P. Berger and T. Luckmann's *The Social Construction of Reality* in 1967, Young sought to advocate a sociological research orientation in respect of education in which the knowledge transmitted within educational institutions and those institutions themselves would both be perceived to be man-made artifacts subject to historical change and influence. The previous era of research had generated educational reforms which had been advanced in crucial reports such as the 1956 White Paper on Technical Education, the Crowther Report of 1959, or the Robbins Report of 1963, but these reforms had reinforced the notion that the educational system existed to provide trained manpower for a modernizing, technological society. In linking educational development so closely to the needs of the economy the educational sociologists had also been able to justify the provision of equality of opportunity on the grounds that it would enable the country to maximize its human resources, but their reformism did not extend to allowing individuals to challenge the nature of the society within which that equality was permitted to them. Young's work, therefore, arose from a disenchantment with the educational reforms which had been engendered by the structural-functionalist sociologists, and the purpose of his book was to launch a new movement for educational reform which would start from a different conception of the structure and construction of society.

There were, however, inherent difficulties with the collection of essays which Young edited as *Knowledge and Control*. There was, first of all, a tension between contributors in relation to their epistemological positions, and there was, secondly, the difficulty of trying to establish a meta-sociological stance which would be unaffected by educational norms from a base in a department of the sociology of education within an Institute of Education. Both difficulties were quickly identified by commentators. Bill Williamson's contribution to *Educability, Schools and Ideology* entitled 'Continuities and Discontinuities in the Sociology of Education' (1974) clearly identified the two epistemological strands contained within *Knowledge and Control*:

> The new sociology of education operates on two levels or, at least, seems to be preoccupied with two kinds of problems. Firstly, there is a concern with what is regarded as appropriate knowledge to be passed on in schools. M. Young's view on this matter is that if we knew more about the selection of knowledge we would know more about the structures of power in society. Secondly, and particularly for those who are more attracted to the inter-actionist social psychologies which are one of the intellectual tributaries to the new sociology, the most important concerns seem to be with the structure of classroom interaction between teacher and pupil.[5]

The first strand which was mainly concerned with the structures of knowledge within society was typically represented by the two contributions to the volume made by Pierre Bourdieu – 'Intellectual Field and Creative Project' and 'Systems of Education and Systems of Thought', whereas the second strand was typically represented by Nell Keddie's 'Classroom Knowledge' in which she analysed the processes of labelling inherent in teacher/pupil interactions. It was Williamson's view that the programme of *Knowledge and Control*, whatever the dominant epistemological emphasis, was doomed to failure because it emanated from an institution devoted to Education and was popular in the Open University where courses were either for teachers or designed with teachers in mind. He wrote of those new sociologists of education who, in his view, were 'trapped in their own institutional location' that they wanted

> to understand the ideology of education without having first worked out its political economy.[6]

The new sociology evidenced, for Williamson, a political naiveté which could not have been shared by a Marxist, and would be likely to tend in a Marxist direction:

> Marxist writers such as Althusser have never entertained the illusion that a capitalist society is capable of sustaining an education system which promotes equality. Nor have they ever doubted that schools are transmitters of bourgeois ideology or that teachers were the active agents of this transmission. But it has taken the new sociologists a little longer to raise fundamentalist questions of this kind and then in the language of social phenomenology. I suspect, in fact, that the most important effect of the new sociology and the theory of social world building which goes with it, is to force students and teachers alike to consider the whole basis on which they act and to contemplate a radical reconstruction of educational institutions. In this respect the analytical language of the new sociology is almost Marxist.[7]

Two other contributors to *Educability, Schools and Ideology* – Roger Dale and Geoff Whitty – reacted in a similar way to Williamson in suspecting especially the social psychological epistemological strand of neglecting the influence in inter-actionist situations of forces of objective power. Dale had collaborated in 1972 with his Open University colleague, Geoffrey Esland, on *The Construction of Reality*.[8] His contribution to *Educability, Schools and Ideology* entitled 'Phenomenological Perspectives and the Sociology of the School' was a re-working of a paper which had appeared in the *Educational Review* in 1973[9] in which he had tried to give a guide to the literature on phenomenology which was then so popular. Dale provided a valuable exposition which outlined the virtues of phenomenological sociology – that it sets out to describe the experiences of everyday life and begins with data rather than with grand theories – but he expressed the reservation that too many phenomenological sociologists were inclined to regard an 'insider's' definition of a situation as sufficient. Expressing this same point more generally, Dale commented:

> The major weakness of the phenomenological approach is that it is concerned with the 'how' and not the 'why' of the social world. . . . Somewhat ironically, it can be argued that phenomenological sociologists concentrate in the surface structure rather than the deep structure of social life. They emphasize the immediate experiences and subjective meanings of everyday life; they do not seek to reveal the nature of the system of social relationships which governs the way those meanings are distributed within societies.[10]

The immediate respondents to *Knowledge and Control* did not realize that Bourdieu's work was attempting to come to terms with precisely these issues of the relationships between subjective and objective meanings, exploring the processes of reciprocity whereby those objective meanings which are subjectively created are also constituting elements of the subjectivity. As

Williamson predicted, the obvious recourse for those in search of some objective components within a process of inter-subjective exchange was to a Marxist framework within which an economic base could be believed to have absolute status. Whitty, like Esland a product of the graduate seminar group in the department of Sociology at the Institute of Education, London, made this point specifically in his contribution to *Educability, Schools and Ideology*. In 'Sociology and the Problem of Radical Educational Change: Notes towards a reconceptualization of the "New Sociology of Education"' which was based on parts of his MA thesis, Whitty commented:

> I also want to suggest that a return to the work of Marxist-oriented writers may, in particular, permit us to formulate (via the notion of circumstances) a critique of knowledge as it is constituted which focuses more precisely on those aspects which may be considered 'dehumanising' without rejecting all constituted knowledge as invalid – and without celebrating the act of 'doing knowledge' at the expense of any consideration of the created product.[11]

Dale and Whitty were typical representatives of the mid-1970s reaction to *Knowledge and Control*. They distrusted the 'Keddie' strand of the book and found themselves driven to the conclusion that inter-personal constructions of reality are inevitably the reflections of conflicts of power within capitalist society. The framework of thinking is unequivocally announced in the introduction to the 1976 Open University reader, *Schooling and Capitalism* which was edited by Dale and others:

> Under a capitalist mode of production there is an unequal distribution of power. It is therefore in the interest of those who hold power to ensure the perpetuation of capitalism. The maintenance of existing social relations of production is crucial and is achieved not only through direct work experience but also through the whole range of social institutions, which take their basic form from the contribution they make to such reproduction. This collection of papers is assembled to show how the capitalist mode of production influences one social institution, schooling.[12]

By 1977 Young himself appears to have been partly Marxized by association with Whitty. Together they edited *Society, State and Schooling. Readings on the Possibilities for Radical Education* in that year. The fact that the first essay in the collection is a re-publication of Whitty's 'Sociology and the Problem of Radical Educational Change' sets the tone for the whole volume and Young's 'Curriculum change: Limits and Possibilities' follows suit. More clearly than in 1971 Young differentiates between traditional philosophy of knowledge and its alternative. He uses Maxine Greene's 1971 article in 'Curriculum and consciousness'

> where she describes the dominant view of the curriculum of educational philosophers, such as Hirst and Peters, in terms of 'a structure of

socially prescribed knowledge, external to the knower, there to be mastered'; which she compares with her own phenomenological view of the curriculum as 'a possibility for the learner as an existing person mainly concerned with making sense of his own life-world'.[13]

and he labels the former 'curriculum as fact' and the latter 'curriculum as practice'. Whereas *Knowledge and Control* was seeking to represent the inadequacies of structural-functionalist sociological research in the field of education, the emphasis has shifted here towards an explicit attack on the assumptions of Young's colleagues in the department of Philosophy at the Institute of Education. As a result of this clearer identification of the epistemological opposition, Young is able to articulate more precisely his position in relation to the two epistemological strands of *Knowledge and Control* which were both different versions of 'curriculum as practice'. At the beginning of his article, Young states:

> I shall suggest that 'curriculum as fact' needs to be seen as more than mere illusion, a superficial veneer on teacher's and pupils' classroom practice, but as a historically specific social reality expressing particular production relations among men. It is mystifying in the way it presents the curriculum as having a life of its own, and obscures the human relations in which it, as any conception of knowledge, is embedded, leaving education as neither understandable nor controllable by men. The alternative conception of 'curriculum as practice' can equally mystify to the extent that it reduces the social reality of 'curriculum' to the subjective intentions and actions of teachers and pupils. This limits us from understanding the historical emergence and persistence of particular conceptions of knowledge and *particular* conventions (school subjects, for example). In that we are limited from being able to situate the problems of contemporary education historically, we are again limited from understanding and control.[14]

For Young, 'curriculum as fact' conceals the fact that the knowledge which is transmitted at any time is the product of human agency in analysable historical conditions and circumstances. By contrast, however, 'currriculum as practice' contains the inherent danger that knowledge might become limited solely to the current products of exchanges between 'teachers' and 'learners' in circumscribed 'educational' contexts. Young's ideal is that there should be a constant reflexive recognition that all knowledge which currently has 'objective' status has been subjectively produced in the past and is undergoing a continuous process of modification as a result of subjective exchanges which occur in all sectors of society. It follows that Young's Marxist-tending theory of knowledge cannot rest content with offering a critique of existing 'curriculum as fact' but must move towards the generation of the present social conditions which would enable the theory to become practice. Consequently, Young argues that

Radical changes based on a theory of 'curriculum as practice' are likely to face very quickly the practical experience that curriculum is not *just* teachers' and pupils' practice, but that it involves also the views of parents, employers, administrators and so on, about what education should be.[15]

or, again, that

A more adequate theory of curriculum as *practice* would not restrict practice to that of teachers, nor of teachers' practice to their activities in the school and classroom. If the educational experience of both teachers and pupils is to become a realistic possibility of human liberation, then this is going to involve many others who have no direct involvement with the school, and much action by teachers and pupils that would not be seen as either confined to school or, in conventional terms, necessarily educational at all.[16]

The introduction to the section, 'Beyond Critiques', in which Young's essay appears – presumably written collaboratively by Whitty and Young – criticizes Young's contribution for being too imprecise about the nature of the politicization of education which it was recommending. The introduction favours, instead, the overt detail of the article by Frith and Corrigan entitled 'The Politics of Education' in which, it points out, those authors

stress the need to focus on the content and control of education, and argue that classroom struggles have to be articulated by socialist teachers in the context of working-class politics if they are to be more than easily-crushed diversions.[17]

It is clear from a comment of that sort that, by 1977, Young's attempt to sustain his vision of an intellectually reflexive society had been overtaken by the impetus for direct political action. Halmos's perception, also of 1977, that his dreams of a personal service society were being shattered by a resurgence of direct political activity could have been shared by Young in respect of his hopes for the 'new directions in the sociology of education'.

Identity and Structure: Issues in the Sociology of Education (1977), edited by Denis Gleeson, was a collection of essays which sought to 'build upon and develop from' the achievements in the sociology of education since *Knowledge and Control* but it sought to do so on the basis of an explicit assertion that the pendulum needed to swing back from the earlier optimistic idealization of the capacity of individuals to negotiate social change:

While rightly emphasizing that society is neither an external fact nor the functionally agreed sum of its parts, 'new directions' have tended to idealize the 'negotiable' potential of the individual and have swung the pendulum to the opposite, and equally unacceptable extreme. Such a position has exaggerated the individual's power to transcend external circumstance and moreover has wrongly implied that difficult situations (in school, court, hospital, prison, etc.) might be 'brought off' simply through acts of negotiation.[18]

Indeed, although Gleeson's collection tries to remedy some of the deficiencies of the context-free inter-actionist phenomenology disliked by Young, Dale, and Whitty without embracing a Marxist solution, it also includes a contribution from Brian Davies which is offered as a 'cautionary note on the further development not only of the theory but also of the practice to which this volume is addressed',[19] but which stands as a harsh epitaph on the 'new sociology' movement. Bernbaum's book of 1977 – *Knowledge and Ideology in the Sociology of Education*[20] – had already effectively declared the movement dead, but Davies's 'Phenomenological sociology and education: radical return or magic moment?' resolutely buried it:

> There should be no doubt that the present name of the game involves not a few people who, having been led excitedly from interactionist youth (the best way of knocking Parsons there was) into 'phenomenological' ferment and mistaking its pursuit of essence for radical promise, new, new directioned (nothing more vehement than the double convert) to mainstream historical 'radicalism' in Marx, attempted to avoid its conservative partyism in favour of its 'early' versions, alas only to find that later Marxism has no place for education except as mechanical reproducer of social relations. They accept the logic, *pace* Bourdieu and Althusser, and settle for educating as the most automatic job in the world under any settled regime, energies liberated for the struggle at large (it's a good job is teaching.) The crudest explanations of how educational process 'works' are reinvoked, now under the label of 'political economy'. Gintis *et al.*, for example, tell us that Parsons and Dreeken were right all along. These are intended to ensure that the danger of any belief that education may through the mass transmission of differential knowledge produce a less exploitable pluralistic society is firmly grubbed out by sloganized appeals to the inevitability of class warfare. The minimal cost of possessing the most radical chic is the assassination of painfully compiled empirical truth if there be any taint of its authorship outside the true faith. Thus was social and political necessity always justified by those who claim to have found the heart of the struggle.[21]

This cruel judgement of the proponents of the 'new sociology' nevertheless offers an accurate summary of the ideological progression from 1971 to 1977 which constituted the context within which the BA/BSc by Independent Study was developed within the School for Independent Study – a course development for which I was largely responsible. Like Ian Cunningham, I joined the DipHE extended working party in January 1973, and, as was the case for Cunningham, my previous experience meant that new influences were introduced into the DipHE discussions. I had read English at Cambridge and had then undertaken research there under the supervision of Raymond Williams and, partly, of Robert Young and Mary Hesse of the Cambridge department of the History and Philosophy of Science. This supplementary supervision was necessary because my research was an attempted analysis of the relationship between natural philosophy and literature at the end of the 18th century through the specific exploration of the thought and writing of Joseph Priestley and Samuel Taylor Coleridge. My doctoral thesis was completed in 1972[22] – two years after I had begun to teach English Literature at the newly designated North-East London Polytechnic to students who were taking the University of London external BA General degree. The thesis maintained an uneasy methodological balance between a structuralist approach and one which traditionally still accepted the notion of individual intention. It culminated in an analysis of Coleridge's *The Ancient Mariner* in which I argued that the shooting of the albatross 'unawares' was represented as a materialistically determined act which, therefore, was morally neutral while the mariner's sense of guilt was socially constructed from the conjunction of the crew's reaction to the event and the mariner's disposition to adopt and internalize that reaction. The structure of meaning assigned to the killing of the albatross was a superimposition on a pure event which was, for the mariner, experientially neutral. I went further to suggest that this interpretation of Coleridge's poem was also the key to his developing aesthetic theory and the key to an understanding of the relationship between 'literary' and 'scientific' discourses. These discourses were not to be crudely differentiated on the grounds that one is 'self-expressive' and the other is positivist and impersonal. Coleridge's literary artifacts were to be seen as 'meta-discourses' within which he could juggle with languages which had become divorced from their empirical or experiential bases and could create a world of artificial meaning which itself attained an objective status. It followed from this work that my main intellectual interest became the pursuit of a sociology of literature which would not, like the Marxist approach, take refuge in a belief in some irreducible, socially unconstructed facts. As its response to Eric Robinson's disposition to make the polytechnic a centre for applied learning, my department set about the task of developing a CNAA submission for a degree course in Communications to replace the Humanities teaching for the BA General. I found that my reading of the literature of the sociology of mass communications at this time also provided me with a model for analysing literature sociologically. Between 1972 and 1975 I studied part-time at the London School of Economics where I did research on the early development of the Chicago School of Sociology.[23] This work both provided me with an essentially pragmatic perspective on the evaluation of literary or communication texts and also caused me to reflect upon the institutionalization and professionalization of a new body of knowledge – sociology – and its adherents in a new institution of higher Education – the University of Chicago – between 1895 and 1920. In those years, R. E. Park and E. W. Burgess transformed the everyday social knowledge of late 19th century philanthropists into the specialized knowledge of social scientists.

It was with something like this baggage of ideas that I joined the extended working party after the Course Development Unit had rejected the proposals for a Communications degree, with which I had been associated, on the grounds that the proposed course was too theoretical. My daily experience of working at NELP had already brought home to me how complacent and privileged had been my own prior academic education and I had no difficulty in accepting the opposition to academicism expressed by the educational reformers. It was also logical that I should adapt my interest in the intellectual origins of Chicago sociology to suit the orientation of the DipHE working party towards a conception of the educational process as one in which skills and competence might be acquired. An allegiance to Dewey's instrumentalism was the result and for several years I sought to apply Deweyan educational progressivism to the context in which the new DipHE was emerging. This meant that, following William James, I regarded the acquisition of knowledge as a process whereby individuals might select from a pre-existent 'stream of consciousness' that knowledge which they might require to satisfy their psychological needs; and it also meant that, following John Dewey, the criterion of the validity of that knowledge was its effect in action. In practical terms, I regarded the Central Studies component of the DipHE as a de-schooled situation which was analogous to the 'social laboratories' or 'educational settlements' of institutions of higher education at the turn of the century. Here the staff were to assist students in learning from controlled group actions in 'real life' community situations. The choice of a special interest study was the real interface between the common-sense knowledge of students, grounded in everyday experience, and the traditionally structured organized knowledge of the educational institution. Berger and Luckmann, and through them, Schütz, caused me to see the students' choice of special interest study as a problem of relevance rather than of problem-solving. Increasingly what was at issue for me was a redistribution of knowledge within a pluralist society where all individuals might have the right to make their own knowledge selections rather than a skill-based critical attack on knowledge itself. Between 1973 and 1976 the Unit and the School assumed a common hostility to what Young was to call the 'curriculum as fact' approach of Peters and Hirst. But it was a reading of Hirst's 'Liberal Education and the Nature of Knowledge' which showed me that an acceptance of his cogent dismissal of the philosophy of competence or transferable skill did not entail an acceptance also of the crude elitist educational control which seemed to be implicit in his advocacy of the transmission of the knowledge of the forms of knowledge. One particular passage of Hirst's article presented the argument against 'transferable skills' which I had quickly come to accept in the first years of operation of the DipHE, while equally exposing the weaknesses of his own adopted position. Hirst had written in 1965:

> On logical grounds, then, it would seem that a consistent concept of liberal education must be worked out fully in terms of the forms of knowledge. By these is meant, of course, not collections of information, but the complex ways of understanding experience which man has achieved, which are publicly specifiable and which are gained through

learning. An education in these terms does indeed develop its related abilities and qualities of mind, for the mind will be characterized to a greater or less degree by the features of the understanding it seeks. Each form of knowledge, if it is to be acquired beyond a general and superficial level, involves the development of creative imagination, judgment, thinking, communicative skills, etc., in ways that are peculiar to itself as a way of understanding experience. To list these elements, picking them out, as it were, across the forms of knowledge of which they are part and in each of which they have a different stamp, draws attention to many features that a liberal education must of course include. But it draws attention to them at the expense of the differences among them as they occur in the different areas. And of itself such listing contributes nothing to the basic determination of what a liberal education is. To be told that it is the development of effective thinking is of no value until this is explicated in terms of the forms of knowledge which give it meaning: for example in terms of the solving of problems in Euclidean geometry or coming to understand the poems of John Donne. To be told instead that it is concerned with certain specified forms of knowledge, the essential characteristics of which are then detailed explicitly as far as possible, is to be given a clear understanding of the concept and one which is unambiguous as to the forms of thinking, judgment, imagination and communication it involves.[24]

My experience in trying to secure entry, in 1975, for the first NELP diplomates to the third year of existing taught degree courses confirmed that Hirst's negative position was correct. In trying to 'list' a set of 'transferable skills' the DipHE staff were endeavouring to extrapolate intellectual skills from their contexts and, in doing so, were trivializing them. In so far as the practice of the students had followed the ideology of the staff there was no possibility that their 'generalizable' competence in 'method' or 'process' might have equipped them with the capacity to cope with advanced context-specific intellectual studies. Similarly, the Popperian rhetoric, which involved an attack on accumulated knowledge, also very quickly wore thin. Nevertheless, Hirst's positive solution was completely unacceptable. As the opening sentences above indicate, he offered the forms of knowledge as a substitute for the *theoria* of the Greeks. He proposed that it was the function of education and of teachers to initiate students into the language of the discrete forms of knowledge. In this process the minds of students would be necessarily moulded by the distinctive features of those forms of knowledge into an awareness of which they were being initiated. Thus there would be a moral effect from this process of initiation which would be equivalent to the moral effect which the Greeks believed followed naturally from the harmony of the individual mind with the universe. Hirst's problem, however, in trying to re-instate Greek *theoria* was that he had to acknowledge that the forms of knowledge were man-made. They were 'the complex ways of understanding experience which man has achieved'. It was clear, therefore, that Hirst tacitly assumed that some people might modify the forms of knowledge while other people – the majority – would be expected passively and uncritically to acquiesce in the knowledge structure which would be offered to them for edification. Teachers and educational institutions were to operate as gate-keepers maintaining moral and intellectual control over students by collud-ing in misrepresenting provisional forms of knowledge as if they were abso-lutes. It was this recognition that Hirst's conception of a 'liberal education' was intrinsically authoritarian that enabled me to define more carefully the opportunity for selecting knowledge which was being offered to students within the School for Independent Study. Independent study gave students the opportunity to react directly to experience and to generate their own understandings rather than to be initiated into the disciplines which were only previous tentative understandings which had become reified and insti-tutionalized as systems of control.

Knowledge and Control came as a breath of fresh air as an endorsement of my developing view that it was the authoritarian social control over course con-tent that constituted the strongest deterrent to the democratization of British higher education. I realized, however, that the influence of American pragmatism towards an emphasis of individual selectivity of knowledge led remorselessly to a radical individualism. I was not happy with Dewey's instrumentalist criterion of validity. In practice it increasingly seemed to lend support to the incipient experientialism of the part-time DipHE in that the validity of 'objective' knowledge was measured by reference to its func-tion in promoting the self-development of the knowing person. I remained convinced that there were objective things to be known and that the essence of independent study should be that it would provide access to that objectiv-ity rather than reduce it to self-knowledge. It is not surprising that my sym-pathies lay with the epistemological strand of *Knowledge and Control* mainly represented by Bourdieu and Bernstein. Bourdieu's 'Intellectual Field and Creative Project, in particular, suggests the philosophical orienta-tion which led to the distinctive character of the submission to the CNAA for the BA/BSc by Independent Study. Bourdieu's essay was congenial because it arose out of the same late 1960s tension between structuralism and intentionalism as had my own doctoral research.[25] Individual intentions constitute objective structures but, equally, those individual intentions are themselves partially constituted from an internalization of objective structures, or, as Bourdieu puts it:

> The creative project is the place of meeting and sometimes of conflict between the *intrinsic necessity of the work of art* which demands that it be continued, improved and completed, and *social pressures* which direct the work from outside.[26]

The construction of knowledge was no different from the creation of a work of art. Although people should not be initiated into an existing structure of intellectual explanation, it was inevitable that individual projects would both be partly constituted by it as well as partly modify it. Equally, individual projects would only modify an existing intellectual field if they sufficiently engaged with the language of that field to secure legitimacy within it. Bourdieu illustrated his notion of 'legitimacy' within an intellectual field with a brief social historical reference:

> Intellectual life was dominated throughout the Middle Ages, during part of the Renaissance, and in France (with the importance of the court) throughout the classical period, by an *external* legitimizing authority. It only gradually became organized into an intellectual field as creative artists began to liberate themselves economically and socially from the patronage of the aristocracy and the Church and from their ethical and aesthetic values. There began to appear *specific author-ities of selection and consecration* that were intellectual in the proper sense (even if, like publishers and theatre managers, they were still subjected to economic and social restrictions which therefore continued to influence intellectual life), and which were placed in a situation of *competition for cultural legitimacy.*[27]

This analysis seemed doubly applicable to the situation of the School for Independent Study as it sought permission from the CNAA to introduce the BA/BSc by Independent Study. In the first place, the polytechnic experi-enced the CNAA as an 'external legitimizing authority'. The course submis-sion involved the polytechnic in securing its own liberation from the CNAA to conduct its internal legitimization of the individual proposals made by students. Hirst's forms of knowledge were recommended in the name of 'education'. It was an important part of the BA/BSc's challenge to the 'educa-tional' control of the CNAA that it wanted to encourage students to see that the course offered them the chance to by-pass 'educational' validity by estab-lishing the independent legitimizing validity of the intrinsic intellectual merits of their intentions. Just as creative artists had overthrown the control of the Church in 19th century France, so individuals might now overthrow the domination of Education by establishing new intellectual fields.

This background to the development of the BA/BSc by Independent Study has been a personal account of a private meaning. It was my creative project between 1975 and 1979 and it acquired public form almost entirely in the structure which was approved by the CNAA.[28] The significance of the struc-ture is very easily explicable in terms of the philosophical issues discussed above. Students were assigned to tutors of the School for Independent Study in a 'pre-course' within which they developed their individual programmes of study. The 'pre-course' was envisaged as a de-schooled context within which students would be helped to define their inquiries (their 'creative projects') and to justify these inquiries in relation to the current state of relevant explanation. Students were explicitly asked to justify their proposed pro-grammes, and these justifications were to be of the pedagogical style to be adopted, the proposed location within or in relation to the educational insti-tution, the proposed assessment, as well as the proposed content of study.

Intellectual justifications were required, in other words, not just of the intrinsic value of the proposed content but, additionally, of the complex set of circumstances and conditions which would constitute the proposed experience. The students' proposals were to be submitted to a Registration Board which was required to respond in a manner which matched the complexity of the justifications. The Registration Board comprised representatives of the School for Independent Study, representatives from each of the faculties of the polytechnic, and external examiners with expertise which would 'cover' the fields of the faculties. The Board was expected to make two kinds of legitimizing decision. It was first expected to judge whether each proposal was legitimate within the terms of the intellectual field with which it was engaging, and, secondly, whether the proposed student package was a legitimate equivalent to those activities which would normally carry social recognition as worthy of the award of an Honours degree. In order to make these judgements, the Board was expected to involve itself in a process of negotiation with students in respect of their proposals. Students were required to submit an interim proposal which would be the basis of negotiation before the submission of a final proposal for decision. It was intended that the 'subject specialists' on the Registration Board would be prepared to consider the content of their specialisms as provisional or problematic and, equally, to regard the institutional framework within which these specialisms were transmitted as an intrinsic factor of their provisionality. At the same time, the fact that the Board was required to maintain an adherence to the concept of an Honours degree meant that negotiated Board decisions might only gradually modify the public meaning of 'disciplines' or educational institutions by slowly mediating the 'grass-roots' intentions of individual students.

The structure of the BA/BSc by Independent Study enforced a differentiation from the DipHE in two important respects. Firstly, it enabled students to shake off the burden of an imposed ideology of 'competence'. A programme of study proposed by a student to enable him to develop competence would need to be intellectually justified as rigourosly as a proposed 'academic' programme. Secondly, the Registration Board for the degree was actually involved in legitimizing individual student proposals, whereas the Validating Board for the DipHE only sampled statements produced by diploma students in order to offer public endorsement of the processes of the course. Diploma staff judged whether the statements prepared by students proposed appropriate means by which those students might reach their own self-determined ends, and the Validating Board scrutinized the staff judgements without exercising any power in evaluating the legitimacy of the course's overall objectives. By contrast, the Registration Board was required to make a significant public judgement of each individual student proposal. In short, the Validating Board performed a public relations function while the Registration Board performed a public legitimation function.

The essence of the importance of the Registration Board was that it assumed the relativity of knowledge and the plurality of values and sought to provide a forum in which channels of communication and negotiation remained open between those people who were socially defined as 'teachers' and 'learners'. By 1977, as we have seen, the philosophical support for the activities of the Registration Board in the thinking of the 'new sociology of education' had collapsed. By 1977, the political potential of 'reflexivity' and negotiated curriculum content had been discredited. It was partly because the wind had gone out of the sails of the philosophical debate that the course eventually secured approval in 1979 after struggling in the period from 1976. One of the staff of the school heavily involved in the operation of the degree in this period – Maggie Humm – attempted to shift the rationale of the course in a Marxist direction and her account of the course sounded a new note in her contribution to the papers assembled to describe the 'NELP Experience of Independent Study'. She wrote:

> Independence is then neither simply the institution of libertarian ideas nor an account of the philosophy behind them. The point of the degree is not to institute ideas, but to develop, in the student, the ability to 'know' alternatives, through a libertarian ideology. . . . We can only break the interlocking of capitalism by developing structures within capitalist society within which to exercise freedom.[29]

But the dominant trend was as described by Brian Davies – towards an acquiescent, mechanical and a-political implementation of procedures. It is now easy to see that in the early 1970s there was an apparent affinity between the aims of the educational reformers and those of the supporters of the 'new directions' sociology of education. Both movements could be seen to be opposed to a controlling academic elite which conspired to restrict democratic access to educational and, hence, occupational opportunity. Superficially, therefore, the BA/BSc submission of 1976 appeared to be a logical extension of this common opposition. This impression was rapidly shattered when the first Registration Board for the degree, meeting in July 1976, only accepted a proportion of the proposals which had been submitted to it by students who had just successfully gained the DipHE. The educational reformers suspected that the Registration Board might simply be, or become, an instrument of the oppressive academicism which they were fighting to destroy. This suspicion has persisted as the degree has steadily resisted the encroachments of the movement for reform. The degree has been able to avoid the debate on access because eligibility is only for those who have completed the first two years of an Honours degree, a DipHE, or other carefully negotiated equivalent qualifications. The degree operates with a firm framework within which the assessment proposals of students are permissible and therefore resists engagement with the debate on student 'profiles'. The degree has not allowed itself to become attached to the 'Education for Capability' campaign – ensuring, indeed, that it was only the DipHE rather than the degree or the school which received an award under the Recognition Scheme in 1982. The degree, finally, has resisted the notion that 'independence' lies in the capacity to pursue a programme of independent study successfully. Instead, it has argued that the DipHE exists to enable students to acquire the competence which will enable them to propose a programme of study to be undertaken within the degree, while the structure of the degree itself is the guarantor that the substantial content of the proposed studies merits recognition equivalent to that which is bestowed on any Honours degree course.

The argument advanced against the 'new directions' movement was that it was politically naive – that it was foolish to suppose that curriculum negotiations could be anything other than reflections of unequal power relations. The same argument might properly be advanced against the degree. It has maintained its political momentum as a result of its dependence for its student intake largely on those students who were initially attracted to the DipHE. By the same token, the credibility of the DipHE has been partly sustained by the opportunity provided by the one-year degree to transform the attainment of private objectives into the fulfilment of public standards. Until the end of the 1970s, the educational reformers were too preoccupied in keeping the influence of the personal growth movement under control to worry about the distinctive approach to independent study which was developing through the degree. The confluence of educational reformism and person-centredness since the beginning of the 1980s has tended to isolate the tradition of independent study which has been associated with the degree since its inception and which was reproduced mechanically in the submission for a MA/MSc by Independent Study approved in 1984. In its isolation, this tradition comes under attack from two main positions – from 'new paradigm research' and from 'post-modernism'. It is against these two philosophical props of current educational reformism that new counter-arguments must now be advanced. I shall argue in my last chapter that there are pressing political reasons why 'modernist' values should now be reasserted to stem the rising tide of irrationalism.

Notes

1 M. S. Archer, 'Egalitarianism in English and French Educational Sociology'. *European Journal of Sociology*, XI, 1, 1970, p. 129.
2 ibid. p. 119.
3 M. F. D. Young (ed.), *Knowledge and Control. New Directions for the Sociology of Education*, Collier-Macmillan, London, 1971, p. 2.
4 ibid. p. 2.
5 M. Flude and J. Ahier (eds), *Educability, Schools and Ideology*, Croom Helm, 1974, p. 5.
6 ibid. p. 10.
7 ibid. p. 8.
8 R. Dale and G. Esland, *The Construction of Reality*, Open University Press, 1972.
9 See *Educational Review* 25, 3, 1973.
10 Flude and Ahier, op. cit. p. 63.
11 ibid. p. 127.

12 R. Dale *et al.* (eds), *Schooling and Capitalism. A Sociological Reader*, RKP with the Open University Press, 1976. p. 1.

13 M. F. D. Young and G. Whitty, *Society, State and Schooling. Readings on the Possibilities for Radical Education*, The Falmer Press, 1977, p. 236. The quotes are from M. Greene, 'Curriculum and consciousness', *The Record*, Vol. F.3. No. 2, 1971.

14 Young and Whitty, op. cit. p. 236.

15 ibid. p. 243.

16 ibid. p. 248.

17 ibid. p. 229.

18 D. Gleeson (ed.), *Identity and Structure. Issues in the Sociology of Education*, Nafferton Books, 1977, p. 2.

19 ibid. p. 11.

20 G. Bernbaum, *Knowledge and Ideology in the Sociology of Education*, Macmillan Press, 1977.

21 D. Gleeson (ed.), op. cit. p. 200.

22 D. M. Robbins, unpublished PhD thesis, *Literature and Natural Philosophy, 1770-1800* for the University of Cambridge, 1972. For a discussion of some aspects of the thesis, see J. Beer, *Coleridge's Poetic Intelligence*, Macmillan, 1977, pp. 104 and 299.

23 Unpublished dissertation (1975): 'The development of sociological theory in relation to race relations at the University of Chicago from 1900 until 1920.' Martin Bulmer has recently raised many of the issues which concerned me in his *The Chicago School of Sociology. Institutionalization, Diversity, and the Rise of Sociological Research*, University of Chicago Press, 1984. He is, however, much more sympathetic to the process of institutionalization than I was in 1975.

24 R. D. Archambault (ed.), *Philosophical Analysis and Education*, RKP, 1965, p. 122.

25 The essay first appeared in France as 'Champ intellectuel et projet créateur' in November 1966, in a number of *Les Temps Modernes* which was wholly devoted to 'Problèmes du Structuralisme'.

26 Young (ed.), 1971, op. cit. p. 166.

27 ibid. p. 162.

28 The Summer number of 1977 of the *Higher Education Review* (edited by J. Pratt and published by T. Burgess) carried an article on the degree by independent study in which I presented an edited version of the 1976 CNAA submission with a few brief comments.

29 *The NELP Experience of Independent Study*, a collection of papers and documents compiled for the first conference on independent study by the School for Independent Study, 18-20 April 1979, p. 115. Available from the archives of the School for Independent Study, Livingstone House, London E15 2LL.

Conclusion

Arresting the 'Great Betrayal'

The 'conclusion' of this book should, on one level, be very clear. It condemns those aspects of the rise of independent study which have militated against intellectual achievement and it hopes to ensure that the anti-intellectual trend may be reversed. The purpose of this concluding chapter, however, is to suggest resonances and significances which go far beyond concern for the future direction of independent study. The educational innovation described in these pages has been in the front line of wider social and philosophical conflicts and this chapter concentrates on these. It starts from the position that the threats to the potential value of 'independent study' all derive from a common anti-rational orientation. The chapter offers a selective account of some 20th century perceptions of the threat of anti-rationalism to civilized values.

The account is selective in three ways. It expresses, firstly, a subjective meaning which I have created out of several independent intellectual explorations. I begin with some reference to Julien Benda's *La Trahison des Clercs*. I first encountered this text as an undergraduate when I was reflecting on the French debate about Romanticism and Classicism, Action Française, and Maurras – all in connection with work on T. E. Hulme and T. S. Eliot. More recently, it was in the background when I undertook research in the late 1970s and early 1980s on higher education institutions in France during the Vichy regime from 1940 until 1944. I move from a representation of Benda to one of Max Horkheimer. His *Eclipse of Reason* is a text which, in the 1960s, helped me to understand the development of Coleridge's thought at the crucial moment of transition in Western European sensibility from an emphasis of 'objective' to 'subjective' reason. Thirdly, I represent some of the ideas of Alasdair MacIntyre. I can remember reading his critique of Marcuse when it appeared in 1970 at the beginning of the period re-experienced in this book, but the stimulus for a new consideration of MacIntyre was provided by his recent lecture in a series given in honour of R. S. Peters.

These, then, are three personal reference points, but there is also an objective, historical logic which explains the second basis for selection. The three authors are presented chronologically. Each text can be seen to have specific meaning within its context which is separate from any meaning associated with my personal explorations. In particular, Horkheimer's text was profoundly rooted in his experience of World War II. It is this location in history which provides the third explanation for the selection of texts – the fact that they offer internal resonances within the book. Halmos's account of the post-World War II oscillation between 'personalist' and 'political' reforming initiatives offers an analysis of the period which generated Horkheimer's text, while that text itself was a deliberate attack on the Deweyan philosophy which had such an influence on the American developments in progressive education and social psychology, culminating in the movements described in Part I of this book. Indeed, the career of Malcolm Knowles which is charted in Chapter 3 offers a vital exemplification of precisely this theoretical connection. Some of these internal resonances express an almost unconscious network of cross-references. The quotations from Benda, for instance, are designed to relate to our common contemporary experiences even though some of these are barely stated in the text – passages, for instance, in which he insists that the glorification of physical prowess or the enforced insertion of the 'clerc' into the economic market place are symptoms of the degradation of reason. Readers are invited to interpolate their own embellished connections.

This conclusion, in other words, only offers suggestive hints towards an account of the background to contemporary irrationalism. A systematic analysis might involve a work of the proportions of Lecky's *History of Rationalism*, but the nuances constitute an important prelude to the attempt to argue from Habermas's work towards practical recommendations to resolve our current malaise. Again, this chapter does not begin to offer a thorough commentary on Habermas's continuing work. It simply tries to bring together his epistemological and sociological perceptions in such a way as to articulate a diagnosis of present tendencies in our society. This account focuses on the fact that 1977 was a crucial point of transition for Habermas and suggests that the same date was equally significant in the United Kingdom and for the Degree by Independent Study. In both cases, it marked a point at which it became clear that epistemologically-inspired attitudes had to be embedded in social practice. This final chapter explores the implications of that realization for the preservation of our essential freedoms. Above all, it is a recommendation that we should be vigilant.

Arresting the 'Great Betrayal'

When Richard Aldington translated Julien Benda's *La Trahison des Clercs* in 1928 he was so unsure of the most appropriate way to render 'clerc' into English that, instead, he adopted *The Great Betrayal* as the English title. This is hardly surprising because Benda himself graphically portrayed the degradation of an ideal while only intimating negatively what might be the characteristics of an uncorrupted 'clerc'. It was the documentation of the betrayal which was so telling and its form was first indicated in a religious reflection borrowed from Bossuet's Élévations:

> I created him to be spiritual in his flesh; and now he has become carnal even in the spirit.[1]

Benda contended that in his time 'political passions' were prevalent and that the clerks had succumbed to these passions. They had, firstly, themselves adopted political passions and, secondly, brought these passions actually into their activities as clerks. Additionally, the clerks had, thirdly, 'played the game of political passions by their doctrines'. Benda supported this claim by showing, first of all, that the clerks now praised attachment to the particular and denounced respect for universals, and, secondly, that the clerks now praised attachment to the practical and denounced the love of the spiritual. It was in his elaboration of this second point that Benda most clearly revealed the assumed characteristics of the true clerk. One manifestation of the new practical orientation of the clerk was his inclination to praise warlike instincts. Benda wrote:

> This teaching leads the modern 'clerk' (we have just seen it in Nietzsche) to confer a *moral* value upon physical exercise and to proclaim *the morality of sport* – a most remarkable thing indeed among those who for twenty centuries have exhorted man to situate good in states of the mind.[2]

Whoever they may actually be, clerks owe their positions to their capacity to exercise pure intellect but are now in the process of disowning their intellectuality. Benda begins again with a direct criticism of Nietzsche in the following passage, but it ends with an indirect dismissal of some of the key phrases of Bergsonian irrationalism:

In Nietzsche, the scorn for the man of study to the benefit of the warrior is only an episode in a desire which nobody will deny inspires the whole of his work as well as the work of Sorel, Barrès and Péguy: *The desire to abase the values of knowledge before the values of action.* To-day this desire inspires not only the moralist, but another kind of 'clerk' who speaks from much higher ground. I am referring to that teaching of modern metaphysics which exhorts man to feel comparatively little esteem for the truly thinking portion of himself and to honour the active and *willing* part of himself with all his devotion. The theory of knowledge from which humanity has taken its values during the past half century assigns a secondary rank to the mind which proceeds by clear and distinct ideas, by categories, by words, and places in the highest rank the mind which succeeds in liberating itself from these intellectual habits and in becoming conscious of itself insofar as it is a 'pure tendency', a 'pure will', a 'pure activity.'[3]

It is not just heroic action which is esteemed by the modern clerk at the expense of thought. Benda argues that the clerks have betrayed themselves by concentrating inordinately on the practical utility of thinking rather than on its intrinsic value. He condemns the teaching of the modern clerks according to which

> intellectual activity is worthy of esteem to the extent that it is practical and to that extent alone.[4]

The traditional commitment of the clerks to the intrinsic satisfaction of intellectual activity without reference to any advantages which it might secure had performed a social function. The clerks had placed before the laymen

> the spectacle of a class of men for whom the value of life lies in its disinterestedness, and they acted as a check on – or at least shamed – the laymen's practical passions.[5]

But the modern clerks have renounced this exemplary integrity. By contrast, Benda argues,

> They proclaim that intellectual functions are only respectable to the extent that they are bound up with the pursuit of a concrete advantage, and that the intelligence which takes no interest in its objects is a contemptible activity.[6]

What had brought about the decline of intellectual disinterestedness? Benda did not offer a detailed analysis but he sensed that a major cause of the degeneration of pure thought was the erosion of the social and economic independence of the clerks. The modern world had made the clerks into citizens and it had become increasingly difficult for them to transcend partial civic interests. Benda could find no solace in the thought that the betrayal of the clerks might only be a temporary aberration for he was satisfied that the trend which he had observed was 'bound up with the very essence of the modern world'.[7] This belief in the irreversibility of the process which he had perceived caused Benda profound dismay, especially since he could clearly foresee its irreversible consequences. He predicted:

> Indeed, if we ask ourselves what will happen to a humanity where every group is striving more eagerly than ever to feel conscious of its own particular interests, and makes its moralists tell it that it is sublime to the extent that it knows no law but this interest – a child can give the answer. This humanity is heading for the greatest and most perfect war ever seen in the world, whether it is a war of nations, or a war of classes.[8]

It was shortly before the end of that war in the spring of 1944 that Max Horkheimer, having taken refuge in the United States from Frankfurt, gave the series of lectures at Columbia University on which he subsequently based his *Eclipse of Reason*, published in 1947. Whereas Benda had considered Nietzsche and Bergson to be the main opponents of reason in the first few decades of the century in France, Horkheimer focused a similar attack on the pragmatist tradition in American philosophy and on Dewey in particular. Horkheimer's first chapter states clearly his perception of the consequences for reason of instrumentalism and pragmatism:

> Having given up autonomy, reason has become an instrument. In the formalistic aspect of subjective reason, stressed by positivism, its unrelatedness to objective content is emphasized; in its instrumental aspect, stressed by pragmatism, its surrender to heteronomous contents is emphasized. Reason has become completely harnessed to the social process.[9]

Whereas Benda had primarily seen his great betrayal as the dereliction of responsibility by a class and only secondarily, but concomitantly, as the degradation of intellectuality, Horkheimer was interested in the philosophical implications of the historical transformations in the status assigned to reason. As the above passage suggests, Horkheimer argued that the emphasis of subjective reason meant that it tended to segregate the subjective from the objective while the emphasis of practical reason meant that it tended to be engulfed by the context in which it was actualized. In both cases the value of rational objectivity has been destroyed. Horkheimer wrote:

> While philosophy in its objectivistic stage sought to be the agency that brought human conduct, including scientific undertakings, to a final understanding of its own reason and justice, pragmatism tries to retranslate any understanding into mere conduct.[10]

The consequences of this retranslation which Benda had anticipated were poignantly suggested by Horkheimer with all the force of immediate hindsight:

> Since ends are no longer determined in the light of reason, it is also

impossible to say that one economic or political system, no matter how cruel and despotic, is less reasonable than another. According to formalized reason, despotism, cruelty, oppression are not bad in themselves; no rational agency would endorse a verdict against dictatorship if its sponsors were likely to profit by it.[11]

For Horkheimer, catastrophic consequences followed from the fact that the pragmatic attitude had destroyed the grounds upon which common value judgements might be reached:

> What are the consequences of the formalization of reason? Justice, equality, happiness, tolerance, all the concepts that . . . were in preceding centuries supposed to be inherent in or sanctioned by reason, have lost their intellectual roots. They are still aims and ends, but there is no rational agency authorized to appraise and link them to an objective reality.[12]

A similar diagnosis of our contemporary disarray in respect of ethical judgements has been offered recently by Alasdair MacIntyre in his *After Virtue, a study in moral theory* (1981). His starting point is that

> The most striking feature of contemporary moral utterance is that so much of it is used to express disagreements; and the most striking feature of the debates in which these disagreements are expressed is their interminable character. I do not mean by this just that such debates go on and on and on – although they do – but also that they apparently can find no terminus. There seems to be no rational way of securing moral agreement in our culture.[13]

By way of illustration, MacIntyre presents rival moral arguments in relation to three commonly debated issues – war and defence, abortion, and the equality of access to health and education. He uses these sets of arguments to demonstrate what he calls their 'conceptual incommensurability'. By this he means that

> Every one of the arguments is logically valid or can be easily expanded so as to be made so; the conclusions do indeed follow from the premises. But the rival premises are such that we possess no rational way of weighing the claims of one as against another. For each premise employs some quite different normative or evaluative concept from the others, so that the claims made upon us are of quite different kinds.[14]

MacIntyre concludes from this that

> It is precisely because there is in our society no established way of deciding between these claims that moral argument appears to be necessarily interminable. From our rival conclusions we can argue back to our rival premises; but when we do arrive at our premises argument ceases and the invocation of one premise against another becomes a matter of pure assertion and counter-assertion.[15]

The force of 'in our society' is important for MacIntyre contends that we have lost the social conditions which alone would make common ethical discourse possible. In a recent lecture delivered at the Institute of Education, London, MacIntyre examined in detail the suggestion that the Scotland of the 18th century was a society in which the necessary conditions were uniquely retained. He justified making this examination before an audience of teachers and educators on the grounds that he contended that the perennially perceived dual functions of the teaching profession – to prepare people for social and occupational roles and also to prepare them to think for themselves – are 'under the conditions of Western modernity' mutually incompatible. The point of the Scottish case-study was to investigate the construction and destruction of a society within which the dual purposes were congruent. Although MacIntyre argued that the Scottish Enlightenment had been successful in creating the necessary 'educated public', he was forced to admit that it was a 'relatively rare phenomenon'

> that a large segment of a whole society should institutionalize its informal debates over the best way for its members to live, so that the conversation of that society is to some notable degree both an extension of and an interchange with the discussions within its universities, so that that same truth is to that degree exemplified in the society at large.[16]

Nevertheless, the intention to make the necessary socially constructive effort is essential if our modern world is to avoid disaster. MacIntyre's vision of the consequences of contemporary modernism, as expressed at the end of *After Virtue*, is as apocalyptic as Benda's prediction. He likens our situation to that of the epoch in which the Roman empire declined into the Dark Ages. A comparable social creativity may still preserve our survival, although the circumstances are even less propitious. 'What matters at this stage,' he concludes,

> is the construction of local forms of community within which civility and the intellectual and moral life can be sustained through the new dark ages which are already upon us. And if the tradition of the virtues was able to survive the horrors of the last dark ages, we are not entirely without grounds for hope. This time however the barbarians are not waiting beyond the frontiers; they have already been governing us for quite some time. And it is our lack of consciousness of this that constitutes part of our predicament. We are waiting not for a Godot, but for another – doubtless very different – St Benedict.[17]

This book has given an account, in Part 1, of some descriptors of educational practice which are now treated as synonymous with independent study. I claimed in my Introduction that the School for Independent Study had not consciously applied any pre-existing model of innovative educational practice and that it had formulated its own understanding of independent study in response to its own particular circumstances. It was an important function of the book to retrieve the various strands of the School's own self-understanding. It has become clear, nevertheless, that two of the three historical strands explored in Part 3 have converged and are in accord with the approaches described under the headings of 'experiential learning', 'self-managed learning' and 'contract learning'. The School's originating educational reformism and its long-standing disposition towards person-centredness are readily accommodated philosophically to the significations of these other, more popular, labels. The reason for this is obvious. These converging trends and movements are all fundamentally irrationalistic and anti-intellectual. They can mainly be traced back to common origins in American social psychology which was itself a product of philosophical pragmatism. They are all current manifestations of the orientations of Bergson, Dewey, and Nietzsche which Benda, Horkheimer, and MacIntyre have identified as the causes of 20th century malaise. In short, I have described, witnessed, and, perhaps, colluded in a modern great betrayal.

It is easily possible to raise objections to the localized components of the interlocking irrationalist structure. Many of these objections have been implicit in my various commentaries. I have every sympathy, for instance, with the stated aims of the Council for the Advancement of Experiential Learning, but it seems likely that there has been an accommodation between these aims and those of educational reformists. In his contribution to Keeton's 1976 volume on Experiential Learning, Melvin Tumin argued that there was a substantial difference between the pursuit of 'functionally equivalent learnings' which involves the exploration of non-traditional means for the achievement of traditional ends, and the pursuit of 'functionally equivalent certification processes' which involves the attempt to secure the recognition of the non-traditional experience as itself credit-worthy without reference to the traditional. He sounded a clear warning that if the work of CAEL were to move in the second direction, it might be at the expense of learning altogether:

> If one does not seek for functionally equivalent learnings, but rather for functionally equivalent certification processes, it may not matter much whether the learning has taken place. If we set up alternative forms of criteria of certification, and if those alternative criteria are accepted as functionally equivalent for occupational location and placement, then we might become increasingly indifferent to what has been learned in the process.[18]

This succinctly and accurately predicts the consequences of the accommodation between experientialism and educational reformism. The movement for educational reform did not simply endeavour to secure wider access to higher education, but it did so, first of all, by advocating changes in curriculum content and, secondly, by attempting to transform the procedures for assessing performance. The movement is now educationally moribund precisely because its neglect of objective learning has tended to reduce educational process to the level of assertion training. ·

The person-centred approach is equally educationally flawed and localized objections can be stated here which also apply to the general ethos of 'self-managed learning'. It seems, for instance, that Boydell himself has come to accept that the person-centred approach which first penetrated education generally from the field of management training should no longer be constrained by the educational assumptions of 'learning'. The movement towards 'self-managed learning' should now more properly be called a movement for 'self-developed self-development' and differentiated from both management and learning. A French publication of 1982 – Louis-Pierre Jouvenet's *Horizon politique des pédagogies non directives* – has acutely analysed the social and political conditions in France which facilitated the colonization of much French educational practice between 1958 and 1978 by predominantly American ideas of person-centredness.[19] Jouvenet argues that the key elements of the Rogerian platform, such as individual freedom and creativity, all presuppose an idealized liberal, pluralist American society as conditions of their existence. At the same time, the political implications of the personal growth movement involve the construction of an a-political 'sociocracy'. The Rogerian movement, in other words, depends upon the existing values of freedom and tolerance to establish an alternative society which is in accord with pre-1787 traditions of absolute freedom. Rogers has himself exposed the inherent contradictions of this endeavour in discussing in *Freedom to Learn for the 80's* the reasons why 'humanistic, innovative educational organizations have a poor record in regard to permanence'. He claims that the main reason is that 'Our culture does not as yet believe in democracy' and that society therefore finds the values of humanistic establishments extremely threatening. But his pessimistic conclusion is a tacit recognition that his freedom requires the sponsorship of the tolerant freedom of the society which he holds in disrespect:

> What we need to learn, it seems, are ways of gaining acceptance for a humanistic person-centred venture in a culture more devoted to rule by authority. Since ours is a pluralistic society, a humanistic option should be given the opportunity to survive. In today's world that opportunity is hard to come by.[20]

A final localized objection can also be made to the appropriation of the adult education movement by the proponents of 'contract learning'. Again, the penetration of the British situation is partly cultural. The healthy British tradition of adult education, manifest this century in the development of the W.E.A. and of extra-mural departments and boasting advocates of the calibre of R. H. Tawney and A. D. Lindsay, has been contaminated by the personalist assumptions of the American tradition. Yet, as Keith Percy argued in a paper to a recent SRHE conference on Continuing Education in Higher Education:

> Empirically, there is little evidence that adults wish to have different curricula from other students and a strong impression that they would

fear for the credibility of their degrees if they did. Similarly, there is little evidence that adults, any more than other students, wish to negotiate their own course content, although in the small number of independent study schemes in higher education adults have been proportionately over-represented.[21]

These piecemeal objections relate individually to some of the weaknesses of 'experiential learning', 'self-managed learning', 'contract learning', personalism and person-centred dominated educational reformism. They do not get to the heart of the problems of contemporary anti-intellectualism, and, indeed, they run the danger of seeming to offer a regressive conservatism as the only alternative. In moving towards a positive response to anti-intellectualism, however, it is my contention that an interpretation of independent study which is an extension of the third strand operating in the development of the School for Independent Study offers the hope of a contribution to social welfare and political health which is the product of a genuine educational reform.

There is no doubt that the responses of Benda and MacIntyre to their own pessimistic diagnoses of our condition are reactionary. Separated by a period of 60 years, those responses are also remarkably similar. Benda did not explicitly articulate a response, but the ideal characteristics of the clerks emerge from his description of those things which they have forsaken. Benda considered that one explanation for the new political attitude of the clerks was that it resulted from

> the decline of the study of classical literature in the formation of their minds.[22]

But *La Trahison des Clercs* was reactionary in a way which was much more fundamental than in its nostalgia for lost classical scholarship. Paradoxically, as one commentator, Robert Niess, has indicated, Benda's idealization of the social function of the clerk has aspects in common with the anti-democratic features of the thought of Nietzsche which he generally opposed. As Niess puts it:

> Curiously, however, although much of the book is devoted to a condemnation of Nietzscheism, which Benda tends to see everywhere, as he does Bergsonism, nevertheless it seems undeniable that the theory and concept of the *clerc* owes a great deal to the idea of the superman as Nietzsche expressed it – the celibate and 'free' superintellectual whose glory comes largely from his resistance to the corrupting effects of a corrupt and bourgeois society.[23]

There is a similar ambiguity about MacIntyre's response. Chapters 14 and 15 of *After Virtue* are devoted to making the case for reviving a tradition in which 'the Aristotelian moral and political texts are canonical' in deliberate opposition to the influence of the Nietzscheans. Although MacIntyre regards such a revival as necessary for the survival of civilized society, he does not appear to hold out hope for any saving transformation of mass society. The best that he seems able to hope for is the preservation of a pure Aristotelian enclave existing in social isolation in a fashion analogous to the separation of the monastic orders at the beginning of the Dark Ages. The 'Idea of an Educated Public' which he outlined in his Richard Peters Lecture was not at all an idea of an educated mass but of a minority which would be able to behave and communicate rationally as a community because all of this few would have been initiated into shared assumptions through a common reading of Greek philosophical and political texts. Paradoxically, again, MacIntyre's Helle-nistically inspired ideal community is as detached from the politics of the State as is the ideal Rogerian community of fully functioning persons.

Just as Horkheimer's critique of 'subjective reason' had been entirely philosophical, so his proposed solution showed little awareness of the means by which it might be actualized. He was clear that a conservative reversion to a commitment to 'objective reason' such as Hegel's was neither possible nor desirable. He contended that 'subjective' and 'objective' reason constituted two concepts of reason which

> do not represent two separate and independent ways of the mind, although their opposition expresses a real antinomy.[24]

For Horkheimer, therefore, the task of philosophy

> is not stubbornly to play the one against the other, but to foster a mutual critique and thus, if possible, to prepare in the intellectual realm the reconciliation of the two in reality.[25]

It was this intellectualist definition of the epistemological problem of the competition between 'subjective' and 'objective' reason that was the legacy of the Frankfurt School in the 1940s. I want to argue that it has been Habermas's achievement to suggest ways in which Horkheimer's solution in the 'intellectual realm' might be actualized socially, and I want to argue further that independent study provides procedures which enable that process of actualization. In an interview recently published in English, Habermas has admitted that in the early 1960s he still accepted that the problems which he perceived could be solved epistemologically. The result of this inheritance was, he says,

> *Knowledge and Human Interests*, which was written between 1964 and 1968. I still consider the outlines of the argument developed in the book to be correct. But I no longer believe in epistemology as the *via regia*. The critical theory of society does not need to prove its credentials in the first instance in methodological terms; it needs a substantive founda-tion, which will lead out of the bottlenecks produced by the conceptual framework of the philosophy of consciousness, and overcome the para-digm of production, without abandoning the intentions of Western Marxism in the process. The result is *The Theory of Communicative Action*.[26]

It was in *Knowledge and Human Interests* that Habermas outlined his well-known epistemological trichotomy. His argument is most readily accessible in his Frankfurt inaugural address of June 1965, which is published as an appendix to the book under the title 'Knowledge and Human Interests: A General Perspective'. This paper first represents the traditional philosophical view, derived from the Greeks, that theoretical knowledge – involving the contemplation of the cosmos – is the only knowledge which can regulate human actions because it is freed from 'mere human interests'. Habermas then assesses the sense of crisis which Husserl felt at about the same time as Horkheimer which was expressed in *The Crisis of the European Sciences*. Husserl's view was that the scientific disciplines had degenerated from the status of true theory but he argued this status could be recovered phenomenologically. The objectivist illusions of positivist science could be counteracted by the explicit recognition that knowledge is related to human interests. For Husserl, that recognition itself achieved a liberation from human interest which constituted a resurrection of the Greek ideal of theoretical detachment. Habermas finds Husserl's response to his perception of 'crisis' inadequate because he does not accept that *theoria* owed its influence to the supposition that it had freed knowledge from interest. On the contrary, he claims, it had educational and cultural implications

> because it derived *pseudonormative power* from *the concealment of its actual interest*. While criticizing the objectivist self-understanding of the sciences, Husserl succumbs to another objectivism, which was always attached to the traditional concept of theory.[27]

For Habermas, the error which is exposed by Husserl's endeavours is not that the sciences have abandoned the classical concept of theory, but that 'they have not completely abandoned it'.[28] In the English debate which was contemporary with the appearance of Habermas's book, Paul Hirst's position as outlined in Part 3, Chapter 3 of this book, is inadequate in the same way as is Husserl's. Habermas's epistemological response was to define 'three categories of processes of inquiry for which a specific connection between logical-methodological rules and knowledge-constitutive interests can be demonstrated'.[29] He tries to outline three distinct categories of human interest which constitute knowledge without allowing them to have recourse for cultural authority to any notion of theory which might be thought to have separate or prior epistemological power. The three approaches which Habermas identifies are introduced in the following way:

> The approach of the empirical-analytic sciences incorporates a *technical* cognitive interest; that of the historical-hermeneutic sciences incorporates a *practical* one; and the approach of critically oriented sciences incorporates the *emancipatory* cognitive interest that . . . was at the root of traditional theories.[30]

The essence of the emancipatory interest is self-reflection and Habermas is optimistic about the inherent possibilities of this category. Whereas the technical and the practical interests tend to become reified and to become embodied in oppressive laws, the essence of the emancipatory interest is that it is critical of the other two and endeavours to ensure that they remain answerable to private human values. It is on the basis of the efforts of emancipatory interest and on its success in destroying the ontological illusions which are still cultivated by the other two interests that Habermas is able to envisage any hope for an ideal, emancipated society. But, as he has admitted, the analysis of *Knowledge and Human Interests* was excessively epistemological. He had, however, already published in Germany *Strukturwandel der Oeffentlichkeit* (Structural Transformation of the Public Sphere) in 1962 and it was the line of argument advanced there which has provided the basis for his subsequent embodiment of the epistemological in the social and historical. The main elements of Habermas's historical argument were summarized in an article on 'The Public Sphere' which appeared in 1964. Habermas first defined the meaning which he was assigning to the 'public sphere':

> By 'the public sphere' we mean first of all a realm of our social life in which something approaching public opinion can be formed. Access is guaranteed to all citizens. A portion of the public sphere comes into being in every conversation in which private individuals assemble to form a public body. They then behave neither like business or professional people transacting private affairs, nor like members of a constitutional order subject to the legal constraints of a state bureaucracy. Citizens behave as a public body when they confer in an unrestricted fashion – that is, with the guarantee of freedom of assembly and association and the freedom to express and publish their opinions – about matters of general interest.[31]

He then traces the historical development of the public sphere. The rise of the bourgeoisie led to the 'liberal model' of the public sphere. A class which did not yet possess political power interposed itself as a public sphere between the state and the masses and established for itself an ideology of supervision and mediation. The ideology was enshrined in the modern constitutions of the end of the 18th century. As Habermas puts it:

> In the first modern constitutions the catalogues of fundamental rights were a perfect image of the liberal model of the public sphere: they guaranteed the society as a sphere of private autonomy and the restriction of public authority to a few functions. Between these two spheres, the constitutions further insured the existence of a realm of private individuals assembled into a public body who as citizens transmit the needs of bourgeois society to the state, in order, ideally, to transform political into 'rational' authority within the medium of this public sphere. The general interest, which was the measure of such a rationality, was then guaranteed, according to the presuppositions of a society of free commodity exchange, when the activities of private individuals in the marketplace were freed from social compulsion and from political pressure in the public sphere.[32]

The structures of this liberal model still persist, but Habermas argues that it no longer relates to the actual conditions of 'Social Welfare State Mass Democracy'. As a result of the extended influence of mass media, the bourgeoisie has not been able to retain control over the 'public sphere'. As Habermas comments,

> Group needs which can expect no satisfaction from a self-regulating market now tend towards a regulation by the state[33]

or, again,

> Laws which obviously have come about under the 'pressure of the street' can scarcely still be understood as arising from the consensus of private individuals engaged in public discussion.[34]

The scepticism about the notion of parliamentary representation is just one reflection of the collapse of the liberal model of the public sphere.

This is not the place to attempt an exegesis of the development of Habermas's thought. It is fair to say, however, that these two papers of the early 1960s represent the two main strands of his thinking which coalesced in the late 1970s when he realized most clearly that an exclusively epistemological analysis was inadequate. The fundamentals of these two papers have been retained within a more recent framework which distinguishes between the 'system-world' and the 'life-world'. Crudely, the 'system-world', represents an alliance of the historical state and the technical and practical knowledge-constitutive interests, whereas the 'life-world' is the location within which the mass socially seeks to establish a new public sphere on the foundation of the realization of emancipatory interests. In an essay which has received support from Habermas,[35] Richard Bernstein has argued that Habermas's *The Theory of Communicative Action* offers a dialectical synthesis of these competing orientations. Bernstein says of Habermas that

> He wants to do justice to the integrity of the life-world and social systems, and to show how each presupposes the other. We cannot understand the character of the life-world unless we understand the social systems that shape it, and we cannot understand social systems unless we see how they arise out of activities of social agents. The synthesis of system and life-world orientations is integrated with Habermas's delineation of different forms of rationality and rationalization: systems rationality is a type of purposive-rational rationality, life-world rationality is communicative rationality.[36]

It was precisely because Habermas believed that under the conditions of late capitalism he was witnessing the colonization of the life-world by systemic rationalization processes that he gave his support to protest movements such as those of the students in 1968 and the 'Greens'. He believed that those movements which embodied emancipatory interests were active in restraining the excesses of the system-world. Through these movements communicative rationality might moderate purposive rationality and reconstitute the equivalent to a public sphere in a post-liberal society. As he admits, however, it was in 1977 that his view shifted slightly. He explains the change in the following manner:

> The tense German political situation, which was becoming more and more like a pogrom following Schleyer's kidnapping in 1977, drove me out of the theoretical ivory tower to take a political stand. For the first time I took seriously neo-conservative ideologies which had become fashionable since about 1973. . . . I attempted to clarify the concept of modernity implicit in these considerations, and the departure from modernity, a departure from radical democracy and enlightenment – those ideas which had given rise to the Federal Republic.[37]

He realized that the rationality which he wished to encourage in the life-world as a critique of the system-world was becoming an irrationality which was unconsciously colluding in system-world oppression. Suddenly, Habermas's whole venture looked as if it might be torpedoed. In a recent review, Zygmunt Bauman has described this traumatic transition. Having described Habermas's defeat of Husserl in *Knowledge and Human Interests*, Bauman continues:

> But even as he was pursuing and completing his project, the dominant intellectual mood changed to its opposite, and his theory has now to be defended against quite different adversaries, for whom Habermas's arguments against Husserl and other 'absolutists' are trivially true, yet are far from sufficiently radical. Today his opponents are the theorists of 'post-modernism', who declare any search for 'objective validity' of knowledge to be obsolete and misguided, and want to live in peace with the plurality and relativism which they see as irreversible; . . . The meaning of Habermas's work has thus shifted. Its role now is that of a staunch and resolute defence of the essential values and ambitions of modernity; . . . In this new stage of polemics, the emphasis in Habermas's project has moved to the potential for rational argument, mutual understanding and agreement which has to be present in every act of communication.[38]

Hence Habermas is distrustful of the influence of Nietzsche now in a way in which he was not in 1968[39] and he has, as a result, given a series of lectures in France on the 'discourse of modernity'.[40] He realizes that he had not taken the influence of Foucault and Derrida sufficiently seriously and is now concentrating on a defence of his modernity against these modern irrationalists.

I have argued that 1977 was also a key year in England. It marked the collapse of the movement of ideas which had become associated with the 'new directions in the sociology of education'. It also seemed to mark the discrediting of *Knowledge and Control* which had so overtly influenced the submission from the School for Independent Study to the CNAA for the BA/BSc by Independent Study. The course structure has remained and it has been reproduced in the structure for the MA/MSc by Independent Study but, in the last decade, it has lost the momentum which is only to be derived from the vitality of an ideological rationale. But the emphasis of one strand of *Knowledge and Control* has been revitalized since 1977. That year, for instance, was the year of the appearance in English of both Bourdieu's *Reproduction in Education, Society and Culture* and his *Outline of a Theory of Practice* both of which are conducive to a defence of communicative rationality against post-modernism. The continuity of Bourdieu's thought into the post-modern period offers a pointer to the way in which the original rationale of the BA/BSc by Independent Study can be brought up to date.

I am contending that Habermas misjudged the nature of the threat to the life-world. In the specific context of higher education institutions, it is certainly true that there has been a growing state encroachment upon the orientation of institutions and upon curriculum contents. I have argued that the educational reformism which inspired the proposal for the DipHE at NELP unconsciously collaborated in that encroachment by emphasizing instrumental knowledge and instrumental acquiescence in the needs of the labour market. In about 1977 the movement for educational reform, reluctant to be associated overtly with the obvious strategies of state control manifest in the innovations of the Manpower Services Commission, tried, instead, to develop the bargaining power of the life-world by encouraging the development of the personal competence of citizens. However, this movement had excessively joined forces with the personal growth movement which, fundamentally, wishes to have no direct influence on the system-world at all. I have suggested that Carl Rogers and Alasdair MacIntyre have this in common that they both wish to turn their backs on the system-world as long as it offers them the toleration which will enable them to foster their own different kinds of life-world. The threat to the life-world, therefore, is not so much that it is being colonized by the system-world as that it is itself, in response to that creeping colonization, wishing to cultivate a separate existence. The submission for the BA/BSc by Independent Study in 1976 was at Habermas's epistemological stage. It assumed that the reflexivity of students in devising their own programmes of study was itself sufficient to bring about a change in society and social attitudes. By contrast, it now has to be recognized that the registration process for the course is important because it sustains a channel of communication between the life-world and the system-world. It enables the technical and practical interests of the technocrats and the administrators to be moderated by the everyday values of citizens. When asked recently whether the 'ungovernability' of Western democracies today 'favour a real democratization – let us call it a socialization of politics – or is a victory of technocrats and experts inevitable, a victory of complexity over democracy?', Habermas replied, in part, that he was

> convinced that we want democratization not so much in order to improve the efficiency of the economy as to change the *structures* of power: and in the second place to set in motion ways of defining collective goals that merely administrative or power-oriented decisions

would lead astray or cripple. It can be shown that there are collective needs which cannot be satisfied so long as the decision-making process remains administrative or power-oriented. This is the real reason for demanding their democratization. . .[41]

The process of registration implemented in the BA/BSc and the MA/MSc by Independent Study can only actualize that democratization if the process itself preserves a mediating neutrality between the life-world and the system-world. In the microcosom of the School for Independent Study, what is now needed for its health is the perpetuation of a balance between the personalism represented by the diploma within which students identify those objectives which will fulfil their own social psychological needs and the system-representation of the BA/BSc and MA/MSc whereby students secure a public recognition of their individual programmes which offers them an entrée to the controlling corridors of power. There are no signs currently that educational reform might equalize society either by transforming access to educational institutions or by changing the content of organized curriculum provision. On the contrary, our society seems to be dividing rapidly between those who are initiated into the technical and practical knowledge necessary to occupy positions of control and those who, helot-like, are allowed to enjoy politically impotent, person-centred self-development. The process of registration still holds out some hope that 'independent study' might sustain democratization and not become socially and epistemologically marginalized.

To safeguard this role, the process of registration needs to preserve the possibility of rational judgements of rational proposals. The alliance between educational reformism and person-centredness is currently undermining these joint possibilities by making a post-modernist attack on intellectual judgement and by making a 'new paradigm' attack on the possibility of rational proposals. Jean-Francois Lyotard has offered the most articulate expression of the post-modern attitude which affects the willingness of some staff to condone the legitimation assumptions of the registration process. Lyotard celebrates the collapse of the possibility of judgement in the following way. He defines 'postmodern' as 'incredulity toward metanarratives' and continues:

> To the obsolescence of the metanarrative apparatus of legitimation corresponds, most notably, the crisis of metaphysical philosophy and of the university institution which in the past relied on it.[42]

'Metanarratives' are the pre-requisites for the consensual judgements which must be the hallmarks of the registration process. The stability of a proposal is equally important, but one of the contributions to the immensely popular *Human Inquiry. A Source book of New Paradigm Research* illustrates how incompatible with 'new paradigm' methodology is the notion of a fixed intention which might be specified as a plan at a fixed point in time. The chapter entitled 'A dialectical paradigm for research' parallels a conventional research programme with one which follows 'new paradigm' procedures. Having already searched the literature to refine a problem, the conventional researcher then

> designs a research plan and discusses it with one's supervisor or colleagues.[43]

This is the plan which would then be 'registered'. The process for the new paradigm researcher is collaborative and cannot be fixed temporally as a plan of projected action or thought:

> Some action plan has to come into being. This may require some daring, some risk-taking, some breaking of the bounds. I need to involve others at this stage in the process. PROJECT is essentially an *outward* movement ... But again, at a certain point, plans are *not* what is needed. Action itself is the thing to get into. In action I am fully present, here now. Plans are a mere distraction from the past, and can only hamper and impede. I must be ready to improvise if unexpected reactions occur.[44]

Just as the framework of Habermas's thinking has provided the means to understand the social and political implications of contemporary irrationalism, so the ongoing venture of *The Theory of Communicative Action* provides a continuing supply of ammunition to sustain an intellectual resistance to the irrationalism itself which threatens to destroy the democratic potential of the registration process.

For 'registration process', furthermore, read 'the function of institutions of higher education'. The history and the philosophy which have been documented in these pages are not of parochial concern. They do not just relate to the further development of three courses in one department of one polytechnic. In an article published by *The Times Higher Education Supplement* shortly before the recent General Election entitled 'Crawling from the wreckage', Raymond Williams drew attention to the fact that when the expansion of education was being debated in the 19th century there was then a public conflict of 'traditionalists' and 'modernizers'. The former 'old humanists' were those represented by Robinson and Burgess as the 'academics'. The latter were the 'industrial trainers' who represented the narrow vocationalism now exemplified in government training schemes. But, Williams argues, there was always a very different third group – 'the public educators':

> These, then as now, were keen to admit and encourage the new kinds of knowledge and skill which a changing society, as well as changing systems of production, urgently required. But they insisted, also, that there were no simple and reliable lines of transfer between new kinds of knowledge and skill and their actual realization in any complex general society.[45]

It is this third strand which is currently threatened, although Williams is convinced that it is inconceivable that it could be endangered since

The real context of every important project, including those which have traditionally been privileged and protected, is now inescapably public and general. There are boltholes from this condition: in some currently richer society; in private contract with paranational corporations; in accommodation, by privatization, to some temporarily popular political tendency. But the society as a whole is and still will be here, and no recognizable system of higher education can survive without it.[46]

I find it difficult to share Williams's optimism. The 'boltholes', surely, are prevailing. Shortly there may be no such thing as 'society as a whole' but instead a divided society of 'haves' and 'have-nots'. Increasingly the danger is that higher education institutions will either become exclusively the servants of the state or system-world – producing the manpower to maintain the control and the prosperity of the 'haves' or become exclusively the servants of the intellectually disenfranchised majority who inhabit the life-world which has no channel of communication with its systemic oppressor. The signs are that institutions might tacitly become functionally differentiated along these lines. The process of registration becomes the model for institutions. They, as much as the process of registration, must cherish an intermediary status. If the process, or the institutions, were to lose independent status and succumb to the pressures of either system or life world, the significant opportunity for recreating a 'public sphere' of a whole society would be lost. It is for this reason that the rise of independent study, interpreted as an opportunity for the exercise of communicative rationality, is crucially desirable, whereas the continuing rise of a personalist independent study must, to use Brecht's word and for similar reasons, be 'resistible'.

Notes

1 Bossuet, *Élévations*, VII, 3. quoted in J. Benda, trans. R. Aldington, *The Great Betrayal*, London, 1928, p. 29.
2 Benda, trans. R. Aldington, 1928, op. cit. p. 106.
3 ibid. p. 119.
4 ibid. p. 121.
5 ibid. p. 122.
6 ibid. p. 122.
7 ibid. p. 142.
8 ibid. p. 145.
9 M. Horkheimer, *Eclipse of Reason*, New York, OUP, 1947, p. 21.
10 ibid. p. 48.
11 ibid. p. 31.
12 ibid. p. 23.
13 A. MacIntyre, *After Virtue, a study in moral theory*, Duckworth, 2nd edition, 1985, p. 6.
14 ibid. p. 8.
15 ibid. p. 8.
16 A. MacIntyre, 'The Idea of an Educated Public', being the first Richard Peters Lecture delivered at the University of London Institute of Education on Wednes-

day, 30 January 1985, p. 16. I am grateful to Graham Haydon of the Philosophy of Education Department of the University of London Institute of Education for giving me access to Professor MacIntyre's script in advance of its publication.

17 MacIntyre, *After Virtue*, 1985, op. cit. p. 263.
18 M. T. Keeton and Associates, *Experiential Learning, Rationale, Characteristics, and Assessment*, Jossey-Bass, London, San Francisco, Washington, 1976, p. 44.
19 The book is written on the assumption that non-directive pedagogy is now past history. The preface, written by Guy Avanzini, comments: 'La pédagogie non directive est désormais, à la fois, sortie de l'école et entrée dans l'histoire. Après le prestige dont elle bénéficia jusqu'en 1974, rares demeurent les classes où on la pratique,' : L-P. Jouvenet, *Horizon politique des pédagogies non directives*, Privat, 1982, p. 10.
20 C. R. Rogers, *Freedom to Learn for the 80's*, Charles E. Merrill Publishing Co., 1983, p. 250.
21 C. Titmus (ed.), *Widening the Field. Continuing Education in Higher Education*, SRHE & NFER-Nelson, 1985, p. 46.
22 Benda, trans. R. Aldington, 1928, op. cit. p. 138.
23 R. J. Niess, *Julien Benda*, Ann Arbor, Univ of Michigan P., 1956, p. 151.
24 Horkheimer, op. cit. p. 174.
25 ibid. p. 174.
26 P. Dews (ed.), *Habermas. Autonomy and Solidarity*, Interviews, Verso, 1986, p. 152.
27 J. Habermas, trans. J. J. Shapiro, *Knowledge and Human Interests*, Beacon Press, Boston, 1971, p. 306.
28 ibid. p. 307.
29 ibid. p. 308.
30 ibid. p. 308.
31 J. Habermas, trans. S. & F. Lennox, 'The Public Sphere', *New German Critique* (3), 1974, p. 49. The article appeared originally in German in Fischer Lexicon, *Staat und Politik*, new edition (Frankfurt am Main, 1964).
32 ibid. p. 52.
33 ibid. p. 54.
34 ibid. p. 54.
35 See Dews, op. cit. p. 153.
36 R. J. Bernstein (ed. and int.), *Habermas and Modernity*, Polity Press, 1985. p. 22.
37 Dews, op. cit. p. 105.
38 Z. Bauman, 'The adventure of modernity' – review of Dews, op. cit. in *The Times Literary Supplement*, 13 February 1987, p. 155.
39 See Dews, op. cit. p. 132.
40 J. Habermas, *Der Philosophische Diskurs der Moderne*, Frankfurt 1985.
41 Dews, op. cit. p. 67.
42 J-F. Lyotard, *The Post-modern Condition: A Report on Knowledge*, trans. G. Bennington and B. Massumi, Manchester U.P., 1984, p. xxiv.
43 P. Reason and J. Rowan (eds), *Human Inquiry. A Sourcebook of New Paradigm Research*, John Wiley & Sons, 1981, p. 97.
44 ibid. p. 97.
45 R. Williams, 'Crawling from the Wreckage', *The Times Higher Education Supplement*, 5 June 1987, p. 13.
46 ibid. p. 13.

Index

The Society for Research into Higher Education

The Society exists both to encourage and co-ordinate research and development into all aspects of Higher Education, including academic, organizational and policy issues; and also to provide a forum for debate, verbal and printed. Through its activities, it draws attention to the significance of research into, and development in, Higher Education and to the needs of scholars in this field. (It is not concerned with research generally, except, for instance, as a subject of study.)

The Society's income derives from subscriptions, book sales, conferences and specific grants. It is wholly independent. Its corporate members are institutions of higher education, research institutions and professional, industrial, and governmental bodies. Its individual members include teachers and researchers, administrators and students. Members are found in all parts of the world and the Society regards its international work as amongst its most important activities.

The Society discusses and comments on policy, organizes conferences and encourages research. Under the Imprint SRHE & OPEN UNIVERSITY PRESS, it is a specialist publisher, having some 40 titles in print. It also publishes *Studies in Higher Education* (three times a year) which is mainly concerned with academic issues, *Higher Education Quarterly* (formerly *Universities Quarterly*) which will be mainly concerned with policy issues, *Research into Higher Education Abstracts* (three times a year), and a *Bulletin* (six times a year).

The Society's committees, study groups and branches are run by members (with help from a small staff at Guildford), and aim to provide a forum for discussion. The groups at present include a Teacher Education Study Group, a Staff Development Group, a Women in Higher Education Group and a Continuing Education Group which may have had their own organization, subscriptions or publications; (eg the *Staff Development Newsletter*). The Governing Council, elected by members, comments on current issues; and discusses policies with leading figures, notably at its evening Forums. The Society organizes seminars on current research for officials of DES and other ministries, an Anglo-American series on standards, and is in touch with bodies in the UK such as the NAB, CVCP, UGC, CNAA and the British Council, and with sister-bodies overseas. Its current research projects include one on the relationship between entry qualifications and degree results, directed by Prof. W.D. Furneaux (Brunel) and one on questions of quality directed by Prof. G.C. Moodie (York). A project on the evaluation of the research standing of university departments is in preparation. The Society's conferences are often held jointly. Annual Conferences have considered 'Professional Education' (1984), 'Continuing Education' (1985, with Goldsmiths' College) 'Standards and Citeria in Higher Education' (1986, with Bulmershe CHE), 'Restructuring' (1987, with the City of Birmingham Polytechnic) and 'Academic Freedom' (1988, the University of Surrey). Other conferences have considered the DES 'Green Paper' (1985, with the Times Higher Education Supplement), and 'The First-Year Experience' (1986, with the University of South Carolina and

Newcastle Polytechnic). For some of the Society's conferences, special studies are commissioned in advance, as 'Precedings'.

Members receive free of charge the Society's *Abstracts*, annual conference Proceedings (or 'Precedings'), *Bulletin and International Newsletter* and may buy SRHE & OPEN UNIVERSITY PRESS books at booksellers' discount. Corporate members also receive the Society's journal *Studies in Higher Education* free (individuals at a heavy discount). They may also obtain *Evaluation Newsletter* and certain other journals at a discount, including the NFER *Register of Educational Research*. There is a substantial discount to members, and to staff of corporate members, on annual and some other conference fees.